A FIELD GUIDE TO
SPIRITUAL WARFARE

A FIELD GUIDE TO SPIRITUAL WARFARE

The Power to Pull the Impossible
From the Heavenly Realm

MICHAEL J. NORTON

DESTINY IMAGE® PUBLISHERS, INC.
P.O. Box 310, Shippensburg, PA 17257-0310

"Speaking to the Purposes of God for This Generation and for the Generations to Come."

This book and all other Destiny Image, Revival Press, Mercy-Place, Fresh Bread, Destiny Image Fiction, and Treasure House books are available at Christian bookstores and distributors worldwide.

For a U.S. bookstore nearest you, call 1-800-722-6774.
For more information on foreign distributors, call 717-532-3040.
Reach us on the Internet: www.destinyimage.com.

ISBN 13 Trade Paper: 978-0-7684-3642-6
ISBN 13 Hard Copy: 978-0-7684-3643-3
ISBN 13 Large Print: 978-0-7684-3644-0
ISBN 13 E-book: 978-0-7684-9040-4

For Worldwide Distribution, Printed in the U.S.A.

1 2 3 4 5 6 7 8 9 10 / 14 13 12 11

DEDICATION

I would like to dedicate *A Field Guide to Spiritual Warfare* to my mom, Betty Norton. I know you are leading the (Mark 16) M16 cheer section *from Heaven!*

To my wife, Lisa, who is my spiritual strength: together we expect miracles in each and every battle we fight.

To my three boys, Matthew, Ryan, and Josh, who have lived through some pretty crazy things in our house, and who accept the supernatural as being normal.

To the M16 Intercessors, Elyssa, Heidi, Leah, Diana, Lisa, Conni, Nina, Lynn, Jason, and Bekah: through your prayers and your faith to pull from Heaven, the impossible has bowed to the name of Jesus, and captives are set free.

To my good friend Jimi: when you pedaled to my house on that cold January day, did you ever imagine the path would lead us here?

To the men who instructed me and shaped me—Bob, Mark, and Gary: I am honored to be able to give to others what you have sowed into me.

Acknowledgments

Jesus—all the glory of every victory and miracle goes to You. Words can never express Your steadfast mercy and Your grace.

Charles Norton, my father—for realizing my need to absorb the Christian classics. Thanks for the Josephus and the Chesterton books.

Julia Loren—thanks for proofing and editing. You were the divinely appointed editor to make this project a reality.

Lisa Norton, my wife—thanks for being my interpreter, my editor, and for every red pen mark you had to make in checking my work.

Bob Johnson—for the "Worship and Warfare" meetings and for Night Strikes! My spiritual life was deeply changed forever.

Mark Neitz—thanks for volunteering me to be a team leader for Night Strike years ago. Thank you for sharing your spiritual dream of Guyana and the South American Amazon with me.

Destiny Image staff who worked on this project—thank you for letting me share this message and reach the people who may need the miraculous touch of God.

My family, and extended family—thank you for being extremely supportive of the ministry.

Endorsements

A Field Guide to Spiritual Warfare: The Power to Pull the Impossible From the Heavenly Realm is a cutting-edge field guide that has evolved from many years of confronting the forces of darkness. You will not find unpracticed theory or callow theology, but rather a proven, effective model in bringing release to the captives.

Jimi Merrell
Pastor of Prayer and Outreach
Valley Christian Center, Dublin, CA
Co-Founder of Dreamfusion.org

As darkness increases, it is important to let Jesus "retool" us for the ministry ahead. Mike Norton's book, *A Field Guide to Spiritual Warfare* does just that. This guide gives us insight and equips us to let the light of Jesus dispel the darkness in people's lives once and for all. Mike does an excellent job of explaining and training us to let go of old methods of evangelism and deliverance, exhorting us to follow the leading of the Holy Spirit as Jesus sets people free from the prisons that bind them. I recommend *A Field Guide to Spiritual Warfare* to be embraced by evangelistic teams everywhere.

Cindy McGill
www.hopefortheharvest.com

CONTENTS

FOREWORD

P lease allow me to begin by saying how truly honored I am to write the foreword for this book. This is especially true because I know the author and have seen firsthand how he walks out, on a daily basis, all that he has written. I have known Mike for several years and have watched him as a student; now he is the teacher. In the beginning of our relationship, he was hanging on to my every word; I now hang on to his.

I have been in full-time ministry for over 25 years. During that time, I have read many books pertaining to deliverance—some very complicated, some very weird, and others just plain whacked. I believe that this is the best book I have ever read on this subject. It deals with a very difficult topic and makes it palatable for the reader. Mike has done an exemplary job in dealing with this topic and making it simple to understand, while also teaching readers, with power, how to move in miracles.

Mike has cut his teeth for this ministry by working in one of the toughest cities in America: San Francisco. It is the only city of its size in America that has never experienced revival. Mike has taken the message of the Gospel of Jesus with me and several others to the streets of this great city. These tools were not honed in the fire of the Church, but in the hellfire of the streets. We have learned that the Father loves the 99 and rejoices with them continually, but His heart is after the one. That is where we spend the majority of our time: going after the one.

Whereas other books give the impression that you must be called to this type of ministry, this book is for every believer. It is a must-read if you plan on sharing the love of Jesus with the lost or have a desire to help the believer get set free.

Another refreshing note about this book is that Mike is not looking for a demon under every rock. His goal in life is to make the Father known. The focus is not to give attention or accolades to the devil or his demons. In fact, Mike doesn't even let them talk. Instead, the focus is solely on Jesus, and all attention is directed toward doing only what the Father is doing. Believe me, this is very refreshing.

Another thing that stands out to me is that these are not theories Mike has come up with, but proven testimonies of the power of Jesus. They were birthed through fasting, intercession, and taking God at His Word. Revelation 19:10 says, *"...the testimony of Jesus is the spirit of prophecy."* If these testimonies are happening in Mike's life, they can happen with you wherever you are.

Mike is not only a friend to me, but also a partner in ministry. My wife and I are blessed to travel all over the world. Whenever we come across people who need special attention, we immediately set them up for phone deliverance with Mike and Lisa. We have even done this across continents. I affectionately refer to Mike and Lisa as my personal demon-bouncers.

I can hardly wait for this book to be published so I can offer it on my product table at conferences and meetings. This is a message the Church has shied away from. Now the Church can have successful access to it. Thank you, Mike and Lisa.

Bob Johnson
Bob & Kimberly Johnson Ministries
International Speaker/Evangelist

CHAPTER 1

AGAINST THE FORCES
OF EVIL IN HEAVENLY REALMS

*He said to them, "Go into all the world and preach the good
news to all creation. Whoever believes and is baptized will be
saved, but whoever does not believe will be condemned. And
these signs will accompany those who believe: In My name they
will drive out demons; they will speak in new tongues; they
will pick up snakes with their hands; and when they drink
deadly poison, it will not hurt them at all; they will place their
hands on sick people, and they will get well"* (Mark 16:15-18).

The Prodigal City

San Francisco is a very spiritual city. Though residents may
not know Jesus, many gravitate toward one spirit or another.
It is a city of prodigals, people who at one time or another
went to church, but no longer do.

Everyone knows San Francisco as a city that publicly embraces
the erotic tendencies of the flesh. The evidence is found on the
streets, at nearly every turn. The *Satanic Bible* is here, too, and has
its origins in the Haight Ashbury District. Deliverance ministries
still come across adults who had their minds splintered years ago,
when their parents participated in satanic rituals.

Back in 1968, San Francisco hosted the so-called "Summer of Love." Sadly, that summer had more to do with debauchery than with anything resembling real love. Idolatry of the flesh and perversion are flaunted to this day in many public parades and other events. The New Age movement and Wicca are also strongly rooted in the streets of the city named after Saint Francis of Assisi.

The spiritual condition of San Francisco parallels the spiritual state of Europe described by Father Gabriele Amorth in his book, *An Exorcist: More Stories.* Father Amorth is a renowned exorcist; he makes an interesting point about the decline of Christianity and the rise of the demonic in Europe. He writes:

> First: Why, today, is there such high demand for exorcists? Can we make the case that the demon is more active today than in the past? Can we say that the incidence of demonic possession and other, lesser, evil disturbances is on the rise? The answer to these and similar questions is a decisive Yes. Rationalism, atheism—which is preached to the masses—and the corruption that is a by-product of Western consumerism have all contributed to a *frightening decline in faith.*[1]

As people drift away from the Church at alarming rates, demonic activity rises. People in Europe, like those in San Francisco, are spiritual people; however they are embracing idols instead of following Jesus.

Like any major city in America, San Francisco is full of "damaged goods," prodigals, and demonic activity. As I mentioned, the *Satanic Bible* was written in San Francisco. Through the decades, many counterfeit spiritual fads have originated in the area, started by "gurus" who have rejected Jesus and enticed others to follow them.

Are these people beyond God's reach? No. But gone are the days of handing out tracts on the street. Giving tracts to these people is pointless. For one thing, they have been hurt by words spoken over them in church in regard to their sexual behavior. Tracts will not overcome their resentment.

What works in San Francisco is the evangelistic style laid out in the Book of Acts. As we reach out to those on the streets of this city, we see lives set free by the love and power of Jesus. And if we see such results on our city streets, we believe every city can respond to the style of power evangelism we have been blessed to release.

True power evangelism takes an effort few are willing to exert. Yet, if we do not reach out, who will? If we do not stem the decline of Christianity, what will happen to our cities? The mayor of San Francisco, Gavin Newsom, said, "As California goes—so goes the rest of the nation."[2] He was talking about the legalization of gay marriage at the time—and he was right about the "California Effect."

The same is true of San Francisco; as it goes, so goes the nation. But there is a flip side to that coin, and it is encouraging: we believe that if San Francisco can turn to Jesus, so can the rest of the nation.

So, come with me on a journey to the streets of San Francisco. Come and see how you, too, can transform a city, one life at a time. Come with me as we minister on the streets at night. Watch what we do. Then follow me as our ministry, M16, works by day. Discover how you can release the light of the power of God that breaks the hold of darkness.

Walk and Talk Evangelism

For the past several years, I have served as a team leader for Bob Johnson's City Ministries Friday night San Francisco outreach, called *Night Strike*. Every time we go out, we witness phenomenal miracles in healing and deliverance.

Even so, we can rarely walk up to homosexuals and ask to pray for them. The question reopens old wounds of rejection all over again. We know that words speak either death or life. The Bible tells us so:

> *The tongue also is a fire, a world of evil among the parts of the body. It corrupts the whole person, sets the whole course of his life on fire, and is itself set on fire by hell* (James 3:6).

Sadly, when Christians should have spoken life to these people, they said some horrible things instead. The Church forgot to love sinners while hating their sin.

Too many Christians are into sandwich board and bullhorn ministry; too many are quick to point out the sins of others. People already know about their sin; making it public only serves to embarrass the very people we want to reach. It doesn't help those of us who serve as foot soldiers for Jesus, either. It is counterproductive all around—and satan uses the blunder to his advantage.

As street evangelists, we walk the neighborhoods and talk to people. They know we're Christians; yet the people already damaged by word curses often choose to be polite to us. As we talk to them, we pray and ask the Holy Spirit to reveal something about them to us; this method of encounter with individuals and the Holy Spirit on the streets is called prophetic evangelism. Many times what the Holy Spirit reveals is what was spoken over them in Church. What happens next is that people start weeping and deliverance begins.

How we minister to people is important. One of my objectives as a Night Strike team leader is to equip those on my team. I encourage them to try prophetic evangelism. In fact, many people's first experience with the prophetic gifts comes through a Night Strike team leader.

On one such occasion, our team was on the streets in the Tenderloin District of San Francisco. As we walked, we saw a homeless woman slouched over on the sidewalk. She looked the worse for years of wear: Her strawberry blonde hair was a knotted mess. Her dress was tattered and filthy. She didn't have a blanket, but I knew she was going to sleep right there on the sidewalk that night.

I gave the woman a friendly greeting. She broke from her hopeless stare to see who was speaking to her. She was either puzzled or a bit overwhelmed to see a group of six people standing around her. Earlier in the night, we ran out of food and had none to give her, but we stayed on the streets with something even more important to offer: an encounter with Jesus Christ.

As this tired and weathered woman made eye contact with me, I noticed that her eyes were those of a man. She was a transvestite. I asked for her name and she answered, "Tina."

Tina wasn't much for words, but she gave us her undivided attention. I explained that we were out on the streets blessing people. Tina returned a quizzical look. I asked if it would be OK if we said a simple prayer for her. Tina shook her head in the negative and turned her attention back to the dirty sidewalk.

I gave Tina a farewell, "God bless you," and proceeded to lead the team on. God stopped me from taking another step and told me that Tina was one of His children. "Go apologize for what your brothers and sisters said to her." God's voice was loud and clear!

I told my team to wait. I then turned and walked back to Tina, whose expression said, "What now?"

I knelt down to Tina's eye level and told her, "Jesus just told me that you were in church as a child. People in your church said horrible things to you about who you are. Jesus said He loves you and told me to apologize to you for their behavior."

Tina's hopeless eyes began to tear. Still kneeling, I put my hand on Tina's shoulder and told her, "Jesus told me to come back and tell you this. He loves you, and He sees what you're going through."

Tina nodded in tearful affirmation.

It's important to listen to what God tells you. He has a different message for each person on the streets. God meets His children at the level of their individual needs.

The Holy Spirit touched this person firsthand and in a gentle manner. For years, people like Tina thought they were damned by Christ, because of *our* words spoken over them. They have therefore learned to reject Jesus. Now Jesus comes and tells them how much He loves them.

It is incredible to witness the impact of His love. The greatest miracle to witness is a change in heart. Once that begins, we are released to pray a blessing over the person. It means so much to the individual; but it is also the start of the Holy Spirit repairing His Church in the city.

I know a lot of churches would flip at the notion that we are laying hands on transvestites and releasing heavenly favor on them. Don't judge people on the streets by how they are dressed. Look at them through your spiritual eyes and see the prodigal son! God may send many evangelists and ministers to them before they repent and turn to Him. Just make sure you leave a piece of Jesus with them.

Mark Neitz of Night Strike, a good friend and mentor of mine, has an interesting testimony in this regard. It is about a transvestite named Kim. Kim would come down on Friday nights just to hang out and listen to our worship team. Mark talked to Kim for years! He simply engaged in simple conversation and shared the love of Jesus. Mark never sought to enforce any type of agenda. He left it all in God's hands.

One night, at Christmastime, Kim came to a Night Strike and talked with Mark. All of a sudden, she burst into tears and said, "Mark, all of these years you never, ever judged me or made comments about my dressing in women's clothes. You just talked to me as a friend. I really miss my twin boys; I'm grieving the fact that I'm not around them anymore. I want to see them!"

All those years of talking and Kim never mentioned anything about a family. Now, deliverance had begun!

When you love on God's people, don't have an agenda. Bob Johnson has a quotation I really like: "I am called to be a fisher of men. I catch'em and He cleans'em."

Some scars are very deep and take lots of time to heal. Patience is needed; in fact, it is one of the keys of deliverance ministry. If you are a stickler for a timeline, this isn't the ministry for you!

Mark's approach with Kim is the same one we use at pagan fairs and festivals. Many of the people attending these events have already been "churched"—and hurt by the words spoken over them. My wife Lisa and I are on an outreach team that attends Bay Area New Age fairs. We use the gifts of the Spirit to share what we call Holy Spiritual "readings." This is the hottest ticket at these venues! The gifts of the Spirit can cut through any counterfeit magic the enemy can conjure.

With all that San Francisco has become, it is no wonder that some see it as the modern-day Sodom and Gomorrah. Many Christians are ready to call down fire from Heaven upon the place, just as the apostles wanted to do in Luke 9:54. I see San Francisco as the modern-day city of Ephesus. And these are the Acts of the modern-day apostles.

It's for your city too.

Offensive Engagement

The battle cry of Night Strike is "To the deepest, darkest neighborhoods where we're told not to go—that's where we go!"

The Night Strike name reflects a military operation. It is a fitting name; we are God's soldiers and we strategically plan which neighborhood He wants to invade. This approach to ministry, along with the equipping I have received from Night Strike, would eventually influence my Mark 16 (M16) deliverance ministry.

My participation in the San Francisco Night Strikes was formative; it helped forge and sharpen my prophetic evangelism skills. God was leading me into deliverance ministry and preparing me for the deepest, darkest parts of spiritual warfare, where other ministries dare not go.

That is where M16 goes. We will go into a house with demonic activity and engage the enemy. My team and I do not enter these situations blindly, though. Each member of our team is a mature Christian who is equipped for spiritual warfare. Without training in prophetic evangelism and the gifts of the Spirit, this ministry could not be effective. Members of our team know how to communicate with the Holy Spirit. Whether you are evangelizing on the streets or praying in deliverance ministry, talking with the Holy Spirit is crucial.

As I just mentioned, *engaging* the enemy is one of the services M16 provides. We have served eviction notices to powers of darkness and worked with people who are demonically possessed. In each case, we have been a part of witnessing the glory of God.

Very few churches and ministries will take up an offensive strike operation of this kind and stand on their faith to see it bear fruit. Most who have engaged in spiritual warfare know it is *truly* warfare. It costs you something to be prepared for it.

Sometimes the enemy inflicts collateral damage. This is where most ministries back off. Our approach is this: when we are attacked, we stand on our faith. In our ministry, we have learned that you must be more than a prayer warrior, you must be a pray-er who is also a *warrior.*

The enemy hates us for helping others and has attacked us in sick, twisted ways, hoping to get us to back off. Just ask our family members; they are now more versed in spiritual warfare than a lot of pastors with seminary PhDs. My two oldest boys, both in their early teens, have cast out demons. We take them to prayer meetings where we expect to engage the enemy. We are not fearful; we know our God is omnipotent and can deal with the temper tantrums of the enemy.

Make no mistake: you need to have your spiritual house in order before entering this ministry. The enemy goes straight for the jugular vein. He will try to destroy both you and your family.

Here's one example (and keep in mind there are many darker examples I could share):

My wife and I ministered deliverance prayer to a young woman who was under the attack of witchcraft. Unfortunately, the woman wasn't ready to be delivered. The attacks on her were real, but they brought her a lot of sympathy, which she relished. She also enjoyed receiving the deliverance prayer ministry, but not because she wanted to be set free. She enjoyed the attention her oppression brought her.

Lisa and I prayed over the woman. The deliverance prayer ministry team went on the offensive and hit the demon where it hurt, in the spirit realm. The girl twisted and screamed as I read Revelation 20 aloud. The demon wouldn't budge, which Lisa and I thought was a bit odd. Why? Because the demon knew it only had to outlast our ministry prayer session; then it would be able to return to business as usual.

The next day, while driving home from work, my mind went into a trance. I started accelerating into an intersection—against the red light. At the very last moment, I heard God say, "Wake up!"

I snapped out of the trance, hit the brakes, and plowed into the back of another car. I walked away unscathed, but my son's car was totaled.

The point is that this was a demonic attack and it was real. I remember earlier on the day of the accident getting a picture in my head of a demon-possessed lady driving a car. She was looking at me and snarling. I got the message loud and clear. Still, I had a close call.

The demons didn't know me very well, however. I wasn't about to quit. Instead, I went home and went on a 21-day Daniel fast; I prayed for understanding and for the blocking of any cracks that allowed the demon to attack my mind that day.

Even as I write this, I remember that I was given a spiritual warfare dream while on my Daniel fast on how to confront this demon. God often uses dreams to reveal the nature of the battle. God will use dreams to aid his warriors in breaking off demonic assignments. Through this dream I severed the assignment of retaliation on me by essentially killing the demon in it.

When you engage in offensive warfare, you encounter manifestations. While praying for several months for a young, demon-possessed man in Guyana, we had shadows manifest in our house. Two nights before I was to leave on a mission trip to Guyana, the Holy Spirit awakened me from a sound sleep at two o'clock in the morning.

This wasn't a, "Hey, Mike, this is God. Get up and greet the day!" kind of experience. God literally had my mind fully awake in a snap (although my body was still adjusting). He had me look at the door to our master bedroom. Through the upper portion of the doorframe, I saw a dark shadow bolt into our room. It flew to the wall across from me and manifested as the shadow of a man.

I jumped out of bed to confront the shadow. I was angry and commanded it, saying, "Get the hell out of my house!" This was not the reception it was expecting. The demon expected me to be afraid and trembling. The shadow bolted out through the nearby window.

There were no hairs standing up on the back of my neck. There was no cold shiver running down my spine. I don't sleep spiritually naked; I go to bed with my armor on and I sleep with the long sword of the Spirit in my heart.

When the unwelcome guest departed, I immediately ran down the hall to my kids' rooms and prayed to break any assignments over them that the intruder may have brought into the house. Then I went back to bed and fell asleep. The enemy used the shadow to try to frighten me out of the fight for a young man's salvation. While I was on the trip to Guyana, my wife had to deal with other manifestations. Among them the enemy set off our fire alarms while she was in the middle of spiritual warfare prayer.

As for the demon-possessed young man, he accepted Jesus and is on the road to full recovery. His case required months of prayer. Our initial prayers were for guidance as to whether we should take on the case. My good friend Gary Paltridge worked on this with me. We were concerned about the young man's condition. He couldn't sit through prayer without demons manifesting and talking. His will was completely compromised; we were concerned that the demons would tell him to kill himself.

That is why Gary and I entered into intercession and prayed about whether we were to proceed. Once that question was settled, we prayed some more—this time about when we should do the deliverance prayer session. At all times, we were in communication with God.

It was because of this young man and the severity of his condition that I decided to set up an intercessor team for M16 Ministries. The intercessor team is comprised of close ministry friends who work in the prophetic and are not afraid to go on the offensive. The young man and his family were soaked in protective prayer from M16 intercessors and the intercessor team from the young man's mother's church.

The use of intercessors in this battle played a crucial role. Keep in mind that just having intercessors doesn't necessarily guarantee a calm and peaceful deliverance. Many factors are in play and each deliverance session is different. What was effective in this case was that all the intercessors and prayer warriors involved were listening and talking to the Holy Spirit.

When our young friend finally walked through the door at the deliverance prayer session, he was already a changed man. The spirits were so beaten up by months of prayer that they didn't even bother to manifest. It was an incredibly peaceful deliverance session as the Holy Spirit came in and blessed him with a gift of grace and mercy. The young man renounced satan and other occult practices. It was truly amazing to see how gently God handled a fragile situation.

As you can see from these testimonies, we are at war. We are not to fear engaging the enemy. However, engaging the enemy without being equipped is not a good idea, either. I believe this is why many churches don't engage the enemy. It is because they are not equipped for this warfare.

I also believe that, as Christians, all of us are re-learning what some of our Church generals (such as Aimee Semple McPherson, Smith Wigglesworth, and Dr. John G. Lake) taught us in the late 1800s and early 1900s. These were warriors of God who knew how to heal people and deliver souls from darkness through the power of the Holy Spirit. I believe that somewhere between the Roaring Twenties and the 1990s we lost what these generals of God had equipped us with.

Grown Men Aren't Afraid of the Dark

I wasn't always the man who could get up out of bed and order a demon to leave my house. Quite honestly, I wasn't afraid of the dark; I was *terrified* of it for 38 years of my life. I share my testimony with other men and women who are afraid or ashamed to admit that they, too, have this bondage of fear.

There is freedom from this nightmare. I am no longer afraid of the dark. I went from fear of the dark to hatred of the enemy who dwells in the dark. This is a common side effect of being delivered from the bondage of fear.

For those who know me, this inside joke is familiar: Darkness is my hunting ground, and the only thing I have to fear of the dark is not knowing where my son left the vacuum cleaner. We have boys in our family who don't always put things away. I have stumbled over the vacuum in the dark more than once.

My fear of the dark has its roots in my early childhood. The enemy tends to attack children because they are vulnerable. He knows that the scars we receive in childhood last longer and tend to compound and do more collateral damage as we get older.

My childhood was incredible; I have lots of fond memories. I was blessed with an amazing family and raised in a devout Catholic home. My father was in the Marine Corps. My mom (as my wife and I believe) had the gift of discernment of spirits. My mom was always seeing spirits in the homes we lived in. For reasons I never understood until later in life, our houses were always haunted.

When I was about three years old, I remember seeing things in our house that didn't fit in my concept of physical reality. Processing the things I saw freaked me out. On one occasion, my mother walked over to her friend's house down the street, with me in tow. She told her friend, out of my earshot, that there were spiritual things going on in our house. I overheard my mother, despite her efforts to conceal the matter. I already knew because I had seen a chair in my room move on its own. From this experience, the spirit of fear took root.

I never wanted to follow in the footsteps of my Catholic mother in exploring the spirit realm. My mom was acutely aware of the supernatural, but she was not equipped in using her gifting. My mom asked deeper questions only so she could understand what she was seeing.

Oddly enough, Catholic Church history is rich with mystics and charismatics. A recent Catholic Church mystic was Padre Pio (1887-1968), a Capuchin priest whose life was marked by the supernatural.[3] There was also a charismatic movement in the Catholic Church in the 1970s. It affected the state of Louisiana, just one state where our family was living at the time. The movement never reached any of the Catholic churches we attended, however.

Because my mother was gifted but not equipped to operate in her gifts, she turned to materials on psychics in the hopes of gaining some understanding of the supernatural experiences she was having. My mother did not understand that she had a spiritual gift from God (specifically, the discerning of spirits). Therefore, she inadvertently turned to ungodly sources and practices.

As my mother explored what she thought were psychic experiences, items and doctrines unpleasing to God entered our home. My mother had her own tarot cards and did readings. On one occasion, while doing a reading for a family friend, she drew the card bearing the symbol of death. Within the month, this friend was involved in a tragic accident in which someone was killed.

I never liked the tarot cards. I sensed at an early age that they were a source of evil. My mom's spirituality had developed a dual nature: one side stood with Jesus, her Lord and Savior; the other dabbled in the dark regions of the spirit realm. It was through a lack of knowledge that this doorway to evil was opened. Even as believers, we can hold the door open for the enemy.

The houses we lived in always seemed to have spiritual activity in them. My mom said the houses had ghosts. There was always the false belief that the ghosts were friendly. I remember when I was in elementary school and we lived in Virginia. I would get in bed, roll myself up tightly in a blanket, and butt myself up to the wall adjoining my bed so I couldn't see what entered my room.

This wasn't an overwrought imagination at work. There was a tremendous spirit of fear present. There were formless figures moving in the darkness of the hallway. Sometimes they whispered quietly. I made sure I fell asleep facing the wall. My greatest fear was that I would turn over and see a face staring at me. And whenever possible once I was in bed, I stayed in bed until daylight.

My mother used to get upset with me when, as a fifth grader, I would yell down to the first-level family room from my upstairs bedroom and ask for a glass of water. Once I was barricaded in my blankets, I would not come out. Most nights were calm; but on those occasional nights when there was activity, I would lie petrified in my bed. Though these occasions were infrequent, even one encounter would bring a cascading spirit of fear upon me. That fear would linger for months.

I didn't know the formless figures moving around in the darkness were demonic. It didn't matter what they were—bad ghosts, demons, whatever—they frightened me. My biggest fears would set in when all the lights in the house were off. Do you remember the uncontrollable excitement of Christmas morning, when you would get up in the early, dark hours way before your parents were awake? I remember one Christmas when I counted down from ten and bolted down the hall and down the stairs so I wouldn't have a chance encounter with darkness. Many times I did this 100-yard dash out of fear that something *might* be there.

Not all of the supernatural experiences of my childhood were scary. During the fifth grade, my catechism class took a Saturday field trip to the National Cathedral in Washington, D.C. I remember standing in one area of the cathedral and feeling an incredible presence of angels. There was a feeling of warmth inside me that I could not describe. It was like nothing I'd ever felt before. There was a sense of being safe and protected. Yet, there was so much more to it that I felt sure it was a touch from Heaven.

I didn't want to step out of that presence. It was the opposite of fear! It *had to be* Heaven. Still, it didn't make sense to me because, according to my belief system at the time, Heaven was where you went when you died. I wondered, "How can I be experiencing this while I'm alive?"

That moment would stay with me all my life. As an adult, I would eventually experience this same feeling whenever God let me know that I was standing in the presence of manifested angels.

During the sixth grade (when I was 12 years old), I received confirmation of my sensitivity to spiritual activity. The United States Marine Corp (USMC) reassigned my father to Okinawa. Our family moved to a suburb of San Diego while my father served in active duty overseas.

Once again, we moved into a haunted house. (For my mom, this seemed to be a standard feature of any home we bought.) It was a beautiful one-story Spanish style home perched on a hillside in a prominent neighborhood. Superficially, the house was great. But something was wrong. I suspect the house was tainted, spiritually speaking, by some sort of ungodly activity that occurred under previous owners.

Our family poodle wouldn't enter the family room at certain hours of the evening. At times, the dog behaved as though someone were sitting on the couch where there appeared to be an empty seat. Once again, I started hearing whispers and seeing shadows moving in the darkness of the hallway. I got the sense that these spirits were different ones from those we left behind on the East Coast. These were not spirits that followed us to San Diego; they were already in the house before we moved in.

The nights of wrapping myself tightly in my blanket and sleeping with my face pressed against the wall resumed.

When I had to go to the bathroom in the early hours of the morning, I would again use my countdown from ten. At the appropriate time, when the right amount of courage rose up inside me, I would fling off the covers and run to the bathroom (which was next to my bedroom). I would turn on every light beginning in my room, down the hallway, and all the way to the bathroom. I made sure my entire path was paved with light.

Upon returning to bed, the only light I would turn off was one light in my bedroom. I believed the hallway would be safe from shadows as long as the hall lights were left on. I would fall fast asleep knowing I was protected by the light flooding into my room.

A few minutes after my mad dash, either my sister or my mother (who was a very light sleeper) would get up and switch off the hall lights, irritated at the interruption to their sleep. I didn't care who was upset as long as I was again wrapped up and safe in my blanket. Often the few minutes of light were all I needed to go back to sleep.

Just under a year later, my father was given new orders to relocate to another military base in southern California. We moved out of the house and rented it to two very liberal women who were partners in a relationship. They made comments to my parents about there being spiritual activity in the house. They summoned the aid of a guru to make contact with the spirits in the house. The spirits responded during the séance by setting the kitchen on fire.

I didn't need this confirmation to tell me what I already knew—supernatural things were happening. The good news was that my father moved the family to our new house, which had no ghosts (shadows). I had my own period of spiritual peace in this new house. My mom, however, dabbled more deeply in psychic reading and divination with tarot cards. She also hired psychics to do readings for her.

Despite Mom's activities in this home, it was a peaceful environment for me. In my spiritual warfare dreams, when God reveals generational issues with my family, I return to this house as my "safe" house.

Throughout my high school years, I experienced alternating cycles of peace and spiritual activity. We lived in two different homes during that period. In the latter, the activity started up once again. My mother was convinced that the spirits of her deceased dogs were coming to visit her. There were nights when I slept petrified and in terror. Just as an earlier house serves as my "safe" house in warfare dreams, this house is the one I go to in my deliverance dreams to deal with my own generational spirits.

As of this writing, there is still minor spiritual activity in my parents' house. By minor, I mean that, on occasion, footsteps are heard in the house. When my mother passed away a few years ago, I found many books by the psychic Sylvia Brown in the house. I prayed over them, broke the assignments that may have come from them, bound the demonic activity associated with these objects, and blessed my mother. Then I destroyed the books and a Ouija board. (Just recently, after my father proofread this manuscript, I learned that the Ouija board had originally entered the house as a toy, subtly, like a Magic 8 Ball or some other deceptive toy.)

Having survived a spiritually tumultuous youth, I entered college and pursued a degree in physics and mathematics. I also pursued a beautiful woman, whom I married. In my college years, angels started appearing to me in the physical realm. I knew they were angels because I had the same overwhelming feeling I experienced in the National Cathedral. This time, however, I could see the angels, who appeared in the form of people, right in front of me. I didn't tell anybody about it; I thought people would think I was crazy. It was best to keep these incidents to myself, or so I thought.

The Fighting 777

Do not forget to entertain strangers, for by so doing some people have entertained angels without knowing it (Hebrews 13:2).

Over the course of the next decade (the 1990s), I had several strange encounters with angels. One of the most memorable occurred at a McDonald's drive-thru in the summer of 1998, I believe. I was driving my old 1967 Camaro convertible. It was in the process of being restored, so it was a permanent convertible that always had the top down.

While I waited in line to pick up my order, three men approached me from the driver's side of my car. Gaudy neon colors (luminescent greens, yellows, and pinks) were popular in the 1990s. The three men who approached my car wore neon-colored caps and fanny packs. Their attire was the kind meant to mock the tourists who wear it. It was a comical picture, one that I believe was designed to get my attention.

One of the three men spoke to me, saying, "We need $20." In California, it is common for panhandlers to camp out at intersections and work restaurant parking lots. Californians are conditioned to this reality. My initial reaction was to tell the man I wasn't going to give him the $20. I looked up at him and at his friends. Their dress was truly bizarre, yet I sensed that they weren't tourists at all. And they spoke perfect English.

That was when I was overcome by the sensation I'd had at the National Cathedral years before. These men were angels! I reached in my pocket and handed the man a $20 bill.

The man who had done all the talking looked at me and told me, "You'll never know how or where, but we'll be there to help you when you need us."

Then the three men walked off—and vanished. With my 20 bucks! I don't know what their assignment was or why they needed my cash. I always wondered whether God was having fun with me while fulfilling a need for someone else who truly needed the money at that moment.

I never told anyone about this encounter until much later when I was comfortable opening up and talking about angels. Then, around the year 2001, I had another strange encounter in which I took an angel for a ride in my car. How did I know he was angel? Two things occurred during this visit: First, I thought I knew this guy. It was as if he had been a long lost friend whose name I couldn't remember. The second clue was that he vanished after we were through talking.

Again, I was afraid to tell my family about the incident because I thought they would have me locked up or put on medication! It took me two days to share my experience; but it so shook me that I had to tell someone. Finally, I divulged it, right after the blessing of our dinner. There was a moment of silence and it was clear that Lisa was upset with me—not because she thought her husband was going crazy or because she didn't believe me, but because I didn't tell her about the incident the day it happened.

What I learned from this experience was that satan likes to talk us out of our miracles. Fear of what people would think of me kept me from trusting my own family. Instead of sharing the testimony, I hid it. There was a phenomenal testimony from this angelic encounter: I was delivered from my decades-long bondage to the fear of the dark!

My encounter with the angel who rode in my car made me understand that he was quite capable of grabbing a scary shadow, holding it in a headlock, and doing whatever he wanted to do to it. This spiritual moment was pivotal; not only was the fear gone from that day on, but I also believe I met my guardian angel.

During a deliverance prayer session in 2009, I felt the presence of this same angel. I asked the Holy Spirit the angel's name. I was told that his name was *Raphael*. Now my good friend and partner in ministry, Jimi Merrell, makes fun of me and says that my guardian angel is a ninja turtle.

I have seen the angels from the McDonald's drive-thru experience on several other occasions in the past few years. I call them the Fighting 777. In April 2007, I was on my way to a Night Strike. I usually drive a number of people to this outreach, but on this occasion, schedules didn't mesh, so I drove alone.

When I arrived at the Bay Bridge toll plaza in my wife's Durango, I joined the line of cars inching toward the tool booths. (I had not yet purchased my Fast-Trak, a convenient device that allows you to drive straight through the plaza and pay the toll electronically through your bank account). As I awaited my turn to hand the attendant my money, I looked in the rearview mirror and saw that the Durango was full—of angels. One of them told me to take the commuter lane; then the angels vanished! They were having some fun with me.

What I didn't realize until later that evening was that I would be ministering to a homeless woman who lived on the streets. Her name was Lisa. After I prayed for her, she pulled me off to the side and shared a frantic message with me.

Lisa said, "I know I am not going insane. The other day, I was in the parking lot of a supermarket and my sister pulled up in her truck. But it wasn't my sister. It was an angel who gave me food. It was my favorite food, too. I am not crazy; you have to believe me!"

I prayed over Lisa again. I told her that I believed her and asked her, in turn, to believe me: "I have some friends with me who are going to help you. I am releasing them to you now. You will know who they are when you see them. They are going to open a new door in your life. You need to step through the door when they open it. It's important that you do. Do you know what I am talking about?"

Lisa nodded and said she knew what I was talking about.

Another angelic encounter happened on the very first Night Strike I attended in February, 2007. I had just met Bob Johnson the night before, at a Worship and Warfare meeting he held on the last Thursday of every month. I told him about recent spiritual warfare events in my life. Bob said he could recommend numerous books to me, but he also suggested that I could get some firsthand equipping in spiritual warfare on the streets at a Night Strike. I took Bob at his word and attended the Night Strike scheduled for the very next night.

That night's team was led by Night Strike veterans, Wayne and Diane La Cosse. We were no more than 15 minutes into our ministry walk in the Tenderloin District when I found myself involved in my first deliverance ministry prayer session. It was an exciting moment; God revealed my heavenly citizenship and my resulting authority over the demonic realm. It was the start of my true training by the Holy Spirit in deliverance ministry.

It was an initiation of another kind: God taught me a hard lesson about people who do not want to be healed and made whole. An evil spirit manifested when one woman was prayed for. The prayer session was powerful, but so was this woman's rejection of the Holy Spirit. Her demons just hissed and howled at us.

Diane, who led the deliverance prayer session, had us break it off because of the degree of this woman's rejection. My heart sank; I was literally on the verge of tears. Why didn't she take the hand up to freedom that was being offered to her? Her reaction did not look like the deliverances I had seen in the Bible; there people were healed and made whole.

Yet, God chose to reveal this form of rejection of His Spirit on my very first night in training. It was an emotional experience for me as we shut down the deliverance prayer and walked off.

A few blocks away, we encountered an old woman. As she walked boldly toward us, we asked if we could pray for her. The woman responded, "Yes, please pray that I find a place to live."

I couldn't help noticing that the woman was dressed exactly like my grandmother dressed for church. The woman's clothes were dated; they were 1970s, old church-lady style. The woman was wearing a leopard-skin-looking hat like my grandmother always wore. She had the same green felt coat and white gloves that my grandmother always wore to church.

As Diane held this woman's hands and started to pray, the woman looked over and made direct eye contact with me. She let go of Diane's hands and reached out for me to take her hand. As I did, I got that National Cathedral angel feeling all over again. The woman didn't speak to me. She squeezed my hand and I got this prophetic message: "Everything is going to be OK. We (angels) are here on the streets tonight, too."

Talk about an emotional roller coaster! I was so touched I thought I would cry for joy.

Over the course of nine months (from November 2006 to July 2007) many incredible, supernatural things happened to me. At the end of this nine-month training period, I was released by the Holy Spirit to enter deliverance ministry.

July 2007 was also when I finally shared with my father what was happening in my life. When I told him the story of the angel who was dressed like his deceased mother (she went on to glory in the 1980s), the testimony shook him in a good, Holy Spirit way.

M16 Ministries

In December 2006, I had no clue what a deliverance ministry was. My early Catholic upbringing surfaced and led me to research the rites of exorcism. I thought only the Catholic Church dealt with demons. Having been raised in the Catholic Church, I assumed I had citizenship in it, I guess the way Paul had Roman citizenship.

My attempts to speak with Catholic exorcists and have them share with me what they knew failed. I received no replies from anyone in the Catholic Church. My efforts were heartfelt, but fruitless.

There is a country song, "Get Right With the Man", by Van Zant, that says, "If you wanna make God laugh, tell Him your plans." I know God got a good laugh out of these early efforts to connect with exorcists. When I was nearly exhausted and had frustrated myself by looking for non-existent answers, the Holy Spirit sent me on His path and showed me what I needed to do.

My pursuit of exorcism wasn't totally silly. I was almost on the right track. God was speaking to me and I was trying to process what I was hearing. Through the Holy Spirit's guidance I was set on the right track. I know now that my calling from the very beginning was to boldly engage the enemy. The enemy knew this and tried to derail me. The enemy failed.

When we named M16 Ministries, Lisa and I were looking for a military name. That's what we do; we go into the enemy's camp, share the Gospel, heal the sick, and cast out demons. When I said our mission statement out loud, I said, "Wait! That is Mark 16!" M16 is both our name and our mission.

Now I go in with great concern and enthusiasm to help those who feel they have nowhere to turn in their battles with the forces of darkness. If it is God's will, I will walk into a house presumed haunted by a malicious spirit and I will order it to leave. We have also assisted people with supernatural sleep disorders, including nightmares, levitations, and episodes of being touched or dragged out of bed. Each of these fights has opened the door for us to share the Gospel and the glory of God.

The M16 battle cry is "Make the impossible bow down to the name of Jesus!" My favorite cases are the ones in which it is clear to all that only God can provide the solution. I hate the enemy because I know what he and his minions do to people. Yet, he is not allowed to do as he pleases. Things may get a little ugly, but we are citizens of Heaven. We have dominion in this world through our inheritance in the Lord Jesus Christ.

Each and every one of us has been given authority over sickness, death, and the demonic through our Lord, Jesus Christ. The first Adam lost our dominion, and the second Adam restored it. That dominion, that *authority*, is back in our hands.

I have dominion. You have dominion. It was given to us to be used. Its purpose is to break the power of the enemy and increase the Kingdom rule and reign of Jesus Christ. You, too, have been called to minister where you live. Come on! Let's take back the streets from the enemy and let's win.

Let's make the impossible bow down to the name of Jesus!

Endnotes

1. Gabriele Amorth, An Exorcist: More Stories (San Francisco: Ignatius Press, 2002), 12, http://www.amazon.com/Exorcist-More-Stories-Gabriele-Amorth/dp/0898709172/ref=sr_1_1?ie=UTF8&s=books&qid=1279653047&sr=8-1#reader_0898709172 (accessed July 20, 2010).

2. "California Supreme Court Legalizes Gay Marriage," cbs5.com, May 16, 2008, http://cbs5.com/local/gay.marriage.ruling.2.724840.html (accessed July 20, 2010).

3. "About Padre Pio," The Padre Pio Foundation of America, http://www.padrepio.com/ (accessed July 20, 2010) and William M. Carrigan, "Padre Pio, Cappuchin Priest," padrepio.net, http://www.padrepio.net/ (accessed July 20, 2010).

CHAPTER 2

IN THE BEGINNING WAS JESUS

*For our struggle is not against flesh and blood, but
against the rulers, against the authorities, against the
powers of this dark world and against the spiritual
forces of evil in the heavenly realms* (Ephesians 6:12).

To accomplish the expansion of the Kingdom of God, to
reach the lost, to minister deliverance to the captives, we
must understand the context in which spiritual warfare is
waged—and has been waged over the millennia. It is imperative
that we understand the spiritual entities involved and the spiritual principles governing the battle.

To understand this spiritual war, we have to look at Jesus
and His creation, both inside and outside of time. We must also
become aware of the two distinct warring kingdoms and their
biblical roles. What we are talking about is history itself—that is,
His story.

Two thousand years ago, Jesus walked the earth as the incarnate God! Jesus is the central figure in a violent, spiritual war
that has a beginning and a future ending. Mankind has an active
role in this war. Whether by choice or omission, every human
being takes sides in it.

Jesus' role, both in warfare and in history, transcends time. So many Christians think of Jesus as the baby in the manger or the suffering servant hanging on the cross. Yet, Jesus is so much more. He is also the King of kings, the Prince of Peace, the Bridegroom of the Church, and more.

The enemy in this war is satan and his legion of fallen angels, called *demons.* Satan and his kingdom were defeated through the finished work of Christ (see Col. 2:15). Still, they battle against the Kingdom of God and His people.

To reveal the origin of this war we will now look at a series of biblical events that extend before and beyond our notion of the universe and even time itself. The Bible doesn't explicitly provide a concise timeline of what occurred. Yet, through His prophets, God has revealed in various books of the Bible events that provide understanding of the fall of satan and the Fall of Man.

In...the Beginning

Genesis, the first book of the Bible, gives us the foundations of the creation of the universe, the earth, the Garden of Eden, and mankind. Genesis records the beginning of time.

The first verse in Genesis is very familiar; nearly everyone has heard it: *"In the beginning God created the heavens and the earth"* (Gen. 1:1). You might remember that several verses of Genesis 1 were read by the orbiting Apollo 8 astronauts during a Christmas Eve, 1968 broadcast from space.[1]

We know from the Book of Genesis that God exists outside of creation and the universe. God gives glimpses, through the Scripture's record of the prophets and Jesus, of what happened outside of time before the creation. The apostle John opens his Gospel this way:

In the beginning was the Word, and the Word was with God, and the Word was God. He was with God in the beginning. Through Him all things were made; without Him nothing was made that has been made. In Him was life, and that life was the light of men. The light shines in the darkness, but the darkness has not understood it (John 1:1-5).

Here we have a scriptural reference to a beginning that apparently pre-dates the *beginning* mentioned in Genesis chapter 1. John's Gospel gives us a peek at the *absolute beginning.*

So, what is the Word mentioned in John 1? The Word is the revelation of God. John 1:14 tells us that the *"Word became flesh."* When John speaks of the Word incarnate (made flesh), he is talking about Jesus Christ. In the beginning was Jesus. There were no angels, no universe, no time.

Keep in mind that man thinks in linear terms. For us, time has a beginning and an end. Yet, God does not think in this manner. He does not have a beginning; there is not a date on which He was created. Before the universe was, God already was; long after the universe ends, God will still exist.

What we seek is an absolute beginning of creation. But even the scope of creation as we know it exists outside of time, if we consider the angels' creation.

However, we can't define a beginning for the Holy Trinity since He is eternal. In his Gospel, John uses a poetic style of writing to express Jesus' role as part of the Holy Trinity. The Trinity is the Father; the Son, Jesus; and the Holy Spirit; they exist outside the scope of the creation of the angelic hosts and outside the creation of the universe. In the *absolute beginning...*was God.

God Creates the Angels

Before the earth and universe were created, God created spiritual beings called *angels.* They are created beings under the authority of Jesus. An interesting revelation of their point of origin can be found in the Book of Job:

Where were you when I laid the earth's foundation? Tell Me, if you understand. Who marked off its dimensions? Surely you know! Who stretched a measuring line across it? On

> *what were its footings set, or who laid its cornerstone—while the morning stars sang together and all the angels shouted for joy?* (Job 38:4-7)

Angels were present and shouted for joy when God laid the foundations of the earth. The angels were created to serve (minister) through many different tasks: worship, revelation, guidance, and protection, to name a few. We know God created the seraphim; cherubim; archangels; and some very interesting-looking angels, the living creatures, from Ezekiel 1 and Revelation 4.

In creating the heavenly hosts, we know God was setting the foundation for the creation of man. The prophet Isaiah describes seraphim as angels that proclaim the glory of God. Isaiah 6:2 describes the seraphim as six-winged angels flying above the throne of God. The duty of the seraphim is to continually glorify God (see Isa. 6:3).

Another class of angel, the *cherubim*, appears in both the Old and New Testament. The cherubim take their position beside the throne of God (see Ps. 99:1; Isa. 37:16). The duty of the cherubim is to protect the glory of God (see Heb. 9:5). The cherubim are the angels represented on the top of the Ark of the Covenant (see Exod. 37:7-9). After the Fall of Man, the cherubim guarded the Tree of Life in The Garden of Eden (see Gen. 3:24). The Bible describes cherubim as having hands, feet, wings, and many eyes. It is possible the living creatures in John's Book of Revelation are a form of cherubim. The Bible tells us lucifer was the anointed cherubim (see Ezek. 28:14).

The archangel seems to be the highest position an angel can hold. The archangel is God's messenger and enforcer of judgments. There appears to be only one angel specifically identified as an archangel, and that is Michael, from Daniel 10:13.

> *But the prince of the Persian kingdom resisted me twenty-one days. Then Michael, one of the chief princes, came to help me, because I was detained there with the king of Persia* (Daniel 10:13).

The Book of Jude identifies Michael as an archangel.

But even the archangel Michael, when he was disputing with the devil about the body of Moses, did not dare to bring a slanderous accusation against him, but said, "The Lord rebuke you!" (Jude 1:9)

It is speculated that lucifer was an archangel before he was cast out of Heaven. There is also speculation that Gabriel, the messenger angel sent to Mary was an archangel.

The angel answered, "I am Gabriel. I stand in the presence of God, and I have been sent to speak to you and to tell you this good news" (Luke 1:19).

No scriptural reference clearly identifies Gabriel or lucifer as holding the angelic title of archangel. Another archangel, Raphael, is mentioned several times in the Roman Catholic canonical book of Tobit[2] (also known as *Tobias*, which, in the Protestant tradition is considered an apocryphal book). Raphael is often identified in Catholic tradition as the angel who stirs the waters at the pool of Bethesda, in John 5:4 (KJV). Scripture itself does not make any reference to a specific angel.

For an angel went down at a certain season into the pool, and troubled the water: whosoever then first after the troubling of the water stepped in was made whole of whatsoever disease he had (John 5:4).

There are also references to Raphael (or *Rufael*) in another apocryphal volume, the book of Enoch (quoted in Jude 14). Four archangels are most identified in the book of Enoch: Michael, Gabriel, Uriel and Raphael.[3] I don't want to venture into pure speculation on this point of who is and who isn't ranked an archangel. Nor will I reference the books of Tobit and Enoch any further, because they lie outside the Bible canon. I merely present them because their names surface when researching archangels.

Angels have multiple duties that expand beyond the scope of our small list here and even beyond our wildest comprehension. I will leave you with these generalities as we move on to explore the Kingdom of God.

The Kingdom and Domain

God created the universe and reigns over it. The apostle John's Book of Revelation, chapter 4, gives us a glimpse into God's throne room. John tells about the four living creatures (angels) in the throne room who give glory, honor, and thanks to the one who sits on the throne. God set up Heaven to rule His Kingdom, His realm and domain.

We see that there is a hierarchy in this Kingdom. Colossians 1:16 tells us:

> *For by Him all things were created: things in heaven and on earth, visible and invisible, whether thrones or powers or rulers or authorities; all things were created by Him and for Him.*

This gives us some perspective of the powers and authorities assigned to angels. Two angels of authority stand out in the Scriptures: Michael, the archangel, and lucifer, for whom the title *archangel* is speculative. We know that Michael eventually casts lucifer and his fallen angels out of Heaven (See Revelation 12:7-9). As already mentioned, the archangel appears to be the highest angelic rank.

In Joshua 5:14, the commander of the Lord's army first appears to Joshua. The Lord's army is made up of angels; however, the commander of the Lord's army is not an angel. Joshua bows face down to him, clearly recognizing that He is God. In Paul's letter to the Philippians, we see this amazing proclamation:

> *...that at the name of Jesus every knee should bow, in heaven and on earth and under the earth, and every tongue confess that Jesus Christ is Lord, to the glory of God the Father* (Philippians 2:10-11).

Heaven is clearly set up to govern or reign. It is the picture of perfection in a ruling kingdom. It includes the throne of God as well as God's government and hierarchy of angels. From the verses in Philippians we also see that the angels cast out of Heaven must *still* bow down to Jesus. Despite the angelic rebellion, hierarchy and ranks remain. All must bow to the name of Jesus!

Lucifer, the Anointed Cherub

As we continue to explore the historical context of the spiritual warfare in which we are engaged, the fallen angel lucifer commands our attention in more detail.

The prophet Ezekiel reveals important information about lucifer. In fact, Ezekiel 28:11-14 gives more information about this angel than any other Bible passage. Lucifer was perfect in beauty and given more wisdom than any other created being (see KJV). The Scripture says that this angel walked in Eden in his splendor.

> *You were in Eden, the garden of God; every precious stone adorned you: ruby, topaz and emerald, chrysolite, onyx and jasper, sapphire, turquoise and beryl. Your settings and mountings were made of gold; on the day you were created they were prepared* (Ezekiel 28:13).

God covered him in gold and jewels. He was the one and only anointed cherubim:

> *You were anointed as a guardian cherub, for so I ordained you. You were on the holy mount of God; you walked among the fiery stones* (Ezekiel 28:14).

As a cherub he guarded the glory of the throne of God. This is the only evidence given in the Bible of an angel having an *anointing*. This means lucifer was chosen by God with divine favor. The speculation that lucifer was an archangel may have its basis in Jude 1, because the Bible never expressly calls lucifer an archangel. If he was an archangel, however, he may have held two key positions in Heaven.

In any case, lucifer represented absolute perfection in God's creation:

> *Thou hast been in Eden the garden of God; every precious stone was thy covering, the sardius, topaz, and the diamond, the beryl, the onyx, and the jasper, the sapphire, the emerald, and the carbuncle, and gold: the workmanship of thy tabrets and of*

thy pipes was prepared in thee in the day that thou wast created (Ezekiel 28:13 KJV).

Most of the information regarding lucifer and his fall come from Isaiah 14 and Ezekiel 28. In other books of the Bible, lucifer is referred to by his more common names: satan, the serpent, the deceiver, the prince of the earth, and others.

The Rebellion of Lucifer and the War of the Angels

The job of lucifer in the Kingdom of God was to be the protector of the glory of God (see Ezek. 28:14). God created His angels to have free will. Instead of protecting the glory of God, lucifer became jealous of God. Lucifer became overly proud because of his beauty and coveted the throne of God for himself. Lucifer chose to rebel and attempted to seize creation.

The prophet Isaiah tells us about the deadly "I wills" that caused lucifer to sin:

> *You said in your heart, "I will ascend to heaven; I will raise my throne above the stars of God; I will sit enthroned on the mount of assembly, on the utmost heights of the sacred mountain. I will ascend above the tops of the clouds; I will make myself like the Most High"* (Isaiah 14:13-14, emphasis added).

Lucifer set in motion a scheme to take the throne of God for himself. He no longer wanted to glorify God, but desired to rule over creation in God's place. Ezekiel tells us that lucifer was filled with violence and sinned. His wisdom was corrupted by his rage and pride.

No exact details of the rebellion are given, except for this explanation given in the Book of Revelation, which is referring to a pre-creation war in heaven:

> *And there was war in heaven. Michael and his angels fought against the dragon, and the dragon and his angels fought back. But he was not strong enough, and they lost their place in heaven. The great dragon was hurled down—that ancient serpent called the devil, or Satan, who leads the whole world*

astray. He was hurled to the earth, and his angels with him (Revelation 12:7-9).

The number of angels participating in the rebellion was equal to one-third of the ranks, Again the revelation is referencing a pre-creation war and not End Times.

His tail swept a third of the stars out of the sky and flung them to the earth (Revelation 12:4).

The rebelling angels exercised their free will and they chose to rebel against God. Their transgression was to willfully revolt against God. Their sentence: to be driven out of Heaven.

Jesus tells us in Luke 10:18 that He *"...saw Satan fall like lightning from heaven."*

Satan's uprising failed and the archangel Michael removed the rebelling spirits. When lucifer was banished, he was referred to as satan (the accuser), the dragon (Revelation), and the serpent. Satan was cast down to the earth (see Isa. 14:12). But he awaits judgment to burn in hell. Some of his demons are in the gloomy dungeons of hell, awaiting judgment (see 2 Pet. 2:4). Some are roaming the earth. We know satan is the prince of the earth and is currently free to roam it. But there is a lake of fire prepared for him, his demonic army, and wicked human souls:

Then He will say to those on His left, "Depart from Me, you who are cursed, into the eternal fire prepared for the devil and his angels" (Matthew 25:41).

And they will go out and look upon the dead bodies of those who rebelled against Me; their worm will not die, nor will their fire be quenched, and they will be loathsome to all mankind (Isaiah 66:24).

The sentence pronounced upon those rebellious angels is an irrevocable sentence. There is no salvation plan for them. They will burn for eternity once the wicked (non-repenting) men and angels are sentenced for eternity.

Creation of Adam and Eve

The angels were present when God created the earth (see Job 38:7). Over a period of six days God created the heavens and the earth. I am not going to enter a debate here as to whether these are God-days or actual earth days. God knows! However, somewhere in time from when the earth was created to before the creation of man, the rebellion of lucifer occurred. Remember that according to Ezekiel 28:12-13,

> *You were the model of perfection, full of wisdom and perfect in beauty. You were in Eden, the garden of God....*

Lucifer, not satan, walked in The Garden of Eden even before the creation of man. To put this into perspective, lucifer walked in the Garden prior to the angelic rebellion. When he was thrown out of heaven he became satan. It is satan who tempts Adam and Eve in the Garden of Eden.

On the sixth day of the creation, God created the man, Adam, and the woman, Eve, in His own image (see Gen. 1:27). The angels were not created in God's image. It is conceivable that we are created in His image because we have a body, soul, and spirit. This Trinity-like composition is often seen as one in which the body represents the incarnate Jesus, the soul represents the Father, and the immortal spirit represents the Holy Spirit. Each of us is a created spirit being who also possesses a body and a soul.

In the creation, God did something incredible: He gave mankind dominion to rule over the earth. Mankind, like the angels, was granted a free will. With that free will came the moral responsibility to obey God. When Adam was placed in The Garden, God commanded him not to eat from the Tree of the Knowledge of Good and Evil (see Gen. 2:17).

Two specific trees, each with spiritual attributes, are identified in Genesis 2:9: the Tree of Life and the Tree of the Knowledge of Good and Evil. Man was permitted to eat from the Tree of Life, but was forbidden to eat from the Tree of Knowledge of Good and Evil (see Gen. 2:16-17).

As long as Adam and Eve obeyed God, they were free to walk in The Garden in the presence of their Creator. We know that Adam and Eve were created innocent and were not ashamed of their nakedness. The Book of Genesis tells us that God walked in the cool part of the day to seek out His children, Adam and Eve (see Gen. 3:8).

God loves His children and created the concept of the family. He would also be the role model of fatherhood—the ever-present loving Father.

The Fall

In Genesis 3:1-5, we find Eve and the serpent (lucifer) talking in The Garden. Notice the transition from lucifer the anointed cherub walking in The Garden of Eden in Ezekiel 28:13 to the serpent (satan) in Genesis 3. Having been cast out of Heaven, satan had power, but no authority at this point.

He was not a talking snake sticking its head out of the Tree of Knowledge of Good and Evil. Nor was he the medieval red devil with horns and hooves. This is satan, formerly lucifer, in all his created splendor. He was the perfection of beauty. Eve was probably mesmerized as he spoke with her, captivated by his beautiful smile. He was a serpent because he was crafty in his ways. He smiled at her on the outside; yet inside he absolutely hated her.

Lucifer hated God. He hated how God spent so much time with Adam and Eve. He hated the fact that God created the universe for Adam and Eve. All this was supposed to be his—satan's. He was supposed to rule the universe, but his rebellion failed. God gave man what satan thought was rightfully his.

Crafty satan had a plan for Adam and Eve. He knew first-hand the consequences of rebellion and disobedience to God. The punishment is spiritual death; he and his army of demons are doomed for all eternity. Satan's plan in The Garden was to make sure Adam and Eve would be imprisoned with him for all eternity.

Eve fell for satan's convincing words:

"You will not surely die," the serpent said to the woman. "For God knows that when you eat of …[the forbidden tree] your eyes will be opened, and you will be like God, knowing good and evil" (Genesis 3:4-5).

See how satan appealed to Eve; he convinced her of the appeal of the fruit and the benefit to be gained from it. She saw that *"…the fruit of the tree was good for food and pleasing to the eye, and also desirable for gaining wisdom…"* (Gen. 3:6). Satan convinced her that God had deceived her about the tree. He told her God didn't want her to possess the same level of wisdom He has. Satan, the father of lies (see John 8:44), probably convinced her that he had eaten from the tree to gain his superior wisdom.

Wasn't this the same sin that led to satan's disastrous procla-mation: *"…I will make myself like the Most high"* (Isa. 14:14)? No mat-ter what satan's selling point was, Eve should never have listened to him. The devil didn't make her do it. She invited the devil's lies and acted of her own accord. God commanded Adam and Eve not to eat from that tree, yet she stubbornly opposed the will of God. Genesis 3:6 states that Adam was right there with her. He didn't try to stop her.

Then Adam ate the fruit (see Gen. 3:6). Their innocence was now gone, and the two stood in front of each other, naked and ashamed.

One can only assume that satan was exuberant over the suc-cess of his scheme. How easy it was to execute! Now, he would be known for all eternity as the one who destroyed God's plans for creation.

Satan could rejoice at his evil deed because he had abso-lute hatred for everything in creation and even for the Creator Himself. Those beings created in God's own image were now doomed to spend eternity in the pit. They became subject to the same spiritual death that awaited him—an eternity separated from God's presence. In this act of defiance, satan usurped the authority given by God to Adam. He deceived mankind into surrendering their dominion to him.

Check and mate.

Next, we see God walking through The Garden looking for Adam and Eve (see Gen. 3:8-9). God knew what had happened. Adam and Eve hid behind a tree, ashamed of their nakedness. What happened when God questioned them? They both laid blame elsewhere and lied like little kids (see Gen. 3:12-13).

I wonder what would have happened if they had owned the situation and asked for forgiveness? Instead, Adam blamed God the Father for creating a beautiful woman who caused him to sin. Eve blamed satan, in essence saying, "The devil made me do it!"

When Adam and Eve chose to disobey, they willfully chose to sin. In doing so, they chose to live under a curse of satan. By disobeying God, they surrendered their authority and gave it to satan. Adam and Eve took a chance and bet that they would be more like God if they ate the apple. What they got instead was the curse of sickness, death, and disease—not to mention the curse of eternal damnation. They surrendered their God-given dominion in exchange for satan's Ponzi scheme. Like others who fall for illicit schemes, they lost everything!

What unfolds next in Genesis 3 exceeds even the supernatural wisdom of satan.

Banished From The Garden

God is about to banish Adam and Eve from The Garden of Eden. Once more, we see the focus placed on the Tree of Life and the Tree of the Knowledge of Good and Evil:

And the LORD God said, "The man has now become like one of us, knowing good and evil. He must not be allowed to reach out his hand and take also from the tree of life and eat, and live forever." So the LORD God banished him from the Garden of Eden to work the ground from which he had been taken (Genesis 3:22-23).

God said that man must not be able to partake of the Tree of Life. Why? Perhaps eating from the Tree of Life would keep man in his sinful state forever. So God took measures to prevent access to it:

After He drove the man out, He placed on the east side of the Garden of Eden cherubim and a flaming sword flashing back and forth to guard the way to the tree of life (Genesis 3:24).

The Tree of Life appears again in Revelation 22:2, where the tree is said to have properties that would bring healing to the nations. Revelation 22:19 warns against taking words away from the Revelation. We are told that doing so will revoke our share in the Tree of Life.

Man Is Offered Salvation

There's no telling at this point how mad God was with satan. This was the second major wicked event carried out by the anointed cherub.

God would not let satan's efforts go unchallenged. The Book of Genesis tells us that God came into The Garden of Eden to seek out Adam and Eve. God always seeks man, because He loves people. We see evidence of this in the Gospels and here in Genesis. God cares deeply.

So can His heart be bruised when man falters? Can He feel sorrow? I think He did in this awful moment when satan's wicked plan went into motion.

Yet, God had a plan. He would set things straight, dish out consequences for Adam and Eve, and put His creation back on track. In Genesis 3:15, God announced His plan in what amounts to the first prophecy found in the Bible:

And I will put enmity between you and the woman, and between your offspring and hers; He will crush your head, and you will strike His heel (Genesis 3:15).

The word *enmity* is not often used in contemporary language. *Enmity* involves the kind of "hatred or ill will,"[4] that implies future repercussions. In essence, God told the deceiver, "I will show you My wrath by coming into this world through the line of a woman."

Who is this woman? She is Mary, the mother of Jesus. The line of Mary is important because in Old Testament history, God promised that the Savior would be a descendant of King David (see Isa. 11:10). In Jeremiah 22:30, however, God cursed Jehoiachin, the last reigning king from the line of Solomon (David's son). Under this curse, no more kings would be in Jesus' family tree.

Meanwhile, Jesus' earthly father, Joseph, descended from Solomon's line. For the prophecy to hold, Joseph's seed could not be involved in the birth of Jesus. Well, God's promise regarding the Savior who would be a son of King David stood. We see in Luke 1:32 that Mary appears to be a direct descendant of David. God kept His promise!

In Luke 1:35, the Holy Spirit comes to Mary to fulfill the prophecy foretold in Genesis 3:15, a prophecy clearly referring to Mary and her son, Jesus.

It is Jesus who then comes to deal with satan firsthand. It is Jesus who crushes satan's head at the cross. It is Jesus who is sent to earth from Heaven by the Father, to be our sacrifice. It is the Holy Spirit who led Jesus into the desert to face all the temptations satan could throw at Him. Satan even tried to barter with Jesus, offering Him dominion over the earth, if Jesus would bow to him. This is Isaiah 14:14 all over again: *"...I will make myself like the Most High."*

Imagine saying, "God, you will bow down to me"! Satan wanted the Creator to bow down to a created being. It's no wonder the deceiver would make such a ludicrous offer; Scripture tells us that satan's wisdom was corrupted by his own vanity (see Isa. 14:13-14).

Jesus could have easily destroyed satan in the desert or cast him into hell. But Jesus was going for the jugular. He was going to endure the painful prophecy for all of mankind and take away the curse satan handed us in Eden. Not only did Jesus endure torture and then crucifixion; but He also confronted satan in hell, face to face (see Col. 2:15).

Through the miracle work on the cross, Jesus restored our dominion, crushed the angelic army of darkness (snakes and scorpions), and gave us authority over them:

> *He replied, "I saw Satan fall like lightning from heaven. I have given you authority to trample on snakes and scorpions and to overcome all the power of the enemy; nothing will harm you"* (Luke 10:18-19).

Not only did we get dominion and authority, but we were given the choice to spend eternity in Heaven with God. All we have to do is ask Jesus for it (see Rom. 10:9-10,13).

Seek Ye First

You just read the Christmas and Easter stories and a brief history of the universe all rolled into one. (Not many Christmas pageants start at the beginning of pre-history.)

Here is why this background is so important: we need, first of all, to understand why Jesus came to earth; then we must recognize our authority in Him. In spiritual warfare, it is God who battles for us; therefore, it is imperative to know that Jesus is the King of kings and the Creator of all that is.

There is no moral plurality in religion. Buddha cannot make the claims Jesus did. Buddha won't give you eternal life. Instead, Buddha will bring you to the lake of fire. There are no past lives. There is no psychic energy and there are no levels to be attained.

These are the lies of satan. There is only one way to salvation: Jesus Christ.

Seek Jesus and His Word—not the miracles, signs, and wonders. If you seek Him and share His Gospel, the miracles, signs, and wonders will follow.

Endnotes

1. Dr. David R. Williams, "The Apollo 8 Christmas Eve Broadcast," NASA, http://nssdc.gsfc.nasa.gov/planetary/lunar/apollo8_xmas.html (accessed July 21, 2010).

2. *Douay-Rheims Bible,* Tobias 3:25; 6:16; 8:3; 9:6; 11:4; 11:7; 12:15; DRBO.org, http://drbo.org/index.htm (accessed July 21, 2010).

3. Rev. George H. Schodde, PhD, *The Book of Enoch: Translated From the Ethiopic With Introduction and Notes,* (Andover: Warren F. Draper, 1882), http://www.hermetics.org/pdf/enoch.pdf (accessed July 19, 2010).

4. Merriam-Webster Online Dictionary, 2010, Merriam-Webster Online, s.v. "enmity," <http://www.merriam-webster.com/dictionary/enmity> (accessed July 26, 2010).

CHAPTER 3

AUTHORITY IN CHRIST

No temptation has seized you except what is common to man.
And God is faithful; He will not let you be tempted beyond
what you can bear. But when you are tempted, He will also
provide a way out so that you can stand up under it
(1 Corinthians 10:13).

Unfortunately, one of the most grossly misunderstood and, thus, misquoted Scriptures dealing with spiritual attacks upon the believer is First Corinthians 10:13, quoted above.

How is it misunderstood? Here is an example of what members of M16 Ministries commonly hear: "I thought God wouldn't give me anything more than I could handle. I definitely can't handle this!"

The fact of the matter is that God will never push you beyond what you can handle—but satan will. Scripture tells us that satan is like a roaring lion who wants to kill us (see 1 Pet. 5:8).

When Christians are under attack, they seldom refer to the second part of the Scripture in First Corinthians 10:13: *"...He will also provide a way out so that you can stand up under it."*

What way out did God provide? Why, it's our authority over the powers of darkness!

When those undergoing spiritual attacks need assistance from M16, we generally do two things: The first is to share who we are in Jesus. It doesn't matter whether the people needing help are unbelievers or 20-year-strong Christians. Either way, we let them know that God is going to do something about their situation. We remind them that God is bigger than any problem satan can manifest.

The second thing we do is to remind those who have accepted Jesus into their lives that they have supernatural authority over every spiritual attack.

Ready or Not?

One interesting prayer session Lisa and I were involved in occurred while ministering to a middle-aged woman named Elaine, a very successful career woman who was living with the dark secret of demonic oppression. The oppression was severe enough that worship music would aggravate the spirits and cause them to manifest and speak.

Ironically, we first met Elaine at a previous prayer meeting. She came up and asked for prayer for God to equip her in deliverance. I assumed at the time that Elaine wanted equipping in order to minister to others. Looking back at that first prayer session with Elaine, I remember that she kept interrupting us (in a friendly manner) as we prayed. What I didn't know was that she was living in torment. A religious spirit had convinced her that she could deliver herself from tormenting demons.

When Lisa and I pray for people, we often "read their mail"; in other words, we often receive words of knowledge relating to their situations. We don't do this to pry into people's lives; we ask the Holy Spirit to give us words of knowledge or prophetic words that will build them up. In Elaine's case, a demon was purposely interrupting us as we prayed. Something was clearly wrong.

I told Elaine that Lisa and I were involved with several prophetic and deliverance ministries, including our own M16. We believe in working in the gifts as much as possible, so we work with a lot of ministries. I told Elaine about Gary Paltridge's Kingdom of Grace ministry which was meeting on the following night. I suggested that it would be a great place for people who wanted to learn how to minister in deliverance.

The Maranatha meetings of the Kingdom of Grace ministry are powerful times of deliverance. We have seen oppressed people literally bolt out of the meetings because the demons couldn't stand to be in the presence of the Holy Spirit.

On the particular evening when Elaine came to Maranatha, I remember receiving discernment during the worship music. It came in the form of the churning stomach I get when demons get ruffled. I then noticed that Elaine was struggling. She was trying to keep her demons on a leash while they were clawing to get out of that place.

Elaine endured the worship, but the demons had taken all they could take. When it came time for prayer, they manifested. We ended up having to take Elaine into a private prayer room so others could receive their prayer. Lisa, myself, and two other prayer team members started deliverance prayer with Elaine. One demon that had manifested challenged us and said, "I know who Jesus is, but who are you?"

A woman on our prayer team responded, "We're in the family [of Christ]!"

The demon hissed at that response. This demon had every intention of becoming violent with us. Through operating in the prophetic, the Holy Spirit revealed to me that the spirit now speaking to us was a spirit of murder. The Holy Spirit also revealed that Elaine's father had been murdered; this was a generational demon.

The evil spirit knew it was trapped in a room with people who were filled with the Holy Spirit and knew their inheritance and *authority* in Jesus Christ. That's a bad spot for a demon to be in!

The deliverance session for Elaine was long. Late into the evening, at nearly 11 o'clock, we started shutting it down. We battle demons on our own terms and not on theirs. We had made progress with Elaine and thought she would return for a private prayer session. Instead, she was embarrassed about her lifelong secret being exposed and never returned to be completely set free.

Religious spirits can affect people's thinking. The one oppressing Elaine convinced her that only she could deliver herself. The demons that had been tormenting her were trapped and bound at this prayer session; she could have been set free. However, Elaine wasn't ready to be set free. We didn't push her into it.

Since that night, I have met up with Elaine at church conferences on two separate occasions. I never discuss the deliverance with her. She knows where to come when she's ready to be set free.

If you know your authority in Christ, demons will literally run through walls to get away from you. Elaine's demons did not want to be in the same room with us because they, too, recognized our authority.

Nevertheless, if you submit to fear, you will surrender your authority back to satan. I cannot emphasize this enough.

The Promise of Inheritance

Romans 8:17 describes our position in the family of Christ:

If we are children, then we are heirs—heirs of God and co-heirs with Christ, if indeed we share in His sufferings in order that we may also share in His glory.

Many people misinterpret this verse and say that we should co-suffer with Jesus. This is absurd. For one thing, it is satan who brings suffering, sickness, and disease. Secondly, it is Jesus who came to destroy the works of the devil.

If your plan is to "co-suffer" with Jesus, then satan has sold you a great big lie. Jesus wants you healed. What Paul's letter to the Romans really says is this: if we are led by the Spirit of God (the Holy Spirit) and we confess that Jesus died to take away our sins, then we are co-heirs with Christ. Not co-sufferers. It was Jesus alone who suffered for our transgressions through his torture and crucifixion. When Jesus said, "It is finished," in John 19:28, He bowed His head and gave up His spirit. It was finished! No more suffering for transgressions. It's all grace and mercy now. Our inheritance gives us sonship. That means that we are princes and princesses in His Kingdom. With these Kingdom titles come Kingdom authority.

> because those who are led by the Spirit of God are sons of God. For you did not receive a spirit that makes you a slave again to fear, but you received the Spirit of sonship. And by Him we cry, "Abba, Father." The Spirit Himself testifies with our spirit that we are God's children. Now if we are children, then we are heirs—heirs of God and co-heirs with Christ, if indeed we share in His sufferings in order that we may also share in His glory (Romans 8:14-17).

Whenever we work with people who are being spiritually attacked in their sleep (through constant nightmares, nightmares that manifest into physical attacks, or manifestations of shadows), we have them read Romans 8 aloud. We know from experience that evil spirits cannot stand that chapter, especially when the Word of God emboldens the person being attacked. Deliverance ministers can come to your house and drive out spirits night after night; but what drives a tormenting spirit away and keeps it away is when the people being attacked know their Kingdom authority in Christ.

You will notice a pattern with our approach to driving out dark spirits. First, we share the Gospel with the person who is under attack. There is only one road to salvation and freedom, and that is through Jesus Christ. In the San Francisco Bay Area and now many parts of our country, we have divine pluralism: people believe there are many ways to salvation. Some churches in the Bay Area honor all gods. This is a flat-out lie. There is only one God and one way to salvation—the Way is Jesus Christ!

When we go into people's houses we are polite and respectful. We inform the people who requested our help that we are going to call on the Creator of the universe, Jesus Christ, to help them. One hundred percent of the time the people are so distraught that they allow us to pray with them in this way. We share the Gospel and have never had anyone refuse to hear it. That is, unless a spirit manifests in them right away. That's a different story.

We present the Gospel with gentleness and respect. We don't attack the person's religion. We let the Holy Spirit handle the situation. He's a big God, and this is one of His children. When a spirit is forced out into the open by the presence of the Holy Spirit, it is already defeated. When victory comes, we ask the individual whether he or she would like to accept Jesus as Savior. After a victorious battle, and after witnessing the authority of the prayer team over the enemy, the person will usually accept the invitation. This is important because people need the infilling of the Holy Spirit to empower and strengthen them as they get back on their feet, spiritually and emotionally.

The next step in the people's spiritual recovery is teaching them about their own spiritual authority. We begin with Romans 8. People have called me up, excited about the fact that they are finally getting some sleep. The attacks begin to subside because they are spending quality time (while awake and tormented)— reading Romans 8 aloud.

Who are you in Christ? You are a son or daughter of the Father. You are a co-heir with Christ!

Dropping the Ball on Authority

Many churches don't teach the true power, authority, and heavenly citizenship we have as believers in Jesus Christ. I, for one, can attest to sitting in a pew for 20 years without truly understanding that I had the power to "pull" healings to earth from Heaven. Nor was I aware that I could inform demons of fear that they had no jurisdiction over my life and had to leave. They had no right to torment me!

Thankfully, there is a spiritual shift occurring in churches as I write this. Beni Johnson, the wife of senior Pastor Bill Johnson, is known for her incredible prophetic and intercessory gifts. She has a great saying: *Shift happens.* Spiritual shift is happening now. I see that more and more churches that once avoided or shunned healing and deliverance are now looking to bring this incredible ministry back into the Church.

It can be a rough ride for a church that makes this transition, mainly because the congregation gets stirred up. This is a godly thing; I have seen God clean up His people when He is invited in like this. Many people who attended church for years but were in bondage are suddenly set free. It is an incredible movement to witness or experience.

Often, we help people who were unable to find sufficient assistance in their own churches. A pastor might be asked to bless a house in which demonic activity is occurring. After the house is blessed, the activity subsides for a day or two; then it resumes. This is common; demon spirits don't like the blessing. The church members call their pastor for assistance again, but he offers little or no advice. He is unable to explain their authority over demons!

The pastor may not have had many encounters with the spirit realm or seen its power. In reading the Bible, it looks like demons leave at the snap of a finger. We see Jesus and Paul demonstrating to us the power of deliverance. Frankly, I have yet to see anyone healed by my shadow as happened with Peter in Acts 5:15. I would love to have that anointing one day, too.

From my battles in the spirit realm, I know that it can take hours and even several engagements in battle to make the enemy leave. Through experience you develop the discernment to know when the enemy has truly departed. Without this discernment, you can be tricked; the spirits pretend to have left when, in fact, they haven't. This is what some pastors and inexperienced warriors face during battle. They lack the discernment that is honed in actual battlefield experiences in the spiritual realm.

If you are a pastor, I strongly encourage you to teach your congregation about their authority in Christ. It may or may not surprise you to learn how many members of the church body are in bondage and torment. Give them some ammo to fight with!

In the many cases M16 Ministries has been involved in, the people being attacked have the spiritual will to fight, but no understanding of their authority and how to use it. Due in part to the popularity of ghost-hunting television shows, I have run into many do-it-yourself home exorcisms. People use printouts of prayers they have heard exorcists use; some purchase bogus exorcism prayers via the Internet. Yet they are not effective in driving out the demonic spirits. Why? The reason is this: unless you understand your spiritual authority, you are doing nothing more than having a shouting match with the demons.

You can read Scripture, as you should, to clear out the demonic, but without the working knowledge of authority that demons clearly recognize (and they *do* recognize it), the fight will go on and on. It's your Christ-given authority over demons that will force them to leave. Authority comes through studying Scripture, developing a strong relationship with the Father, understanding your identity in Christ, recognizing your power through Him, and praying for and expecting a miracle.

Stand on your faith when you pray!

Apostles and Authority

Webster's dictionary offers several definitions for the word *apostle*; let's take a look at two of them.

> ...One sent on a mission...**a**: one of an authoritative New Testament group sent out to preach the Gospel and made up especially of Christ's 12 original disciples and Paul **b**: the first prominent Christian missionary to a region or group

...A person who initiates a great moral reform or who first advocates an important belief or system ...an ardent supporter...adherent[1]

We are familiar with the first definition, which commonly refers to the 12 original disciples and Paul. Why were these men called apostles, as the New Testament clearly labels them?

The second definition was a common term used in Jesus' time when the Romans would conquer a land. Once the land became Roman territory, the people had to be brought under the system of the Roman empire. This was the job of the Roman apostle. The apostle was a Roman ambassador general charged with converting the culture.

Likewise, as Jesus brought people into His Father's Kingdom, He needed apostles to bring the people into God's system of living. This is why Jesus called the original 12 and Paul to be *apostles* of the Church.

Jesus assigned the original apostles to preach; He also gave them authority over demons, sickness, disease, and death (see Matt. 10:1; Mark 3:14-15; Mark 6:7-13; Mark 16:15-18; Luke 9:1). The apostles Matthew, Mark, and Luke made their assignments and authority perfectly clear in their respective Gospels.

These assignments did not end with the first 13 apostles. Jesus called for His people to preach the Gospel, heal the sick, cast out demons, and raise the dead. Here's how it works: We preach the Gospel and the Holy Spirit heals the sick of their physical, emotional, and spiritual ailments. We are also called to cast out demons and raise the dead. This is the commission Jesus gave us:

> He said to them, "Go into all the world and preach the good news to all creation. Whoever believes and is baptized will be saved, but whoever does not believe will be condemned. And these signs will accompany those who believe: In My name they will drive out demons; they will speak in new tongues; they will pick up snakes with their hands; and when they drink deadly

poison, it will not hurt them at all; they will place their hands on sick people, and they will get well" (Mark 16:15-18).

I believe our authority in Jesus is one of the most overlooked topics in our churches today. When Christians who are being spiritually attacked request our help, our first job is to equip them with an understanding of their God-given spiritual authority. Faith and authority are keys to victory in any spiritual battle against the forces of darkness.

Authority to Heal

My participation as a team leader with Night Strike ministry in the city of San Francisco has boosted my faith in the area of healing. Because of what I have witnessed on the streets, I *expect a miracle* when I pray! Team members who come out to pray for the homeless see skin diseases disappear (they heal the lepers). We have also seen terminal diseases go into remission through prayer.

A particular testimony exemplifying these experiences comes from a team in Texas that flies to San Francisco and participates in Night Strike at least once each year. One night, the Texas team prayed over a homeless woman who had HIV/AIDs. She was ill, filthy, and had been out on the streets for some time. She had no job and her diagnosis was terminal.

Kathy, a woman on the Texas prayer team, led the prayer of healing over this woman. Kathy reported that the woman was in tears; she didn't think anyone would care enough to pray for her. She was just one of many people who received prayer on the streets that night.

After a night of street ministry, the team flew back to Texas. The following year, they returned to San Francisco for another Night Strike ministry. During the day, they took buses so they could pray in different areas of the city. While standing at a bus stop, they saw a woman across the street dressed in professional clothes excitedly waving to get their attention. Kathy looked at the woman and sensed some vague familiarity about her. Still,

Kathy couldn't place the woman and assumed it was a case of mistaken identity.

The professionally dressed woman bolted across the street and greeted the team from Texas as they boarded their bus. She even boarded the bus with them.

The well-dressed woman said to Kathy, "Oh, my God! It is you! You don't recognize me, do you?"

Kathy replied, "No, we're from out of town. We're out here with our church from Texas."

The woman got even more excited. "It is you! You prayed for me last year, when I had AIDs. It went into full remission. You even prayed over me and told me I would get a job."

I have seen this happen numerous times. People we pray for get healed and, sometimes, we find out what happens afterward. Two particular gentlemen from the streets come to mind. One man's HIV is in remission; medically speaking, he should not be alive. Yet, he is walking the streets and in ministry! Another man that was prayed for was fully healed of HIV and is now a pastor!

The key is *authority*. When a church sends a team to minister on the streets with us, we always teach them *how* we pray. We pray with our authority from Heaven. We pray from Heaven down to earth. We pray with our inheritance in mind. We don't pray, "Oh dear God, please, please, help this person." This is groveling. That kind of healing prayer does not reflect who we are: we are sons and daughters of the Most High God!

We speak directly to the source of evil that is causing a cancer or any other infirmity. Infirmity is a demonic spirit and a harbinger of sickness. We confront such spirits on the streets by first asking those who need prayer if we can lay hands on them. Then we pray with our eyes open, because we don't want to miss the miracles. Our prayers start something like the prayer below; then we flow with the Holy Spirit as we pray for specific individual needs:

Cancer (sickness, depression, etc.), in the name of Jesus, I command you out of this body. I command order and restoration, in Jesus' name!

That is using our authority and inheritance from Heaven.

We have seen cysts and tumors vanish, hips healed, asthma and glaucoma healed. I have seen the Holy Spirit cut through the power of drugs and bring people to full attention so we could speak to them.

One warm September evening, I was leading a Night Strike team through the Tenderloin District. A nicely dressed woman approached us and asked us for money to ride the BART train back across the bay to her home in Oakland. Her name was Sheila and she was frantic about getting home to her kids who were unattended. I never give money to people on the streets, but on this night I allowed compassion to color my judgment. I slipped this woman the BART fare she needed to get home to her children.

Unfortunately, the road to hell is paved with good intentions. Not more than 15 minutes later, we saw Sheila struggling to lean against a wall in a building entryway. She used the BART fare money I had given her to get a drug fix. I was irritated at myself for being suckered into her lie.

I was angry at the devil. I walked up to her and prayed. I put my hand on her shoulder and prayed to bind her lying demons and demons of addiction. I guess some prayers can be prayed in anger if they are directed and worded properly. Sheila's dilated eyes started to focus on me as the Holy Spirit moved through her body.

Sheila's mind snapped out of the power of the drug, but her body was left in the torment. She looked down at her shaking hands and then at me. Through a word of knowledge, the Holy Spirit spoke through me. He corrected her for having left her two boys unattended. He revealed what her body really felt like when she got a fix.

She freaked out. Her mind was free of the effects of the drugs, but they were still ravaging her body. I never saw Sheila on the streets after that night. I don't know what became of her. I pray it was her wake-up moment. Since this incident I have never given money to anyone while ministering on the streets.

As I mentioned earlier, the Night Strike ministry has testimonies of ugly tumors disappearing and people being delivered. Mark Neitz, director of City Ministries, and the organizer of Night Strike outreaches, shared a powerful testimony with me. He explained that whenever he was on Market Street in San Francisco, he would see a haggard old woman with a golf-ball-sized tumor protruding from the side of her head.

Several times, Mark and his team tried to approach this woman in order to pray for her. She would curse them in a Slavic language; sometimes, she would become violent.

During one Friday Night Strike, Mark hit the streets with a new team member named Mike. Mike grabbed a cup of soup and darted over to the old woman. Mark was apprehensive about how the woman would react to Mike. There was favor however, and the old woman allowed Mike to serve her the cup of hot soup. Mark stood watching and gave a "thank You" to Jesus. Then he walked over and asked the woman if he could pray for her. She nodded in agreement.

Mark didn't know how long his window of opportunity would last, so he got right down to business. He spoke prophetic words over the woman and told her she would be restored to her right mind. Then Mark asked the woman if he could pray over her tumor. The woman accepted Mark's offer. He prayed for the growth to dissolve, in the name of Jesus. Nothing really happened at that moment. Nevertheless, there was a true miracle on the streets that night: this woman received prayer and salvation!

A year later, the Night Strike crew was in the U.N. Plaza of San Francisco preparing for another night of miracles, signs, and wonders. On this particular evening, a woman greeted Mark. Mark didn't recognize her. She reminded him that she was the woman who used to sit over on Market Street. She remembered that he had prayed for her tumor and she reminded Mark of the prophecy he gave about her regaining her right mind.

Then, with great excitement, the woman showed Mark how the tumor had completely dissolved, just as he had prayed it would. She told him that she was now ministering to people on the streets.

Our Night Strike testimonies of healings and deliverance go on and on. We have the authority to heal. What breaks my heart is that the Church doesn't really walk in her authority. In fact, one pastor with whom I have crossed paths once told his congregation, "When you pray for healing, *don't expect a miracle.*"

That's not the Gospel I know. Granted, I have fought some spiritual battles in praying for healing. Some people get healed in an instant. Some people get healed over time. Some people get healed after lots of praying. Some people don't receive their healing at all, and I don't know why. But each time I pray, I fully expect a healing, and I thank Jesus for it in advance.

Faith Beyond Reason

We Christians have brought too many rationales into our spirituality. If we can't see something, we assume that it doesn't exist. Reason has its place in the physical world; God gave us the ability to reason in this natural realm. However, reasoning has its boundaries. It is ineffective in the spiritual realm.

There are Web sites devoted to reasoning when it comes to matters of our Christian faith. I once had a conversation with a church counselor on a topic that concerned demonic oppression. This counselor printed out a topic on reasoning from one such Web site. The counselor told me there was no such thing as demonic oppression. Sadly, the case she was working on wore her down, because she tried to reason, for months, against an evil spirit attached to one of her clients.

It is the glory of God to conceal a matter; to search out a matter is the glory of kings (Proverbs 25:2).

What is Solomon referring to in this verse? What is to be searched out? What is being concealed?

Call to Me and I will answer you and tell you great and unsearchable things you do not know (Jeremiah 33:3).

Are unsearchable things intangible? If so, then they are beyond our physical senses. God tells us in Scripture after Scripture that our physical realm (our universe) exists within the context of the spiritual realm. The matters we seek must be pulled from the spiritual realm into our existence.

How is this done? Through prayer and faith.

Early in my walk, while I was being equipped for spiritual warfare, members of my church would warn that I was walking on dangerous ground. They would direct me to Acts 19:14-16—the account of the sons of Sceva. These men tried to operate in someone else's faith and got beat up by demons.

On the basis of that Scripture alone, this church body would scurry like cockroaches darting across the floor when the light was turned on. This is nothing more than a case of the Church not being taught its authority in Christ.

How did I learn about my authority? The Holy Spirit showed me. He sought me out and developed a relationship with me. He taught me to listen to Him. God would tell me to do weird things, like get on a light rail train at lunchtime and get off at a certain stop. It was not something I could reason out; it was a matter of obeying Him even when I didn't understand why. In all honesty, I realize now that I doubted that He had been talking to me at all.

I started having these lunch-hour spiritual warfare sessions about three times a month for a couple of months. I would get off the light rail in downtown San Jose and be led by the Holy Spirit to a demoniac. God would have me speak to the person, and the evil spirit would manifest. What God was showing me was my authority over evil spirits. I didn't totally get it. What I was getting loud and clear, however, was that the demons in these people didn't like me and didn't want to be around me. God had a lot of work to do to lead me where I am today. Now I understand that it was God who had been speaking to me all along.

In certain cases, God revealed what different demons looked like. On one occasion, I was in a park with a homeless man. I watched him shuffle several times to different park benches that were the farthest away from me. This guy had tattered clothes and no shoes; his un-manicured fingernails and toenails looked like talons on a demon.

This was the closest I came to seeing the Gerasenes demoniac that haunted the tombs in the Bible (see Mark 5). I greeted the man. He responded to my "Good afternoon." Then his voice changed. In foul language, the demon told me what I should do with myself. At that moment, God opened my eyes to see the demon; it was a small, lizard-looking thing. This guy's life was ruined by a tiny lizard-looking demon that was less than a foot tall.

What is so interesting about this period in my life is that I had not yet been released into deliverance ministry. God wanted to show me the spiritual authority He had given me *before* He led me into ministry. One day, God sent me to another homeless man in San Jose. He sent me, not to cast out a demon, but to show me how much the demon feared me. I had authority in Jesus and I had His protection.

I had a couple of months of expeditions to San Jose and Night Strikes in San Francisco before God released me to drive out demons. The Holy Spirit personally instructed me in my authority. At the same time, God taught me to hear Him. Although I truly believed that I *didn't* hear God, I can see in hindsight that I was obedient to Him. As I stepped out in that obedience, I became increasingly aware that it was God who was speaking to me and working through me.

I was simply learning to move in unity with Him. The more I did so, the more my ability to hear Him increased.

The Holy Spirit and Authority

I strongly urge you to get baptized in the Holy Spirit—especially if you are under attack. You don't need a ceremony or a special prayer by a pastor. I was baptized in the Holy Spirit simply because I prayed for it while on a spin cycle in my home gym!

If you are uncomfortable praying for the Holy Spirit baptism on your own, set aside some time and have your Spirit-filled friends pray over you. Once you are Spirit-filled, learn your prayer language. I cannot emphasize enough the importance of speaking in tongues!

Praying in tongues sometimes requires practice. I started out with a "baby prayer language" that gradually developed into a mature prayer language. Don't be distraught if you're not praying in tongues immediately after the baptism of the Holy Spirit. Start your praying by saying sounds, or anything that may come up. Let go and let the Holy Spirit pray through you. Don't worry about getting it right; just let the syllables or sounds flow and your prayer language will mature. My first utterances were clicking sounds like the bushman made in the movie, *The God's Must Be Crazy*. I thought it was absurd and that it couldn't possibly be my prayer language. But it was! The more I prayed in tongues the more my prayer language matured.

Prayer language is powerful when you're under attack. When you pray in tongues, you are letting the Holy Spirit handle the situation. As your mind, body, and soul get trained to use your prayer language, you will notice it surfacing in your spiritual warfare dreams, too.

People have made the argument to me on several occasions that they don't need to be Holy Spirit-filled to cast out demons and pray for healing. This is true; there is power in Jesus' name. People can cast out demons on that authority alone. What is intriguing, however, is that this argument is posed by fellow Christians who read the Bible. Jesus revealed to His followers that unless He fulfilled the Father's request to go to the cross and defeat satan, the Holy Spirit would not be released to us. Jesus needed to return to the Father to be glorified—and then He sent the Holy Spirit.

> *But I tell you the truth: It is for your good that I am going away. Unless I go away, the Counselor will not come to you; but if I go, I will send Him to you* (John 16:7).

Throughout the Book of John we see Jesus emphasizing the one He calls Counselor, the Teacher, the Spirit of Truth, the *Holy Spirit.* Jesus goes on in John's Gospel to discuss life after His return to the Father. It is the Holy Spirit who would reveal to generations of believers the secrets of the heavenly realms:

> *All that belongs to the Father is Mine. That is why I said the Spirit will take from what is Mine and make it known to you* (John 16:15).

We have the Holy Spirit to teach us and be with us and live in us. The Holy Spirit is the Spirit of God living inside of us.

> *You, however, are controlled not by the sinful nature but by the Spirit, if the Spirit of God lives in you. And if anyone does not have the Spirit of Christ, he does not belong to Christ. But if Christ is in you, your body is dead because of sin, yet your spirit is alive because of righteousness* (Romans 8:9-10).

The Father wants His children to be Holy Spirit-filled Christians. According to Acts 1:3, Jesus appeared to His apostles for a period of 40 days after His work on the cross was finished. He commanded them not to leave Jerusalem, but to wait there for the Holy Spirit.

> *Do not leave Jerusalem, but wait for the gift My Father promised, which you have heard Me speak about. For John baptized with water, but in a few days you will be baptized with the Holy Spirit* (Acts 1:4b-5).

The customary example from the Book of Acts for baptizing fellow Christians with the Holy Spirit involves laying hands on them and praying:

> *When they arrived, they prayed for them that they might receive the Holy Spirit, because the Holy Spirit had not yet come upon*

any of them; they had simply been baptized into the name of the Lord Jesus. Then Peter and John placed their hands on them, and they received the Holy Spirit (Acts 8:15-17).

The baptism of the Holy Spirit is an anointing we receive when we ask for the Spirit of God to come dwell inside of us in a greater dimension that affords us greater insight into the realm of the supernatural.

But you have an anointing from the Holy One, and all of you know the truth. I do not write to you because you do not know the truth, but because you do know it and because no lie comes from the truth (1 John 2:20-21).

If the Holy Spirit lives in us, then why are we believers entertaining the argument that we don't need to be Spirit-filled Christians? Reading further in Romans chapter 8, the Word reveals that it is the Holy Spirit who testifies that we are the children of God and co-heirs:

The Spirit Himself testifies with our spirit that we are God's children. Now if we are children, then we are heirs—heirs of God and co-heirs with Christ, if indeed we share in His sufferings in order that we may also share in His glory (Romans 8:16-17).

Talk about a trust-fund inheritance. Hallelujah! Daddy, Abba Father has set up my inheritance! It comes with a Kingdom bank account, eternal life, authority, and documentation. We are citizens of His Kingdom.

But our citizenship is in heaven. And we eagerly await a Savior from there, the Lord Jesus Christ, who, by the power that enables Him to bring everything under His control, will transform our lowly bodies so that they will be like His glorious body (Philippians 3:20-21).

The key wording in this passage regarding our citizenship is that *it is* in Heaven already. It does not say that our citizenship *will be* in Heaven someday. It is a common belief in our churches that you must go to your glory to benefit from this inheritance.

In reality, all the rights and privileges of our heavenly citizenship are available now.

It is the Holy Spirit who takes what is the Father's in Heaven and makes it known to us. First Corinthians chapter 12 outlines the gifts of the Spirit that come from the manifestation of the Holy Spirit dwelling inside of us. Gifts of the Holy Spirit include speaking in tongues, word of knowledge, the gift of prophecy, and spiritual discernment. These gifts are extremely important in exercising our spiritual authority. What is confusing about the gift of tongues is that the Bible specifically identifies three forms of tongues. There is the universal translation form of tongues, found in Acts 2:6-12, and 1 Corinthians 12:10, speaking in different kinds of tongues (languages). There is the prophetic gift of tongues that requires interpretation. (See 1 Corinthians 12:10 and 1 Corinthians 14.) Then there are the utterances of the Holy Spirit, which we all receive, typically with the baptism of the Holy Spirit. The utterances of the Holy Spirit are commonly referred to as your prayer language. The confusion in tongues typically lies in the notion that when we receive tongues we receive all the gifts of tongues. This is not the case. When we receive more of the Holy Spirit through baptism of the Holy Spirit we receive our prayer language. The other forms of the gift are distributed at God's will.

Using your prayer language, that is praying in tongues, is extremely powerful in deliverance and healing ministries. Mark Neitz of City Ministries, Jimi Merrell, and myself were once in a deliverance prayer session where a demon screamed in vulgar language proclaiming its hatred for our praying in tongues. Utterances of the Holy Spirit, the gift of praying in tongues (your prayer language), can also be useful in exposing demons that hide themselves in people.

The gift of discernment of spirits is extremely important in deliverance ministry. Through this gift, the Holy Spirit will warn you when a spirit is present, but not visible. Evil spirits don't like to make their presence known around Spirit-filled Christians because they know they won't win the fight.

I mentioned previously that spirits like to trick the deliverance pray-er, especially a non-experienced pray-er, into believing it has been cast out. Spirits do a great job of conjuring the look of peace over someone who is still in torment. The discerning of spirits is important in evaluating whether that peace is genuine and whether the demon spirit is truly gone. Many times, the Holy Spirit uses a combination of the word of knowledge and discernment of spirits to ascertain whether deliverance is authentic.

The word of knowledge is equally important in determining the entry point of the evil spirit. I don't talk to spirits because they always lie. I ask the Holy Spirit to reveal to me what the root cause of the torment is so the person being prayed for can be made whole.

You remember the story about Elaine, the woman tormented by a nasty demon of murder. In our deliverance prayer session, the demon was uncooperative. I used my Kingdom authority to engage the enemy and asked the Holy Spirit, "What is this foul spirit in front of me?"

I then told Elaine, "This one is responsible for what happened to your father!" Elaine broke down and cried at that moment.

She answered, "My father was murdered."

Details like this will not be revealed if you are involved in a spiritual battle without the Holy Spirit. Spirits of murder and death won't answer too many questions unless they recognize your authority. This true authority comes from being a Spirit-filled Christian.

Isn't every Christian Spirit-filled? Yes, but there is a greater filling, the anointing, when asking for the baptism of the Holy Spirit. Once you ask for that special anointing you're taking one big step into your Kingdom authority. This is where God begins to reveal the spirit realm and the Kingdom of God. Every Christian can experience the supernatural, but when you are baptized in the Holy Spirit, you step into a greater awareness of the supernatural, your inheritance, and your anointing.

Another important gift of the Holy Spirit is the gift of prophecy. Through this gift, we can build up one another in the Body of Christ. During deliverance prayer, I ask the Holy Spirit to reveal something about the person for whom I am praying. Many times the Holy Spirit will reveal a spiritual gift that is being held down by the enemy by way of torment. Often, the gift of prophecy is used by the Holy Spirit to show the person being prayed for that He is present during this session.

Our most effective prayer sessions are with people I don't know. The information the Holy Spirit reveals leaves a bigger impression on them, because they cannot deny that the revelations are coming from God.

Lisa and I were at a church where a woman recognized us as deliverance prayer team members from a house meeting. After the service, the woman asked Lisa to pray over her daughter, who had a rash on the back of her neck. I was wandering around, talking to friends at the time, and made my way back over to my wife. By the time I reached her, she was already praying over the young woman.

I didn't know what Lisa was praying for, so I figured I would jump in and take an opportunity to use the gift of prophecy. When I laid my hand on the woman's shoulder and started praying, I received images in my head of the young woman moving her hands and making creations with her hands as she listened to worship music. The hands were moving to the worship music. I told the woman about the prophetic picture I received of her. She smiled and told me she was a prophetic artist studying at the Supernatural School of Ministry at Bethel Church, in Redding, California.

That prophetic moment built up the young woman and let her know that God was working in her life. That's why I like praying and using the prophetic over people I don't know. When God reveals His involvement in this way, they know they are being touched by Him.

With the baptism of the Holy Spirit you step further into your citizenship and your marvelous, infinite trust fund from Daddy. The account is limitless as long as you are Kingdom-building. When you are Kingdom-building, you are not chasing miracles; you are *expected* to perform miracles.

Miracles come from the Holy Spirit. The greatest miracle of all is the miracle of the repentant heart.

Don't Worry; God Will Cover You

God will reveal more to you as your walk in authority matures. My friends from Night Strike and other deliverance teams here in San Francisco have seen demons manifest, point me out, scream at me from a block away, and then bolt in the opposite direction.

When I participate in New Age and Wicca evangelism teams, I have to have intercessors pray to conceal my authority so that I can participate in these powerful outreaches. Without this prayer, demons would manifest and point me out (along with a few other evangelists), potentially disrupting our ability to minister.

It may shock you that we go to pagan events. But Jesus died for the ungodly:

> You see, at just the right time, when we were still powerless, Christ died for the ungodly. Very rarely will anyone die for a righteous man, though for a good man someone might possibly dare to die. But God demonstrates His own love for us in this: While we were still sinners, Christ died for us (Romans 5:6-8).

Our M16 Ministries team has walked into homes where the owners warned that previous clergyman (presumably, deliverance ministers or exorcists) had been pelted with crucifixes and suffered other forms of attack. One person commented about how different it was when my team entered and the demon bolted to the ceiling.

In deliverance ministry, there is a distinction between the pastoral teaching of the Gospel and the spiritual warfare side of ministry. Some clergy members may not understand the spiritual warfare side of the ministry. I am not putting down pastoral staff here; what I have observed is that most modern clergy have only been truly prepared for the teaching aspects of the ministry. This trend seems to be changing as I see many pastors embracing the ministry of deliverance, which they are learning outside of seminary.

The atmosphere in homes with spiritual activity changes because my team walks in spiritual authority. I can work effectively in this ministry because I know Jesus is real. Jesus is not someone I will meet when I die. I know Jesus now: He's a warrior, He's passionate, and He has an incredible sense of humor.

Knowing Jesus means I have the seal of the Holy Spirit. Just as Jesus had the Holy Spirit in the Gospels of Matthew, Mark, Luke, and John, Romans 1:5 tells me I have apostleship too!

So why did the Sceva brothers get beat up in Acts 19? The reason is that they had the Scriptures, but they did not know their authority. They didn't know Jesus for themselves.

Through Jesus we have the inheritance and the Holy Spirit. We don't get beat up unless we allow it—which means, unless we submit to satan. At the same time, we don't go places where the Holy Spirit has instructed our team not to go. We don't go looking for a fight.

Many times we pray and fast and speak with the Holy Spirit so we are sure to remain covered in His protection and guidance. When we encounter someone whose will is completely compromised by an oath to satan, we might take a month or so of prayer and fasting before we arrange a deliverance prayer session.

We must operate under the authority and guidance of Jesus Christ. When we are told to wait before proceeding with deliverance, we pray for the person until the time comes.

Authority to Raise the Dead

We in America have no doubt that the Holy Spirit raises people from the dead. Unfortunately, we have confined the locations of such miracles to third-world countries, such as those in Africa and South America.

Are we supposed to think that God can only raise the dead in certain places? Do we have to go to foreign lands to bring back the testimony of the Gospel to our corner churches? Or does God raise the dead in America, too?

Why should any of you consider it incredible that God raises the dead? (Acts 26:8)

The apostolic commission is for the whole world, not just missionaries in foreign countries. According to Matthew 10:8, we are to raise the dead. In the state of Washington, there is a ministry that focuses on raising the dead. They are called the Dead Raising Team. To date they have raised several people from the dead. Tyler Johnson, who is a part of this incredible ministry, has relayed to me an amazing testimony from their ministry.

In Redding, California, a baby died in a woman's womb. A few weeks after the baby had been declared clinically dead, doctors were ready to abort it because it threatened the woman's health. The Dead Raising Team (DRT) was called in. They prayed over the woman's womb and the lifeless baby. The team prayed the baby back to life! There is a sad ending to this story. As I followed up with Tyler to document the miracle for the final edits of this book, I was informed the baby only lived for several months. My initial thought was to remove the testimony from this book and put in a happy ending one. But I believe this is a classic example of situations that occur when you're in a healing ministry. Things happen that are beyond your comprehension. People get healed, people get healed whole, and some people don't receive full healings. Nevertheless, the initial miracle did occur.

Tyler gave me some insight into how the team prays. "We believe that sickness is from the enemy, always," he said. (This is the same mindset I use in M16 and Night Strike for healing ministry.) According to Tyler, when someone dies of sickness or due to an accident, DRT classifies it as a "premature death." In other words, satan has interfered with the person's lifespan; the death is outside the will of God.

The DRT takes authority over the situation, because God's will is for us to live full lives. It doesn't matter if the person is 95, lived a full life, and happened to die peacefully of a heart attack while sleeping. Because sickness was involved, the DRT prays to raise the dead.

When the DRT members "pray," they command the person back to life. They are convinced of God's will to do it and they go from there. The DRT goes to morgues, funeral homes, and accident scenes to lay hands on the deceased. They go wherever the dead are found. It sounds a bit morbid, I'll agree, but a baby and a few other people are alive today because of their ministry.

A Prayer for Authority

You may be under spiritual attack right now. It could be a physical attack through a disease or illness, a mental attack with voices or bipolarism, or a straightforward spiritual attack with demonic manifestations. It's all demonic! Sickness, death, and disease are all from satan. Step out in your authority and live a life in which Jesus destroys the works of the devil.

Heavenly Father, I thank You that I am wonderfully made. I thank You, Jesus for the suffering and death You took in my place. Holy Spirit, come into my life and show me how to walk in Your authority. Jesus said You are the great teacher. Show me how I can stand up to fear and command it to leave. Reveal my authority over the enemy. Build me up into the person I was created by You to be. And thank You for giving me authority and dominion over darkness, in Jesus' name. Amen.

Endnote

1.   Merriam-Webster Online Dictionary, 2010, Merriam-Webster Online, s.v. "apostle," <http://www.merriam-webster.com/dictionary/apostle> (accessed July 27, 2010).

CHAPTER 4

EXORCISM AND DELIVERANCE

*I have given you authority to trample on snakes and scorpions
and to overcome all the power of the enemy; nothing will harm
you. However, do not rejoice that the spirits submit to you, but
rejoice that your names are written in heaven* (Luke 10:19-20).

D riving out demons is a part of our apostolic commission; it is not the focus of our faith. Our Kingdom works
include deliverance, forgiveness, salvation, healing,
and reconciliation. The focus of our faith is our living relationship with Jesus Christ. Jesus is the one who crushes the works of
satan.

When discussing scripture and apostolic commissions, office
and anointings, it's always best to engage dialogue with people
you respect. In putting together my description of the apostolic
commission I spoke with Dr. Charlie Self, former senior pastor
of my home church and Dr. Roger Valci, current senior pastor
of my home church. After discussions with them, here is my
reflection on the apostolic commission: I make the distinction
between big "A" and little "a" apostles. Big "A" Apostles are the
original 12 disciples, the literal 12 apostles in the Bible selected
by Jesus. Then there are the little "a" apostles which can be sub-
divided into two categories, the "noun" apostles with titles, those
in a ministry office, as Paul mentioned in Ephesians 4:11, and the

little "a" adjective category of apostles, those with an anointing which include laymen. Or what I call the rest of us!

"It was He who gave some to be apostles, some to be prophets, some to be evangelists, and some to be pastors and teachers" (Eph. 4:11).

The rest of us are called to the little "a" apostolic ministry to advance the Kingdom, heal the sick, cast out demons, heal the lepers, and raise the dead. Don't misinterpret the big "A" and little "a" apostles as one position being more important than another. Both are required in the proper function of the Body of Christ.

When Jesus led me into His deliverance ministry several years ago, there were only a few Web sites dedicated to this kind of work. Now there are probably thousands. Many have jumped on the demon-busting bandwagon.

Jesus' ministry is not exclusively casting out demons! Remember from Chapter 2, Jesus' ministry is to first and foremost preach a ministry of repentance—to turn someone's life around! Then the person who is healed and made whole is supposed to preach the Gospel, heal the sick, raise the dead, and drive out demons. In doing so, every believer gets others to turn their lives around—and they go out preaching the Gospel, healing the sick, raising the dead, and driving out demons. This is Jesus' deliverance ministry, folks!

When I come across a Web site that mentions deliverance and focuses exclusively on demons, I feel the ministry has clearly missed the point. The other oddity I come across is that of deliverance Web sites that describe a team having lead exorcists. This is a Christian hybrid that mimics the *Ghost Hunter* television show model: the team consists of a lead demonologist, lead exorcists, and so forth.

Avoid any such deliverance team that boasts to have an exorcist. Read between the lines; this is an amateur, a fraud, or a person immature in his or her own spiritual walk. An exorcist is exclusively a trained clergy member of the Roman Catholic

Church. Only Roman Catholic and Presbyterian churches have clergy trained in exorcism.

Do you need clergy to evict demonic spirits? No, but sometimes a family or a person may be in no spiritual condition to fight on their own and may require an exorcist. If you are seeking an exorcist, I strongly warn you right now not to allow into your spiritual battle any "exorcist" who is not an ordained and specially trained Roman Catholic priest or Presbyterian minister.

Deliverance prayer ministry achieves the same result as exorcism. In my ministry, I have fought the same battles as an exorcist and have seen victories that show the glory of God. Be sure you have a deliverance prayer person who walks in an anointing of authority. A true deliverance minister is more interested in his or her own personal relationship with Jesus than in casting out demons. Luke 10:20 identifies true deliverance ministers; they rejoice because they know Jesus, not because demons submit to their authority.

There is no lead exorcist title in the Scripture. There is no lead deliverance minister title, either. There is no title at all! So beware. My only title is that I am a son in the Kingdom. And as a son, I am to work to expand the Kingdom. Know the difference between Jesus' ministry of deliverance and modern-day charlatans or misguided apostates. To clarify, misguided apostates are those outside the scope of formal clergy training who self-appointed themselves the title of a demonologist or an exorcist.

Exorcists

As already mentioned, an *exorcist* is a title specifically reserved for trained Roman Catholic and Presbyterian clergy. Anyone outside of this umbrella identifying himself or herself as an exorcist is a charlatan or ignorant person who is not walking fully in the ministry of Jesus Christ. And that is a nice way of putting it.

There is a clear-cut protocol in which a real exorcist is brought into a spiritual battle. Roman Catholic Canon law specifically states that an exorcism is never administered by a lay person. Exorcisms are instituted and administered within the Roman Catholic Church hierarchy. Typically, an exorcism must be petitioned up the ranks of the Church, usually to the bishop, for it to be granted. By the time the request reaches the appropriate level, Church investigations have been carried out to determine the natural, medical, or psychological diagnosis of the person or environment requiring the exorcism ritual.

The charter of the exorcist is to free a person from demonic activity. Since the exorcist is an office in the Roman Catholic Church, the Church is in intercession for the individual during the spiritual battle. Not only is the demon taking on the exorcist in the battle, but the entire Roman Catholic Church as it intercedes with God.

Demonologist

The title *demonologist* is another fraudulent label used in paranormal circles. Again, this is a title and study reserved for trained Catholic clergy. It is the study of theology specifically centered on the one-third of angels who rebelled against God.

Paranormal investigators have hijacked this title and used it to convince people in distress that they are certified to handle demonic activity. Some self-proclaimed demonologists even profess to know the names and sub-worlds of demons. Paranormal demonology is not Roman Catholic demonology. That being said, you need to also be aware that religious spirits may be at work in paranormal demonology teams that include clergy members.

Did you ever hear the apostles call the demons by name? No. Jesus used the word *authority* over and over, didn't He? Jesus may have identified the spirit as a deaf and dumb spirit or a spirit of infirmity, but He never called the spirits by name.

As of this writing, I have had experience in expelling hundreds of demons. The demons *always* lie about their names. Jesus told us the native language of the enemy is lies. So what good is it to know their names? The Holy Spirit knows who they are. I pray and let the Holy Spirit handle them. *Evil spirits or demons* are all you need to know about demonology. What is imperative is this: you must know who you are in Christ and what your authority in Christ is.

Paranormal demonologists do not understand the manners in which demons can manifest. On an online forum, a demonologist posted remarks about making a list of whacko people to avoid. When a woman who was experiencing demonic attacks requested the demonologist's assistance, one of the investigators discovered that the woman would physically attack herself. They labeled her a whacko; her name started their list of people to avoid.

Nearly ten people in the forum responded saying this was a good idea. I added my two cents to the thread; I said that before writing this woman off, someone should contact a deliverance ministry to help her. I identified the situation as demonic oppression and explained that I had witnessed it before. That was, in a nutshell, all I wrote. I am subtle on these forums and do not get into anyone's face. Still, the entire thread was removed from the forum within minutes of my post. The religious spirits at work would rather keep this woman in bondage than see her set free. What do you think these people are going to do for you when you let them into your spiritual battle?

I have had cases in which people were leery of M16 Ministries because we didn't have a lead demonologist. By the time people in need find our ministry, they are already desperate for resolution. They have already corresponded with so-called demonologists. Nevertheless, they are blown away by the authority my wife and I and other team members exercise over demonic activity. Our team literally changes the atmosphere in the house by calling on the Holy Spirit for help.

Know the Bible and know Jesus! You won't need the fancy title.

One more thing to consider in regard to titles: from our case experiences, a lot of demonologists are New Agers who believe they are psychic and practice universal, one-size-fits-all religions. Don't allow them into your problem; it *will* get worse. Psychics talk to demons—not ghosts!

Deliverance Prayer or Rites of Exorcism

If you are Roman Catholic and your house is marked by spiritual oppression, should you seek out an exorcist?

Deliverance prayer is clearly part of Catholicism. Some Roman Catholic Churches even have prayer and healing ministry teams staffed by parishioners. I have taken some charismatic Catholics out on the streets with us, where they prayed for healings. The prayer team handed out St. Francis medals to the homeless people they prayed for. These prayer warriors are the right people for a deliverance ministry. They understand their authority in Christ.

There is a hierarchy in the Roman Catholic Church that functions to take the deliverance prayer as far as the prayer team can—even to the eradication of the evil spirit. However, if the clergy step in to take over, then the deliverance team operates in unity with the clergy. The Roman Catholic deliverance prayer team may even be the first step in determining whether an exorcist is needed.

For non-Catholic denominations, there are deliverance prayer teams in quite a few churches now. A Holy Spirit-filled deliverance team will shut down demonic activity and drive out forces of darkness. And a good deliverance prayer team is networked with other churches and other deliverance prayer teams. Our own M16 Ministries is networked with several ministries and works a lot of demon-related cases in California, in other states, and in some cases, in other countries. We have fought the same battles against the forces of darkness as exorcists do. We serve the same Father in Heaven! There is one glory! And all the glory goes to Him!

One common occurrence I have noticed is that, when we are called out to a location where there is demonic activity, people expect us to recite exorcism rituals. We don't. We pray and let the Holy Spirit take on the fight. We're just there to pray, share the Gospel, and ask the Holy Spirit to come. Every deliverance prayer session is different, so we must be prepared to move as the Holy Spirit directs us.

It is during this time of flowing with and listening to the Holy Spirit that many people we help get touched by God. They witness the Holy Spirit working through us and the impact is life-changing.

No matter if you call for an exorcist or deliverance team, the end result will be based upon whether or not you want to be healed. This requires taking steps of responsibility and owner-ship in your own spiritual life. Do you really want the torment to end? Go to church, get saved by Jesus, and start reading the Bible. As you push out the darkness with the light of Jesus Christ the evil *will* leave.

Darkness cannot tolerate the light of Jesus Christ. This is my experience and sound advice from over a hundred cases involv-ing deliverance and the demonic. The first step is to get saved by the blood of Jesus Christ; the next step is to get delivered and be made whole again.

Deliverance Prayer Ministry

The role of deliverance prayer ministry is to preach the Gos-pel, heal the sick, cast out demons, and raise the dead. This was Jesus' commissioning of the apostles in Matthew 10:1, Mark 3:14-15, Mark 6:7-13, Mark 16:15-18, and Luke 9:1. Jesus came into our physical realm specifically to destroy the works of the devil (see 1 John 3:8). Romans 1:5 states that through Jesus Christ we received (little "a" adjective) apostleship. Who are the apostles? We the Church are the apostles. We received apostleship through our inheritance as sons and daughters (see Rom. 8:16-17).

There is a lot of confusion as to the primary charter of a deliverance prayer ministry. The primary role of the deliverance ministry is to share the Gospel—not drive out demons. There is a lot of misconception in this ministry, including the fact that people often see *deliverance* and exorcism as being interchangeable words. They are not!

I would stress that a deliverance minister is more of a missionary in your own backyard, or wherever God has sent that minister. There are a lot of sick and brokenhearted people who need to be healed physically, mentally, or both; all of them need to be touched by the Holy Spirit. This is the ministry Jesus had in mind when He commissioned us to build His Kingdom.

Do you see now why I detest the title *lead deliverance minister* found on deliverance Web sites? The lead deliverance minister is the Holy Spirit. As a child of God I move as the Holy Spirit moves. I am not in charge of a deliverance session; the Holy Spirit is in charge.

Deliverance sessions don't always involve demonic activity and manifestations. Sometimes the Holy Spirit just needs to touch people and allow the suppressed darkness inside of them to be released. In this situation, you are just praying for the light of Jesus Christ to invade their darkness. People know their own sins and how they bottle it up inside themselves. It is common for people to receive physical healings from ailments as they release this pent-up sin and darkness to Jesus.

Often, people asked for forgiveness long ago and God forgave them. Yet satan continuously reminds them of their past sin. Our ministry has seen may cases in which sin festers in the form of physical ailments. Anger and bitterness can manifest as arthritis, for example.

There is an intertwining of the physical, mental, and spiritual. Sickness, disease, and death are physical attributes of the demonic spiritual realm. Through our ministry participation with the Kingdom of Grace prayer ministry, we have seen incredible instant healings through prayer. Likewise, with my Night Strike involvement, I have spoken with people on the streets of San Francisco who have incredible testimonies of AIDs going into remission through the power of prayer. Many of these people had exhausted all hopes of being well again.

People who have received prayer through our M16 ministry sessions have experienced back healings. One man who was an invalid walked because of a prophetic word from my teenage son. These were prayers of healing and forgiveness; no casting out of demons was involved. Some people get healed instantly, some over time, and some don't receive a healing.

In deliverance prayer ministry, I have seen responses during prayer sessions in the areas of depression, bipolar disorder, and the hearing of voices. Voices can be successfully shut down by deliverance prayer—if the person wants them shut down.

The healings I have highlighted were carried out in a prayer meeting environment. The brokenhearted, the sick, and the weary in these cases were invited to hear the Gospel of Jesus and were then prayed for. Through the Kingdom of Grace ministry, we have seen Christians, non-Christians—and even those who came to declare the meetings heretical—receive healings from the Holy Spirit!

Night Strike is essentially an open-air church and deliverance ministry. As such, we often minister to prostitutes standing in front of strip clubs or building doorways. I ministered to one prostitute and shared with her a word of knowledge regarding how many children she had and at which homes the children were currently residing. I remember specifically telling the woman that her younger daughter was living with her sister and her older daughter was living with her mother.

The woman broke down and cried. She asked how I knew these things about her. I told her, "Jesus is talking to me right now and *He loves you.*"

The woman was given a taste of the Holy Spirit. I was then allowed to pray for her. Notice how the Holy Spirit works. I wasn't instructed to tell the woman that she is a sinner who is going to hell. God would never say that to one of His children. I was instructed to show her that God is real and loves her very much. This is deliverance ministry.

When Lisa and I participate in ministry at New Age and pagan expos, we give people a taste of the Holy Spirit. It's incredible to watch New Agers experience a cleansing touch from God. As they weep, they ask, "What is this?" We tell them that what they are feeling inside is the presence of God, the Creator.

"He is touching you now," we say.

This is deliverance ministry. I want you to clearly understand that the commission of this ministry includes driving out demons, but it's not the focus. The focus of the ministry is bringing people to Jesus.

Being Released to Minister

When God called me to seek hidden mysteries in November of 2006, I had no idea what deliverance ministry was. My wife and I had attended a really nice community church for over 20 years. My wife had actually attended this church all her life. We were active in the ministries at the church and plugged into the church body.

When God revealed the spirit realm to me, He rocked my boat spiritually. I was freaked out. What I learned immediately (and you may have learned at some point) is that not many churches are equipped to deal with the spirit realm. This is true whether the activity is that of angels, demons, or the Holy Spirit Himself.

Hindsight is 20/20. Looking back now, I know I was handed an invitation by God to seek Him more deeply. Often, He will do that by revealing the activities of the demonic. Overnight, I had very deep questions for which I needed answers. I am stable-minded and being plugged into the church helped. The senior pastor knew me as a stable person for years; this helped my credibility factor when I cautiously revealed to him what I was witnessing and experiencing as God revealed to me demonic beings and the presence of angels.

I was no longer satisfied with my spiritual level. It was an uneasy feeling, but God stirs us up inside to move us in the Spirit. God created inside of me a spiritual discontent. Romans 5 shows us how God uses our tribulations to grow us closer to Him:

Not only so, but we also rejoice in our sufferings, because we know that suffering produces perseverance; perseverance, character; and character, hope (Romans 5:3-4).

God sent people my way to guide and mentor me. In December 2006 I went through an entire week during which I constantly heard demonic chatter. It wouldn't shut off. It was borderline maddening. My first divine appointment was a phone call from a friend in the women's Bible study my wife attended. This woman was the connection minister at our church. I put her to the test on this one. She called to talk to my wife one evening, but my wife wasn't home. Through divine appointment, my wife's friend flat out asked me about the spiritual activity going on with me. I jokingly replied, "In all your connections, do you know an exorcist?"

My wife's friend replied, "No. But I know someone who knows a lot about spiritual warfare."

She told me she would have to call me back with the woman's number. When she called back with that phone number, a demon literally screamed in my ear and disconnected the call. I was flustered; I didn't know spirits could do that. I had to call back Lisa's friend and get the phone number.

This led to my first divine appointment involving a mentor. The woman I was put in contact with was named Lisa. Her first bit of advice involved my authority in Christ. An hour after I exercised my authority, the information superhighway of demonic chatter shut down. Just hours earlier, I stood in my front yard in tears, wondering how I was going to spend the rest of my life with these maddening voices in my head.

Our new friend Lisa was also the person who told me to get baptized in the Holy Spirit. More divine appointments occurred over a period of a year as God led me to be equipped in spiritual warfare.

In January 2007, one such divine appointment led me to the doorstep of Bob Johnson's City Ministries. Bob Johnson used to hold a "Worship and Warfare" meeting on the last Thursday of the month. I don't know if I was quite ready for Bob Johnson at the time; he was off the charts when it comes to doing great things in Christ! Yet, I knew I had to move forward and seek Jesus on this path in which He had placed me. Looking back, I don't know what would have happened if I had chosen not to attend Bob's "Worship and Warfare" meeting.

The meeting was pivotal. I met people there who had the answers I was looking for. Some were people who could interpret dreams, like Daniel and Joseph did (see Dan. 2 and Gen. 41). There were also people who were equipped in spiritual warfare. I went from feeling awkward to feeling right at home in less than 40 minutes.

As I mentioned in Chapter 1, Bob gave me sound advice after the meeting. He told me he could give me a list of books to read or I could go out on a Night Strike and learn spiritual warfare firsthand. I took Bob's offer and attended my very first Friday Night Strike the following evening.

I shared a portion of this testimony in the first chapter. Now I'll elaborate on what it means to have the Holy Spirit teach you deliverance. It began on Day One of my classroom training with the Holy Spirit. Our group approached a woman, probably in her mid-thirties. We gave her food and asked to pray for her. She said, "Sure," and allowed us to lay hands on her. Immediately, she went into these strange spasms. Her back contorted violently and she fell to the ground.

This initial encounter taught me and some of the others on the team about our authority over the demonic. I knelt down next to the woman and placed my hand on her shoulder to pray for her. The manifested demon looked at me and screamed with foul expletives, saying that my hand was burning it. This moment built my faith to learn deliverance.

Diane led the deliverance ministry. We started casting out the demon manifesting through this woman. The demon pushed us away from the woman by screaming and yelling that she was being raped. Demons are masters of interference and distraction.

As I mentioned in the first chapter, God showed me that not everyone is healed from demonic oppression. I mentioned this in a class I taught during a conference. Three people got up and walked out before I could finish my sentence. Nevertheless, in deliverance ministry the person being prayed for must *want* to be healed!

During the next couple of months of Friday Night Strikes, the Holy Spirit taught me how to engage the spirit realm. I felt awkward giving testimony after testimony at the "Worship and Warfare" meetings. I think I was stereotyped as the demon-busting guy. But God was working on me and revealing my authority.

Yet, after several months of standing in front of manifested demons and praying over people in the streets, I still hadn't seen any deliverance! It was frustrating. I would pray to God and ask, "What is going on?"

He told me that in the summer I would see someone set free. On occasion He would let me evict a few spirits. But I didn't witness a person being set free during this time. God was equipping me to know my authority and to know His voice. I would ask if I could free a person from the demon and God would tell me, "Not yet."

I was being trained by God Himself to hear and obey. After all, it is God who heals, not us. Now compare the supernatural training I received from the Holy Spirit to the training demonologists get from YouTube videos or books.

Finally, in the summer of 2007, I was released into deliverance with a prayer team from City Ministries. I finally broke through into my authority to release the oppressed. God released me just as He told me He would! This is a very important point that everyone entering any form of ministry needs to pay close attention to: God will train you and prepare you for your ministry. You must listen to God and understand *when* you are being released to your ministry.

Deliverance ministry is all about listening to God. I have seen too many Christians diving into deliverance ministry without being released into it. The problem is that some individuals are spiritually immature in their walk and are unable to take correction from their deliverance ministry peers. I took lots of correction from my peers and mentors. It was my willingness to take correction and be molded by God that showed my peers I was suited to minister with their prayer team.

By doing this I was also showing God I was willing to operate in unity with other people. My actions demonstrated the fact that my interests were in healing and salvation, rather than the ministry itself. God is more interested in the minister than in the ministry. The Father will not put you into a position you are not ready for.

Take the time to listen to God, learn from Him and from the people He sends your way. Then ask the Father when you are to be released into the ministry. The reason I am involved in so many ministries is because God sent me to be equipped by many people. Lisa and I invested time in our training. As we built relationships, other people in ministry became comfortable working with us and mentoring us.

Being Mentored and Mentoring

To this day, Bob Johnson and Mark Neitz at City Ministries mentor me in learning to hear God's voice. They have pushed me (in a healthy way) to understand that I can grow in the gifts of the Spirit, including the word of knowledge, the prophetic, and healing. Looking back, God put the exact people in my life that I needed at the time. I look up to both of these godly men; they are good friends of mine.

We need mentors, especially if we are called to specific areas of ministry. It is wise to learn at the feet of those who have gone before us. It helps us to avoid repeating beginners' mistakes, and it allows us to build on the knowledge they have gained.

It was through another divine appointment at this time that I met Gary Paltridge and his Kingdom of Grace ministry. I mentioned Gary earlier; he is an incredible minister of Jesus Christ. He and I ministered to the young demon-possessed man whose case I described in Chapter 1. Gary's Kingdom of Grace ministry is a great healing and equipping ministry. We have witnessed phenomenal healings and deliverances together. Gary keeps it simple and shares the Gospel. The miracles, signs, and wonders follow as the Holy Spirit moves through the people in his Maranatha meetings.

As my wife Lisa and I earned more favor with the Holy Spirit and being obedient, we were released to prayer ministry with Kingdom of Grace.

Can you see the pattern here? The Holy Spirit plants Kingdom seed in us. He then waters us and sends some of His gardeners our way to make sure we have good vines. If you are entering this ministry, you will need those gardeners. I cannot recommend strongly enough being mentored. Mentoring assisted my wife and me so that we became equipped to take on bigger battles.

Now, I can mentor people who are entering the ministry or learning about their authority in Christ. At the same time, I have a support group of mentors around me—a group of people I can trust. And I know that my mentors have mentors of their own. Mentoring provides for good checks and balances in the ministry.

My mentoring is a constant and ongoing process that will never be completed. I want to keep moving forward and growing so I can see everything my God wants to show me. I thank God for the incredible men and women He has placed in my life. I know there is room for more mentors whom God will one day send my way.

The person I was, spiritually speaking, in 2006 is no more. Everything changed when God called me to this ministry. I then allowed Him to change me and mold me into the person He needed me to be—one who is deeply connected to Jesus and others and more grounded in wisdom, the Word, and the power of the Spirit. I will continue to allow Him to mold me.

Through this process of growing spiritually, my entire family and I have witnessed outstanding miracles. It goes back to Matthew 6:33: *"Seek ye first the kingdom of God..."* (KJV).

Cessationism and Deliverance Ministry

Many Web sites dedicated to the discussion of Christian rationales and the reasonings of the Holy Spirit argue that the gifts of the Spirit are dead. They say the gifts were only given for the foundation of the Church and were reserved exclusively for the original apostles in the Bible. This belief is known as cessationism.

Under this reasoning, man (who was created in God's image) doesn't interact with God on a daily basis; God no longer comes to heal His people when we release the powers of the Kingdom through prayer.

The problem is with the human thought process; we attempt to rationalize and reason our way through the gifts of the Spirit. It doesn't work. The gifts are what they are; they are supernatural. They're available to everybody. Paul said as much in his letter to the Ephesians:

> *Praise be to the God and Father of our Lord Jesus Christ, who has blessed us in the heavenly realms with every spiritual blessing in Christ* (Ephesians 1:3, emphasis added).

He blessed us with every spiritual blessing! This is the Scripture that leaped off the page as I struggled to learn the workings of the word of knowledge, the prophetic, and healing. I was in the midst of people who were my mentors and who made it all look so easy. "I could never do that," I thought.

At least, I could not until I read the first chapter of Ephesians. That was my breakthrough. I am still not as polished as my mentors in some areas. But I can use the gifts of the Spirit. And each time I do I get built up in faith and dive deeper the next time I am challenged. I know that some of the people I take on Night Strike get overwhelmed when I get a word of knowledge and ask them to try doing the same. But when I push them, many get their first taste of working with the gifts of the Spirit. Some people witness healings firsthand—from their own prayers.

I for one know that the gifts of the Spirit are alive and well today. I have seen the works of the Holy Spirit with my own eyes. No ugly blog commentary or nasty e-mails can sway me otherwise. The Holy Spirit moves through His people and we are His apostles (see Rom. 1:5). We received (little "a" adjective) apostleship through our inheritance as sons and daughters (see Rom. 8:16-17).

The other strong point of contention raised against the ministry of deliverance is the idea that satan can heal people in order to mislead them. This is true; satan does have power and speaks the language of lies. But the signs and wonders our ministries have witnessed are not demonic. These were acts of God. Casting demons out of people and seeing miraculous healings that turn atheists or pagans into believers in Jesus Christ are not acts of satan. If it were, he would be fighting against his own kingdom. We know that kingdom divided against itself cannot stand (see Matt. 12:25).

Another argument used against deliverance ministry is a weak one; it rests on a misunderstanding of Matthew 7:22:

Many will say to me on that day, "Lord, Lord, did we not prophesy in Your name, and in Your name drive out demons and perform many miracles?"

To understand this Scripture properly, you have to read Matthew 7:20:

Thus, by their fruit you will recognize them.

There are and will be imposters who claim to be His servants, but are not. We the Church, the Body of Christ, are seeing the fruits of powerful deliverance ministries. The fruit we bear comes through the ministry of the Holy Spirit. We and the imposters will both be judged by our fruit.

Deliverance ministry is not heresy; it is our commission.

Summary

Let's summarize some key points before we move along: *Exorcist* is a specific title held by a trained clergy member of the Catholic or Presbyterian Church. The charter of the exorcist is to drive out demonic activity and free an individual from demonic oppression. Deliverance ministry is the commission by Jesus Christ for God's children to preach the Gospel, heal the sick, raise the dead, and drive out demons.

Please notice that this commission includes driving out demons, but is not exclusively for the purpose of driving out demons. The role of deliverance is to preach the Gospel and turn lives around. It just so happens that deliverance ministers must do some "housecleaning" when the demonic realm is encountered.

CHAPTER 5

LISTENING IN ON HEAVEN'S WILL

Praise be to the God and Father of our Lord Jesus Christ, who
has blessed us in the heavenly realms with every spiritual
blessing in Christ (Ephesians 1:3).

When we minister on the streets of San Francisco at Night Strikes, the Holy Spirit always keeps a direct line open between us and Heaven. Our Night Strike ministry takes to the streets with an incredible worship team in our ranks. The worship team keeps the atmosphere of an open Heaven as the other teams go their separate ways to minister on the streets.

As I mentioned earlier, I always encourage people who minister with us for the first time to try using the gifts of the Spirit—specifically, the word of knowledge or prophecy. Some people are a bit overwhelmed by their first experience on the streets; others embrace the crazy open-Heaven environment with which the Holy Spirit graces us. Either way, when I minister on the streets, I bear in mind that I am there for those with whom God has set up a divine appointment.

A lot of churches that minister with us have no experience with the gifts of the Holy Spirit. When they witness the operation of the gifts firsthand, it becomes an amazing testimony for them to take back to the rest of the congregation. It builds up their faith and drives home the reality of the gifts God uses to prepare people's hearts to receive the healing and delivering power of Jesus.

I can remember a particular night when my team was in the Tenderloin District yet again. My son Matt and I noticed a woman who was wheelchair-bound. We walked over, learned that her name was Suzanne, and asked if we could pray for her. With her permission, I laid hands on her and waited a moment for the Holy Spirit to share why she needed prayer.

From the superficial look of things I surmised that Suzanne was in a wheelchair due to some sort of sickness. But the Holy Spirit told me she was wheelchair-bound due to a violent attack by a loved one. I also sensed that there was ringing in her head, so I shared with Suzanne what the Holy Spirit told me.

Suzanne revealed to us that when she was 24 years old, her husband poisoned her. She died and was brought back to life in the ER. She also confirmed that she was tormented by a ringing sound in her head.

Matt and I prayed for healing in her back and spine. I also prayed to bind the demon causing the torment of the constant ringing. Matt then prayed for the Holy Spirit to cleanse her body and her blood.

We listened to the Holy Spirit as He revealed the woman's needs. It helped us minister to her effectively; it was also a witness to her of God's love. That is how the word of knowledge works on the streets. We have quite a few of these experiences during nearly every Night Strike.

Gifts of the Spirit

In chapter 12 of his first letter to the Corinthians, Paul outlined the gifts of the Holy Spirit that we have talked about. As you already know, some churches believe the gifts are no longer available to us. Other churches believe the gifts are alive and working today. I, of course, believe the latter.

Romans 8:16-17 establishes our inheritance as children of God and co-heirs with Christ. We have authority as part of this inheritance; this authority is necessary if we are to fulfill our commission to preach the Gospel, heal the sick, raise the dead, and cast out demons. We need some supernatural gifts from Heaven to achieve these Kingdom goals. Using our gifts is part of our Kingdom authority.

> *Now to each one the manifestation of the Spirit is given for the common good. To one there is given through the Spirit the message of wisdom, to another the message of knowledge by means of the same Spirit, to another faith by the same Spirit, to another gifts of healing by that one Spirit, to another miraculous powers, to another prophecy, to another distinguishing between spirits, to another speaking in different kinds of tongues, and to still another the interpretation of tongues. All these are the work of one and the same Spirit, and He gives them to each one, just as He determines* (1 Corinthians 12:7-11).

In 2006 when I was my pursuing my invitation from God to seek deeper things, I was extremely frustrated that my church wasn't teaching about our authority in Jesus or encouraging us to pursue the gifts of the Spirit. Why not? Because at that time, the operation of the gifts of the Spirit frightened members of the congregation. The Holy Spirit is now miraculously changing attitudes in this regard. Today, this church is training people in deliverance ministry!

While I was frustrated about the absence of such training at the time, I was equally apprehensive about leaving my church and testing unfamiliar waters under the guidance of new mentors. At the time, I doubted my ability to participate in anything as incredible as the word of knowledge, the healing of the sick, or prophecy.

The problem, in part, lay in my trying to haul the old trunk of disbelief and non-authority into my new walk. It weighed me down and wore me out. Satan also tried to tell me that I could never do what my mentors were teaching me to do. At times, I thought I might as well stick with casting out demons and leave it at that. But my early mentors warned me that such a limitation would make this new ministry wearisome for me. Then I would risk quitting before I had done what God had truly called me to do.

God was teaching me to find balance and live radically for Him. He placed the right people in my path to run interference and derail the disruptive plans of the enemy. My good friend Jimi Merrell walked me through my baby steps as I learned to move in the word of knowledge. He and his wife Holly Jean have also mentored Lisa and me in dream interpretation.

In my journey, I have gleaned from people who are truly prophetic and I have run into some flat-out charlatans. God's wisdom shows me which of His prophets are the real deal and which ones I should avoid. Those I found to be false prophets have fallen off the prophetic radar screen; I haven't heard from them in some time. Those whom I have learned from are still going strong and have earned the respect of other Christians.

It has also become clear to me that being on a "big" online prophetic mailing list doesn't make someone a prophet. At the time of this writing, San Francisco is ground zero for false prophecies; gross numbers of prophetic words have been published about how the city will be judged with earthquakes, tsunamis, and cleansing forest fires. Lisa and I have had similar dreams and visions regarding San Francisco, but they have taken on deeper meanings. We have learned that God always allows for repentance. This important point seems to be missing from some Internet prophecies. So here is my question: does anyone remember God's response to Jonah as he sat on a hill awaiting the demise of Nineveh? (See Jonah 4:10-11.)

Another stunning misuse of prophecy has come to our attention while ministering to the sick. Lisa and I have prayed for healing for many people with terminal diseases. Some of them were prayed for by Christians who prophesied that they would remain sick for another couple of years. This is not only false prophecy; it actually amounts to speaking a curse over the individual who is seeking prayer.

God doesn't *allow* us to be sick. Nor does He inform us that we will be sick for a long time before He will heal us. When you are praying for someone for healing, never pray that God is allowing this, or you will be sick for a season. That is both false prophecy and a word curse prayer and is the enemy speaking. If you encounter this kind of misrepresentation of God in your prayer sessions, set it right by praying to cancel the curse of the false prophecy.

Word of Knowledge or Prophetic Word?

What is the difference between the word of knowledge (see 1 Cor. 12:8) and a prophetic word (see 1 Cor. 12:10)?

Jesus demonstrated the word of knowledge in John 4:17-18. That is where He spoke with the Samaritan woman at the well. He had never met the woman before, yet the Holy Spirit revealed intimate secrets about her which He, in turn, shared with her. This is the gift of the word of knowledge.

A prophetic word comes from the Holy Spirit and is used to build up a person. It is never negative; the Father doesn't tell His kids things to break them down or hurt them:

But everyone who prophesies speaks to men for their strengthening, encouragement and comfort (1 Corinthians 14:3).

Once, on Night Strike in San Francisco, I ministered to a woman on the street. The Holy Spirit gave me a prophetic word; He told me to tell her that the poems and songs she had written were precious to God. The woman, whom I had never met before, gave me a puzzled look and reached into her purse from which she pulled out a small, leather-bound notebook. The notebook contained the poems and songs she had been writing. The Holy Spirit knew she needed encouragement in her gift. God was well aware of all her hard work.

If you wish to pursue the gifts of the Spirit, remember to operate in humility, gentleness, and respect for those into whose lives God has called you to speak. The people I know and respect who operate in these gifts and whose "vines" have produced good fruit never use the words, "Thus saith the Lord," when they prophesy.

Listening to God

God speaks to us. In our modern culture the enemy has successfully mislabeled those who hear from God; he brands them as lunatics, cult followers, or tormented souls who hear demonic voices. Some of our churches have aided and abetted the enemy by declaring that people who claim to hear God are heretics. But John 8:47 says: *"He who belongs to God hears what God says. The reason you do not hear is that you do not belong to God."* The Old Testament concurs:

> *Blessed is the man who listens to Me, watching daily at My doors, waiting at My doorway* (Proverbs 8:34).

Here Solomon is referring to wisdom—specifically the wisdom that comes from God. Romans 10:17 tells us that faith comes by hearing the message which is heard through the Word of Christ. How do we hear the message? God must be making some noise if faith comes by hearing.

There are many misunderstandings about those who hear from God; they are widely discredited by those who know little about how God works. It's another smear campaign by the enemy to keep the Church from listening to the Holy Spirit. Don't fall for it. Start by talking to God throughout your day. Watch and see how He talks back to you. He speaks to each person in unique ways, but His voice is always peaceful and encouraging.

> *God does speak—now one way, now another—though man may not perceive it* (Job 33:14).

When the Holy Spirit began teaching me to listen, I would get a message along with some type of strong impulse or reaction that would encourage me to carry it out. One reaction was that my eyes would tear. I seldom cry, but when God spoke to me He used the tear ducts to let me know He was speaking. This doesn't happen as often as it used to: God used this body impulse to train me.

He will do the same for you. You need to learn to listen to Him and your own body for your unique impulses. Each and every one of God's children is different. Once you recognize God's voice, you will be able to listen and act in obedience.

Listening to God is imperative if you plan to enter into deliverance ministry. When you lay hands on people and pray over them, you *must* listen to God. Develop your spiritual hearing to where you can discern God's voice—whether you are praying for a broken bone to be healed or a demon to be cast out!

This is why I don't need to know demonology. God is in control of the deliverance session; the voice of God will give you the information you need in every prayer and healing session. Deliverance ministry is not a ritual or formula like exorcism is. Each deliverance prayer session is unique to the individual and the situation.

My advice to those wanting to enter a deliverance ministry is to seek the Father and His gifts of the Spirit. Don't measure yourself up to someone you heard speaking at a large conference. It's like trying to pick up your first bicycle and race against Lance Armstrong. You wouldn't do that in real life, so why do it in your spiritual life? You need a bike with training wheels first.

At a conference in San Jose, I heard Patricia King give great advice to people wanting to work in the prophetic. She used a Kleenex box as an object lesson. In my research, I found that the analogy came from the book, *The Gift of Prophecy*, by Father Robert DeGrandis, S.S.J.

It goes like this: When you see someone, take one prophetic Kleenex out of the box. This represents one simple prophetic word for someone. It may be the word *blue*, or some other word. That could be the person's favorite color. You might look at the person and ask the Holy Spirit which Bible "character" this person's spirit represents.[1]

Personally, I don't get words of knowledge; I get pictures of knowledge. Learn the language the Holy Spirit is using *with you.* When we give people words from the Holy Spirit, I often draw out what God is showing me on a pad. I have had some really interesting results; some drawings have opened doors for dynamic encounters with the Holy Spirit.

Spend some alone time with the Father and press through with prayer and fasting for the gifts of the Spirit. God may tell you to go out and pray for someone. This is the kind of thing I heard when I was getting started in this. He simply gave me direction. It was up to me to follow His promptings.

A friend of mine named Morgan Bigelow shared a story with the congregation of Promised Land Fellowship in San Francisco. Morgan said God told him to grab his Bible and go out and pray for people. He did as God asked and he went out to pray—but prayed for nobody.

I had a similar experience; God told me to go to Main Street in my hometown and pray for people. I went out as He instructed and prayed for no one. In my case, I chickened out—even though I went all the way down to Main Street to pray. Still, God honored my obedience in hearing Him.

Faith comes by hearing, according to Romans 10:17. I believe this hearing includes the actual hearing of God's voice. The next time I received instructions from God was the time He asked me to take the light-rail to downtown San Jose on my lunch hour (see Chapter 3).

Little by little, God will build you up. I may be off my training wheels, but I am still pressing deeper with the Father. The gifts of the Spirit are released when we go to the Father and ask Him to release them to us.

Evangelism and the Gifts of the Spirit

Father Robert DeGrandis teaches extensively on the gifts. In his book, *Word of Knowledge: A Charismatic Gift,* he explains that the word of wisdom, word of knowledge, and the gift of discernment are provided so we can pray more effectively for healing, through the power of the Holy Spirit. For example, the gift of the word of knowledge takes us to the very depths of a person's being, so that we can see with the Holy Spirit's eyes what is buried in the unconscious.[2]

In *The Gift of Prophecy*, Father DeGrandis defines prophecy as a means by which the Lord communicates His love and His plan for each individual. Father DeGrandis identifies nine basic gifts from First Corinthians 12. They are: wisdom, knowledge, faith, healing, miracles, prophecy, discernment, tongues, and the interpretation of tongues.[3]

Father DeGrandis' central point is that we often treat these gifts as medals. We think they are bestowed for some righteous act, as though when we are good, God gives us a gift. Father DeGrandis says, "The Lord is more anxious for you to yield to the gifts of His Spirit than you are. The gifts are always to do His work and not your work."[4]

When people ask me to disciple them in deliverance, I invite them out to Night Strike to minister to the homeless. Many times their response is, "Couldn't you just call me the next time you have a prayer appointment and take me with you?"

My advice is this: when you step out of your comfort zone to do His work, the Father really enjoys releasing His gifts. The people who work with me in M16 are people I have known from Night Strike for years. When people take me up on my offer to come out to Night Strike and make a commitment to minister on the streets, I am more open to working with them. Night Strike is the perfect opportunity to do His work and operate in all the gifts. On the streets, every prayer is a divine appointment—and you have to listen to God's will.

Praying in Tongues

Praying in tongues (see 1 Cor. 12:10) is one of the most controversial gifts of the Spirit. There is a lot of confusion in the

Church about how the gift is acquired and used. Many people seek the baptism of the Holy Spirit simply to obey Jesus and connect deeply with the Spirit of Truth. One of the great misconceptions I find is the belief that all the people who receives the baptism of the Holy Spirit also receives their prayer language—speaking in tongues—immediately or "automatically."

The Holy Spirit doesn't speak in tongues. It is the person who is baptized in the Holy Spirit who speaks in tongues. We have a family friend who was upset for the longest time because she was baptized in the Holy Spirit and didn't immediately speak in tongues. We had to encourage her to press through to get her prayer language.

I had to do the same. I did not speak in tongues immediately after receiving the baptism. A good friend encouraged me to make utterances. Her advice was to just to start speaking, no matter how weird it sounded. In Chapter 3, I mentioned using syllables or sounds as your first utterances, just to get the ball rolling in your praying in tongues. Let God take over. It is awkward, but you *will* learn to speak and operate in your prayer language.

The value of your prayer language cannot be overstated. If you are baptized in the Holy Spirit and the enemy is attacking you, I strongly urge you to mobilize your counteroffensive and pray in tongues. When you do, you invite the Holy Spirit to manage the battlefield. With Him in control, you are on your way to spiritual victory!

Doctrinal conflicts arise when the gift of tongues is discussed. Not all churches and denominations agree on the issue. My advice is to obey the doctrinal rules of your church. Many churches believe praying in tongues requires an interpreter when tongues are used in a public setting. The gift of interpretation of tongues is used in these cases (see 1 Cor. 12:10b). Some churches believe that in their sanctuaries praying in your prayer language, which is speaking to God, requires an interpreter. My personal view is that there is a misconception here on which of the three forms of praying in tongues is being used here. Using your prayer language in spiritual warfare means you are talking to God and not to the demons.

Obey the will of your church. The purpose of the gifts of the Spirit is to build the Church, not divide it. In another setting, such as in the confines of your own home at a healing meeting, you have more liberty to use your prayer language. Do you see the distinction? The bottom line is: do not be in rebellion against whatever church you are in.

A close friend who has a powerful anointing in deliverance ministry cast a demon out of a young lady. Signs and wonders in the Church—everybody praise Jesus! Or so you would think. However, the senior staff members of the church were upset because my friend prayed against the demon using tongues without the interpretation of the tongues.

This is a modern-day Pharisaic response, if you will. The Holy Spirit drove out a demon carrying an assignment of death against this woman, yet the church squabbled over the finer points of doctrine. They completely forgot to glorify the Holy Spirit and His precious healing power!

The Gift of Discernment of Spirits

As you walk in your anointing to cast out evil spirits, you will discover that they seek to evade detection. However, they do exactly the opposite with those they oppress: with them, the evil spirits are relentlessly active. They make their presence very much known to those who are living in constant fear and torment.

The spirit realm is invisible, so how do we know if there is a demonic presence in a person or a home? As I mentioned earlier, the Holy Spirit has given us the gift of discernment of spirits (see 1 Cor. 12:10). It is unique to each individual and increases in intensity as you use it. Some have seen spirits in the form of shadows. As the Holy Spirit has taken over my eyesight and allowed me to see into the spirit realm, I have actually *seen* spirits in oppressed people. This doesn't happen all the time, but every so often I get a glimpse. This is one aspect of the gift I wish could be developed further. It would help a great deal in deliverance ministry. But it seems to work off and on as the Holy Spirit deems necessary.

I know I am not supposed to harbor "gift envy," but I have a friend who can see into the spirit realm at all times. Having a background in science and engineering, I put this claim to the test. I would deliberately take people to my friend's prayer meetings that I knew were tormented by specific spirits. My friend would pull me off to the side and tell me right off the bat which spirits he saw on them. He really does see into the spirit realm at all times.

So I am still praying for a deeper release of favor in this area. On other occasions during deliverance, I have felt and seen the presence of angels. I would like this gift switched on full-time, too. That's the coolest thing to see. But I digress.

God called me into deliverance ministry by giving me the ability to hear spiritual "chatter." I have spoken to people who are diagnosed as being bipolar and told them what the voices are telling them at a specific moment. At one house we ministered to a woman who thought she was psychic. I sat on the floor and my wife sat on the couch with the woman. As Lisa shared the Gospel with her, I felt a demonic presence hovering over me. At that moment I heard something, but was caught off guard. I heard only a murmur. I asked the woman, "What did that spirit just tell you?"

She was surprised to learn that I had heard it, too. She said, the spirit said, "Lies! Lies!" Actually, it was more foul and explicit language than that, but you get the idea.

I don't wish to bend theology, but I have a theory that the armor of God is a functional suit like a Holy Spirit "Ironman" suit with gizmos. The armor of God is defined in Ephesians 6:13-17. The helmet of salvation protects us from demonic attacks to the mind. When you encounter a demonic entity or sense something wrong, you might feel a strange pressure in your head, chest, back, or stomach. I believe this is the sensory feature on the armor of God warning that we are in the midst of an evil presence.

When Lisa and I coach other Christians over the phone, we ask them what kinds of sensations they have when activity is taking place or is about to take place. We teach them to listen to their armor. The armor of God warns you when something is manifesting or about to manifest; you can then act on the "intelligence" you receive by praying in tongues even before the activity begins.

When I take Christians on training exercises to houses that need cleansing, I don't tell the students what is wrong in the house. I let them walk around and use their armor and their discernment of spirits to put together the pieces themselves. We don't use *Ghost Hunter* "K2" meters, video cameras, or digital recorders to capture voices. We recognize any fingerprint of demonic activity right away. All we need is the Word in our hearts, the seal of the Holy Spirit, and our faith in Jesus.

Hijacked Spiritual Gifts

A friend of ours was shopping at the local mall when she was approached by a psychic. The woman told our friend that her husband needed to get examined right away, because he had cancer. Our friend was frantic and sent her husband to see a doctor. Lo and behold, he was diagnosed with cancer.

Our friend was frightened by the fact that the psychic foretold the future. I explained that the psychic was simply talking to her demon. This didn't answer our friend's question as to how the demon was able to see future events. The fact is, demons cannot see into the future. This, however, is an illusion they like to project. Demons simply rely on their incredible worldwide web of evil networking to produce information. The demon in this case had not predicted a future event; the cancer already existed. It just hadn't been diagnosed yet.

A psychic uses hijacked gifts of the Spirit. Satan cannot create or distribute gifts, but he can steal them. As Christians, we are forbidden to use divination or speak with the dead (see Deut. 18:10-11). All Christians need to re-read that last sentence. In spite of this biblical prohibition, we see paranormal television shows in which clergy and psychics are summoned to work together to deal with demonic activity. And Christians watch these programs!

It is instructive to see the degree of satan's "wisdom" in pulling us back into bondage. Too often we buy into the idea that if it's on television it must be true! We allow ourselves to be drawn by our curiosity about occultic practices. We explore things we should reject outright.

For example, my initial advice to anyone experiencing demonic activity is to avoid or discontinue contact with so-called psychics. The hardest cases M16 deals with are cases in which psychics are involved. Seldom do we see resolution until the person is literally weaned from the psychic. The demon speaks through the psychic and runs a military-style campaign of misinformation. Psychics don't talk to the dead—they talk to demon spirits! When we die, we go straight to Heaven or hell. Beloved Grandma isn't lingering around in some earthly afterlife, sending you messages from the other side.

Releasing the Holy Spirit

Do not be overwhelmed by what you see at church conferences on the gifts of the Spirit. It is the Holy Spirit who releases the gifts. I think too much emphasis is placed on the people using the gifts and not on the giver of the gifts, who is the Holy Spirit.

The Father in Heaven will release gifts to all His children. We know from Ephesians 1 that we are blessed with all the gifts. Seek the Father in Heaven and ask for a release in this area of your life. I could provide you with a prayer, but it really boils down to quality fellowship and prayer time alone with the Father God. Set aside some time and talk with Him.

If you want to speak in tongues, pray and ask God for your prayer language. Don't worry about what comes out of your mouth.

Just relax and let the Holy Spirit put the sounds on your tongue. As Kenneth Hagin wrote in his book, *Seven Vital Steps to Receiving the Holy Spirit*, the person must do the talking. The supernatural part is what is being said; not which person is talking.[5]

I have provided a simple prayer, below, for the baptism of the Holy Spirit. It is the same prayer found in Appendix B. I would recommend going to a quiet place of prayer, even now. It could be your home, your bedroom, prayer room, or wherever you go for peace to pray to God. You might put on some "soaking" music in the background to invite the presence of the Holy Spirit. Then relax and pray to God for the baptism of the Holy Spirit.

Heavenly Father, I thank You that You love me. I thank You for every blessing You have bestowed upon me and my family. I believe Jesus died on the cross to take away the sins of the world. Today I ask for the gift of the baptism of the Holy Spirit. Jesus said, "If anyone is thirsty, let him come to Me and drink" (John 7:37). My Father in Heaven, I am very thirsty and I have come to drink! I believe in the Father; the Son, Jesus; and the Holy Spirit. Let the streams of living water flow through me. Let my spirit pray to You, Father. Let my spirit sing to You, Father. Let my tongue utter mysteries. Let the gifts I receive build me up and build up Your Church. I praise You, Father, and I worship You with all my heart. I seek You, Father; take my hand and bring me deeper into You each day. I receive the gift of the baptism of the Holy Spirit in faith. I thank You for it. In Jesus' name, I pray. Amen.

Summary

Be realistic about praying for the gifts of the Spirit. Just because you saw a guest speaker operate in the gifts at a conference doesn't mean you will do the same thing after one prayer. Keep in mind that any person who carries an incredible anointing also has an incredible personal relationship with Jesus Christ. God is more concerned with His relationship with you. As you build a deeper relationship with the Father, He will in turn release the gifts of the Spirit.

Operating in the gifts is all about a relationship with the Father who wants to bestow them upon you!

Endnotes

1. Robert DeGrandis, *The Gift of Prophecy*, (Locust Valley, NY:Living Flame Press, 1984), 27.

2. Robert DeGrandis, *Word of Knowledge: A Charismatic Gift*, (Locust Valley, NY:Living Flame Press, 1989), 2.

3. DeGrandis, *The Gift of Prophecy*, 3.

4. DeGrandis, *The Gift of Prophecy*, 5.

5. Kenneth Hagin *Seven Vital Steps to Receiving the Holy Spirit*

CHAPTER 6

HAUNTINGS—EVICTING DEMONIC SPIRITS

M16 battling the forces of darkness? It's in our DNA. Often, when people are delivered from a particular kind of torment, they go back into the fight and minister to others who need to be delivered from the same thing. God instills in us a healthy, controlled anger that we take with us into the fight.

Hauntings can be tricky, especially the cases we receive in which the "victims" aren't Christians. Forget about what you see on *Ghost Hunters* and *Paranormal State*; you don't evict ghosts by burning sage plants. Why? Because according to the Bible, once the work of the cross was finished, the dead go to either Heaven or hell. For instance, the book of Luke reveals what happened when the rich man and the beggar died. Do note, this is an example of the afterlife before Jesus was crucified. The only significant difference is that paradise is not on the other side of the chasm from hades any more. From Luke 16:22-23, here is an example of two men, the beggar, who goes to paradise, and the self-centered rich man who goes to Hades (or hell).

> *The time came when the beggar died and the angels carried him to Abraham's side. The rich man also died and was buried. In*

hell, where he was in torment, he looked up and saw Abraham far away, with Lazarus by his side (Luke 16:22-23).

In Luke 16:22 we see that the beggar Lazarus died and the angels came and took him to paradise. Luke tells us the rich man went to hell when he died. There is no mention of the tormented soul of the rich man lingering around because he feared his judgment. This provides a case example of death and crossing over. What we're examining here are the mechanisms in place by God of what happens when the body of a saint or an unredeemed person dies. There are no lingering ghosts or human spirits as many demonologists claim. God is perfect. You go to glory or judgment when your body dies.

I recently engaged in a debate with a Christian ghost hunter about this topic, and this individual cited that Moses and Elijah, in Luke 9:30, the transfiguration, and worst yet, the Holy Ghost (Spirit) are proof of ghosts in the Bible. This is absolute heresy from ghost hunting's New Age influence leaking into our churches.

Now that masses of people get their spiritual education from television, the job of casting out spirits is trickier. We had a case in which an amateur ghost hunter named Ben sought our assistance in ridding himself of a spirit that followed him home from a site he was investigating.

Armed with electronic equipment, Ben and a group of friends had gone to investigate a house that supposedly had a portal to hell in it. The person whose house it was asked for the ghost hunters' assistance in stopping the activity. As we learned during our interview with Ben, the ghost hunters only came out to play with their electronic gear and see if they could capture voice recordings or videotape activity. There was no real plan to evict demons.

Afterward, when Ben left the premises and got in his car, he felt sick and had the sense that a spirit was riding home with him. Then the activity started in his house, where a black mass would float over his bed and try to choke him.

Ben called a Catholic priest and had his home blessed, but the activity continued. Sometime later, the case landed in our

M16 ministries inbox. We followed up with an interview on the phone. Ben told me he was in contact with a psychic who told him that the "ghost" was a Native American spirit.

Working in the prophetic, on the phone, I told Ben to stop right there and cease all contact with the psychic. I told him that a demon was giving the psychic false information. I told him this wasn't a Native American spirit. That was a lie designed to get Ben and the psychic to speak with the demon. Ben got flustered and told me his psychic was a top-name practitioner who had proven skills in the paranormal.

Again, I insisted; I told Ben he could choose the psychic or he could choose me. It was one or the other.

Ben was in a state of panic. He wanted me to come out and bless his house, even though the Catholic priest had already blessed it. I declined and told Ben the Catholic priest did a fine job of blessing his house. I told him, "It's not your house that needs blessing, Ben. You're the one who needs blessing. The spirit is attached to you, not your house."

Ben had picked up a "cling-on" spirit from the hell gate site. He already had several generational curses and needed to accept Jesus as his Savior. I managed to get him to attend a deliverance prayer meeting. People working in the gifts of the Spirit prayed over Ben and identified his sickness without his disclosing it.

The demon from the haunting site had latched onto another demonic spirit that was already operating in Ben's life. The prayer team worked in harmony with God and broke many generational curses. Ben got prayed over and felt better, but he still didn't take the key step: he didn't accept Jesus as his Lord and Savior.

Things went well for Ben for about a week after the prayer and blessing. Then the spirit became more violent and started knocking items off Ben's dresser. The demon made its presence known to Ben in no uncertain terms. Ben was frantic. Once again, he pleaded with me to come out and bless his house.

God told me there was nothing wrong with the house. Ben simply needed to take the final steps and get saved. I told Ben he had some major decisions to make in his life. I told him, "Either Jesus is your Lord and Savior or He isn't. You need to bring the big guns into this fight!"

I didn't hear back from Ben for about two weeks. Then one day he called. Ben decided to join the Catholic Church down the street from his home. It was the parish of the priest who had first blessed Ben's house. Ben told me that he accepted Jesus and had been baptized. The activity ceased. There is power in a repentant heart; that power completely undermines the powers of darkness!

Many times hauntings are associated with specific individuals. There are unique spiritual dynamics associated with each situation; these need to be identified in order for deliverance to be successful. In haunting cases, you need to ask the Holy Spirit what is going on with the spirits *and* the people being tormented. Ask the Holy Spirit to reveal what needs to be known in order to bring healing to the members of the home.

The difference between a ghost hunter and a deliverance ministry is that the deliverance ministry is there to facilitate not just an eviction of demons, but an inner healing. Who heals the person? Jesus does! But, as always, the person must want the healing.

M16 was brought into a case in which a late-twenty-something psychic woman named Sarah was channeling demonic spirits. She was well aware of the fact that these were spirits and that they were tormenting her.

Sarah's husband was a Christian who had tried several times to get his wife to accept Jesus Christ. One night we received a frantic call from Sarah's husband; in the background of the phone call I could hear demonic laughter. I requested to be put on speakerphone. I prayed and bound the demon manifesting in Sarah—right over the phone.

We managed to bring pockets of peace to the home, but Sarah wouldn't accept Jesus as her Savior. A religious spirit was involved; it kept interfering with Sarah's decision-making. A few weeks after this incident, Sarah decided that she would go to church on a particular Sunday. The night before that church service, the demon shoved Sarah down a flight of stairs at her house.

Sarah then started channeling the legion. Whether it is in reference to the Gerasenes demons I don't know. This is the name Sarah said the demons used to identify themselves. That very night Sarah had a tormenting dream in which she killed her husband with a large knife, for taking her to church. Sarah decided not to go to church and never entertained the thought again. This was a major setback; Sarah needed to accept Jesus so that I could arrange a deliverance prayer meeting and evict the spirits.

I remember the disheartening phone conversation with Sarah's husband. He wanted me to go forward with the deliverance prayer; I told him I couldn't, because the spirits would just return to an empty house in greater numbers. It wasn't my decision or his decision; Jesus wanted Sarah to make the right decision. Despite the full power that had been displayed from Heaven; despite the peace that entered the household after prayer; and despite the fact that Sarah acknowledged all of this, she acquiesced to the demands of the religious spirit that was bullying her.

This demonic spirit would have been tossed out as soon as Jesus' light permeated Sarah's darkness. I still pray for Sarah and know one day she'll make the right decision. She needs to choose between *the lie* and *the truth and the light.* When Sarah chooses the light of Jesus Christ, she will be delivered from her nightmare, and made whole.

Casper Is a Demon

The flood of television shows about the supernatural is creating a surge of misinformation. When reality shows take viewers into haunted houses and capture evidence of spiritual activity, the so-called experts always distinguish between two kinds of beings: deceased human spirits and negative (demonic) spirits.

If you don't know already it, there is no such thing as a disembodied human spirit haunting a house. The shows do a pretty convincing job, however. They use their electronic equipment: digital video recorders to capture shadows, digital voice recorders to capture voices, and electronic measuring instruments to document the activity at a haunted site. If the spirit is "being nice" to the experts, they assume it must be a human ghost.

Satan is using our media to fulfill his own propaganda campaign. The deception is widespread. Many Christians are questioning issues of life after death; they are wondering whether we really can stick around on earth or whether we move on to the reward or judgment of the afterlife. They are wondering, but the real question becomes: is this what the Bible says?

This is a package of lies! When people die they don't linger or get trapped between worlds. We know from the Gospel of Matthew that when we die, we either go to Heaven or hell—and we go at the moment of death. The Gospel of Luke even shows us how the angels carry us off when we die.

> *Then they will go away to eternal punishment, but the righteous to eternal life* (Matthew 25:46).

> *The time came when the beggar died and the angels carried him to Abraham's side. The rich man also died and was buried. In hell, where he was in torment, he looked up and saw Abraham far away, with Lazarus by his side* (Luke 16:22-23).

As I've explained before, so-called ghosts are nothing more than demons. The idea of there being two kinds of spirits is partially true; there are two kinds of spiritual creatures called *angels* and *demons*. Why don't the clergy members who appear in these shows point out the truth?

Father Gabriele Amorth, the lead exorcist of the Vatican, in his book, *An Exorcist Tells His Story*, pretty much said what I am saying: if there is a haunting, the root of the activity is demonic. It isn't Grandma or a deceased family member making a super-natural appearance.[1]

The devil's agenda is clear and he uses clever tactics to perpe-trate it. Often, TV ghost hunters deal with "ghosts" who portray themselves as playful children who like to move a ball or a chair around. These little "child spirits" like to talk to living children in the house. These are demons.

Another recurring theme that satan knows viewers find appealing is the trapped-family-member shtick. The story might involve a family member who was murdered or committed suicide and is now haunting the family abode. Again, these are demons! In the case of suicide, the "haunting" demon is probably the same evil spirit that spoke death to the now-deceased family member in the first place. We know from Scripture that satan loves to dress up his minions and masquerade to deceive us.

For such men are false apostles, deceitful workmen, masquer-ading as apostles of Christ. And no wonder, for Satan himself masquerades as an angel of light. It is not surprising, then, if his servants masquerade as servants of righteousness. Their end will be what their actions deserve (2 Corinthians 11:13-15).

Universal Spirituality

The underlying message satan presents in these ghost-hunting shows is universal spirituality. If the episode is about a Native American spirit doing the haunting, the ghost hunter will use Native American rituals and burn sage throughout the house to evict the spirit.

The irony is that the cast member carrying out the cere-mony is usually portrayed to be a devout Catholic or professed Christian. What satan is doing is creating a kind of equivalence that pushes Jesus down to the level of false gods. It implies that Jesus couldn't handle the situation, but an America Indian spirit could.

When our ministry team is called in to assist in a demonic oppression case, we always run into people who swear by what they see on these shows. They take it as doctrinal truth. However, unless a real Roman Catholic exorcist or a deliverance prayer ministry team is called in, all you are doing is inviting more demons to the torment party!

The other thing satan loves is for the media to portray Christians as being intolerant of other spiritual beliefs. Yet, the reality is quite to the contrary. If you log onto a ghost-hunting forum on the web, it is the Christian faith that is being bashed. This is a rejection of the Holy Spirit. Who is the perpetrator of this slander? Satan.

Just because we don't dive into mainstream mass ignorance doesn't mean we are intolerant or ignorant. It is because of my deep-rooted beliefs and love for my heavenly Father that I will never ghost hunt or work with a psychic. I am simply obeying Scripture. Talking to evil spirits and engaging in divination are forbidden by God:

> *When you enter the land the LORD your God is giving you,* **do not learn to imitate the detestable ways of the nations** *there. Let no one be found among you who sacrifices his son or daughter in the fire, who practices divination or sorcery, interprets omens, engages in witchcraft, or casts spells, or who is a medium or spiritist or who consults the dead. Anyone who does these things is detestable to the LORD, and because of these detestable practices the LORD your God will drive out those nations before you. You must be blameless before the LORD your God* (Deuteronomy 18:9-13, emphasis added).

Perhaps the New International Version of the Bible should read, "do not learn to imitate the detestable ways of the nations you see on television"! God makes it very clear that these mediums and practices are trouble. Yes, mediums can hear spirits— *evil spirits.* They hear them by tapping into demonic power.

Satan is leading people astray. Psychics—even those looking for missing children and assisting the police—are all listening to

demons. It's a propaganda campaign from the enemy; the prem-
ise he is pushing is that not all evil is necessarily evil. Don't fall
for it. Remember the adage that says, "the road to hell is paved
with good intentions."

Nice people go to hell. An alarming number of Christians
are flocking to these shows seeking proof of the supernatural.
Remember, the Pharisees ran around saying the same thing:
"Show us a sign!" (See Matthew 16:1.) Those seeking proof of the
supernatural are getting something more: a cleverly packaged
deception that will eventually dismantle their Christian beliefs.

There is only one way to Heaven and that is through Jesus.
There is only one way to hell and that is by going around Jesus.
It's cut and dried. Satan is attempting to show us that scientific
instruments can detect spirits, yet these tools reveal no sign of
God or angels. It is one more way for him to suggest that God
does not exist.

Remember that in the end times, satan will succeed in
bringing the antichrist to power. This demonically led figure
will receive a lethal head wound and come back from the dead
(see Rev. 13:3). It will most likely be a counterfeit miracle. These
ghost-hunting television shows are preparing the masses for such
a counterfeit. They are just a warm-up for satan's big antichrist
trick!

Answering a Call for Help

Most of the calls M16 receives are from Christians looking for
someone to help in putting an end to demonic activity in their
homes. When we assist these Christians, we work with them on
the basis of the authority they already have in Christ. As long as
the people are seeking resolution and not sympathy, these cases
always end in victory. Forgive me, but I call the sympathy seekers *life-suckers*; they go from ministry to ministry telling their sad
stories again and again, never really seeking and never receiving
victory in Christ.

We get calls from ghost hunters, too. You already read about Ben. Most ghost hunters don't ask us to bless the house they are investigating. They ask us to remove the demon or demons they brought home from the site. I call it the "Disneyland Haunted Mansion Hitchhiking Spirit Syndrome," in honor of the very end of the ride where there are hitchhiking ghosts.

Assisting ghost hunters with their demonic oppression is a lot of work and requires a lot of re-educating. They need to get saved; it's a slow and painstaking process. Jesus doesn't respond to a K2 meter. I have had to cut some of these people loose and let them go their own way. They are adults, and if they don't want to listen to truth, that's their decision.

Evil spirits typically attack these people at the level of a rationale. They cannot see the invisible; this is why satan has them use instruments. He does it to fool them. Many of them will rationalize away a miracle of the Holy Spirit or flat-out shut you down on the phone call. There's truth in a cliché: you can lead a horse to water but you can't make him drink!

A person's first call to M16 Ministries is very important. My wife Lisa and I need to determine from this call exactly what is going on. If the caller controls the conversation and rambles on for hours—it's a sympathy caller who wants my wife Lisa or me to be a personal counselor.

We are not counselors; we are prayer warriors. We know good people who are counselors and we are happy to recommend them, when appropriate. But I don't waste time with sympathy callers. As I said before, they will suck the life out of you. Whenever I encounter these folks, I know generational curses are involved. I also know they usually have no intention of doing anything about those curses.

Some demons demand a lot of sympathy because this is how they torment other Christians. These people don't want to hear anything you have to say and will not let you get a word in edgewise. If these people want to be healed they need both curse-breaking and counseling ministry.

Another common type of call we receive comes from people who see shadows in their homes but are refused help from their home churches. These people always feel the need to say, "I'm not crazy." The dilemma they face is that many churches haven't fully embraced or experienced the spirit realm. However, after we work with these folks, churches often come up with their experts in matters of the spirit realm.

When we receive this type of call, we let the caller tell us what is going on. I don't use a root-cause questionnaire like many deliverance books recommend, so I don't check off involvements or quietly poke around for generational curses. If the people are serious about getting help, they will reveal it all to us during that phone call. The Holy Spirit also allows Lisa and me to operate in the prophetic during these calls. This provides any further revelation we might need. (There is a big, clear difference between this kind of caller and the sympathy-seeking callers previously mentioned.)

During our first phone call, important decisions need to be made. The first decision is the distance factor. Of course, we also need to know whether or not the person is a Christian. With Christians, Lisa and I immediately discuss the caller's authority in Jesus. If the caller is within driving distance (we have now had some good long driving times), we will try to arrange a meeting.

If the callers are Christians, we might meet them at their homes. If not, we try to arrange to meet at a powerful deliverance prayer meeting. The goal is for the caller to be touched by the Holy Spirit. To fight demonic oppression, we need the person to be saved. The first step to salvation is a touch by the Holy Spirit. The next step is their acceptance of salvation in the Lord Jesus Christ. I can pray and pray and pray and fight the demonic, but if the oppressed person doesn't want to be saved, our ministry work will have little effect.

If you are new to deliverance ministry, you need to learn this lesson early on (although I will grant you that we mostly learn our lessons the hard way). I do pray for oppressed people regardless of their salvation, so that they are not harmed. There are times when we work with them for a month or longer. But after a while, it can become obvious that they have their own interpretations of spiritual issues, stemming from a religious spirit. Until they deal with their own spirituality and rein it in based on the truth of the Gospel of Jesus Christ, the oppression will continue.

This is true of most ghost hunters M16 has assisted. There is a religious spirit involved in twisting the truth as these people do (whether inadvertently or not). They rely on the fabricated reality satan provides them through their ghost hunting. Some of these people have sat through powerful Holy Spirit encounters with us. They tell us how the Holy Spirit brought peace to their homes or situations. After a week or so, the religious spirit will unwind and re-explain everything to them. It is really sad, because their liberation is just one correct choice away.

The few ghost hunters who have found freedom from oppression were those who accepted Jesus as their Lord and Savior.

Preparing to Enter a Haunting or Defiled Site

When M16 Ministries receives a request to go into any spiritual battle with the demonic, we pray! We talk with our Father in Heaven about being released into the battle. M16 also has an intercessory prayer team staffed by some incredibly prophetic and mature prayer warriors.

When we're released into battle we ask God how we should pray in this fight. It is the Holy Spirit who heals and saves; we must be operating in unity with the movements of the Spirit. We also pray for protection over ourselves and over the people we are helping. It is a plus to have this protection over us before we enter a site marked by demonic activity.

We once received a call from another deliverance minister who was helping a family close a demonic portal. A group of kids got ahold of a satanic bible and thought it would be fun to read from it. The next thing this family knew, malicious spirits were appearing all over their property. The deliverance minister went to the site and prayed over it. He was hexed by a spirit there and received horrendous dizzy spells for the next couple of weeks until the assignment over him was broken through prayer.

This gentleman asked me how I would have handled it. I told him I wouldn't have gone there without talking to God first. In addition, I would have notified the intercessors to start praying blanket coverage over me. I would also have extended the coverage of prayer at least two weeks beyond the date of the curse-breaking at the site.

You also have to be careful who you let on your team. Many Christians harbor strongholds from which they need deliverance. These people should not be on your team. If they can't deal with their own strongholds, the problem can easily compound during spiritual warfare. When selecting your intercessors, make sure they are mature Christians with some experience in battling the spirit realm.

On the Premises of a Haunting

There are basically two kinds of "hauntings": a house haunted by a demonized object; or a person haunted through demonic oppression.

If a house is under demonic attack and is within driving distance, Lisa and I will jump into the M16 prayer mobile and drive over to the site. When we bless a home, it doesn't matter whether or not the people who live there are Christians. If they're not believers, we consider this to be an evangelistic opportunity to share the Gospel and let the signs and wonders follow! Clobbering a demon and witnessing firsthand the glory of the Holy Spirit is a spiritually life-changing event.

If the people are Christians, we can work with them on their authority to take back their own house. These are opportunities for us to train other Christians in spiritual warfare as well.

As you prepare for these visits, it is always good to fast at least a day before entering the home. If you know full well there is heavy demonic activity in the house, give yourself a few days of fasting and prayer so you can be in intercession and see what God reveals on the matter. Take your time when tackling the forces of darkness. God will reveal issues of timing and tell you what is taking place. Don't be eager to rush in and fight. That's the difference between a mature deliverance ministry and a fledgling one. You will make mistakes; but remember that evil bites back. It's called spiritual warfare.

Remember that Ben the ghost hunter and his friends thought it would be fun to investigate a house with a hell gate—a demonic portal. They were called in to assist the owner of the house. Instead, they experienced firsthand the "Disneyland Haunted Mansion Hitchhiking Spirit Syndrome" and took home some souvenir spirits from the investigation. Sadly, the ghost hunters got more than they bargained for, while the homeowner received no help.

Be careful who you call for help. As a word of advice, I would not voluntarily go to a house with a hell gate unless the Holy Spirit instructed me to do so. What do I mean? If I received a phone call to help someone at a house like this, I would spend a good amount of time in intercession and fasting before stepping foot on the site. The Holy Spirit will shut that hell gate down, but you need to be talking to God to get your battlefield orders. Without talking to God first, my team members would risk bringing home their own "Haunted Mansion Hitchhikers."

Here's a little more advice about hell gates: If someone calls about a hell gate in his or her house, you can be reasonably certain that there is a spike in demonic activity there. But if, by the time you arrive on site, you and your team are not certain there is demonic activity, ask for permission to walk around the property and get a feel of the environment. Half the time when we arrive onsite, we are still wondering whether the people are overreacting to natural noises or house settling.

Whether the call is a false alarm or the house has a genuine hell gate, we are not ghost busters. We don't carry K2 meters or unlicensed nuclear accelerators on our backs. We arrive wearing the armor of God from Ephesians 6 and carrying the gifts of the

Spirit named in First Corinthians 12 and given as part of our inheritance from Ephesians 1.

That's all we really need to enter a site—Jesus. I have been on sites where I was warned the demon would throw stuff at us. But when a Holy Spirit-filled team walks through the door, the demon goes and hides.

We have an eviction notice with that demon's unspoken name on it.

Walking Through Haunted Premises

Walk through the house and listen to the armor of God. Everybody's armor is different and tailor-fitted so you will need to learn how your own armor works. In rooms where oppression is prevalent it is common to feel a thick atmosphere. You might feel pressure on your head or chest; you might experience queasiness in your stomach. Make note of what you feel.

Smell is another sensory system of the armor. Ask other team members if they feel anything; take note of anything they "pick up." Sometimes, I tell the people I am working with that *my spider-sense is tingling.* Remember what you felt in the room and move on. Oftentimes, when you meet with people after the walk-through and you bring up a particular room they hadn't mentioned previously, you get the "Oh yeah—and this happens there...." This gets you more information and gives you credibility, especially in a first-time encounter with non-Christians. If the home belongs to Christians, seeing the gifts of the Spirit in action creates faith-building moments for them.

I have seen shadows manifest during a walk-through. I ignore them, but comment aloud to my team members that we are here to evict evil spirits. This sets the tone by saying, in not so many words, "I'm not impressed with the magic show, nor will I be impressed with any further activity."

And as a side note: we don't show up at night and "go dark" as the ghost-hunting television shows do to sensationalize the event. We show up during the day. If there is oppression in the house, we'll find it.

Be Holy-Spirit Attuned to Defiled Objects

When you are walking through a house, be aware that even ordinary objects can be defiled. Remember Achan and his family who were put to death for hoarding loot from the battle of Jericho (see Josh. 7). Because Achan disobeyed God's instruction, these items were defiled.

Household items are defiled for different reasons. False idols, such as seemingly harmless souvenirs purchased on vacations can harbor demonic activity. These include African war masks, Buddhas, and other idols. Deuteronomy 32:16-17 says that false idols are demons.

New Age books and materials are a big source of spiritual defilement. I had to remove Sylvia Brown's psychic books from my parents' home after my mother passed away. My mother purchased these books because they were featured on *The Oprah Show* (Oprah Winfrey's daytime television talk show).

Psychics use the tools of satan and therefore glorify the enemy. As a result, any material published by psychics is defiled. Ouija boards are also defiled, as are the digital voice recorders that are now used instead of Ouija boards to capture disembodied spirits.

> *Do not turn to mediums or seek out spiritists, for you will be defiled by them. I am the LORD your God* (Leviticus 19:31).

Ouija boards and digital voice recorders are extremely dangerous tools, notorious for opening gateways for demons to cross over. People use both to talk to demons; many people become obsessed with the practice. Thanks to reality shows on the paranormal, the digital voice recorder (when used in this way) has become the Ouija board of our generation. Whatever the method, do not open this door! If you have already opened it, then close it immediately.

If you are on a team doing a walk-through, be very gentle and respectful to the owners and their property. Let the Holy Spirit reveal any defiled objects. Be sure to keep an open mind, but be aware that the enemy will try to deceive you while you are on the premises. People with religious spirits will suspect defilement of the weirdest items. This is the way religious spirits mess with people in order to bring chaos to a walk-through.

Those suffering from demonic oppression can also have a tendency of pointing out "wrong" things about their spouses. You will sense this behavior as being quirky; you might even sense something about the person exhibiting the behavior. Ask the Holy Spirit what is going on. It is so important to operate in the gifts of the Spirit; the Spirit will guide you as you sift through evidence at the "crime scene."

Just do it with gentleness and respect. After all, you are an ambassador of Jesus Christ.

DIY (Do-It-Yourself) Rituals of Exorcism

While helping oppressed ghost hunters, I have noticed that they have a pre-occupation with exorcism prayers and religious rituals. The ritual is a red flag you need to identify. These folks are not trained in exorcism; they won't attend church; yet a religious spirit has fixated them on the rites of exorcism.

These people also burn incense, which interrupts with the smell sensory system. (Demons sometimes manifest with an odor—either a stench or a smell of sulfur.) When I first encountered this incense obsession, I was in the process of blessing a house. I smelled something burning and went into battle mode because I thought a spirit was manifesting for a second time. Instead, it was the owner of the house burning stinky sage incense because the ghost-hunting, charlatan exorcists on TV use incense.

I've mentioned the use of sage before. Psychics use it a lot; it is believed to be a Native American remedy that rids a land of spirits. Again, this is a prime example of the religious spirit mixing religions such as Catholicism and witchcraft in order to dilute the healing power of Jesus. When on a walk-through, you need to shut all this ritual down. Don't let misguided people assist you. Demonic oppression may be manifesting in them to distract you from your walk-through.

Blessing a Home

Once the walk-through is complete, we usually bless the house. It doesn't hurt to give a home a blessing. If we detect any demonic activity, blessing the house will drive it out into the open or identify, through manifestation, which person the spirit is attached to. If nothing manifests the house receives a blessing and everything in the home is consecrated (dedicated, given back) to God, which is the best spiritual position to be in when under an attack.

Chapter 14 of this book is dedicated to house blessing and will help you if you have never blessed a house before. The points here on house blessing are specific to hauntings. It's always good to bless your own home every so often, to make sure no defilement has entered it.

Like everything else I am presenting here, there is no real formula for blessing a home. The goal is to have the owners of the home invite the Holy Spirit into their dwelling and then give the house to Him. Begin in prayer with the family. I usually have the head of the household—the father, the single mom, or whoever it is—invite the Holy Spirit into the home. If it is a nice day, open the front door and let the breeze of the Holy Spirit enter the house.

Be extremely sensitive to the people's property while you are in their home. Also be extremely sensitive to what the Holy Spirit is showing you. Stop and ask yourself questions. For instance, are you standing in a child's bathroom and getting a strange feeling? Is it the bathtub that is making you feel uneasy? Is it the mirror? Perhaps the child is experiencing some self-hatred or anorexia. Now, don't run to the bathroom immediately upon entering a home and look for these things. I present them merely as examples of conversations you need to have with the Holy Spirit when you encounter something.

What is the condition of the home? Is it in utter chaos? Would you be afraid to sit down on the couch or put something down in fear of losing it? Is the house a filthy mess?

Chaos is the environment of demons. Recommend the owners clean up the house immediately and explain the environment of chaos. Explain it in a cordial manner. You want to be able to come back and bless the house when the spiritual environment is right. The King of kings is coming to their home and He loves cleanliness and order.

In the event you are going to a home where you are absolutely positive there is oppression going on, bring a team of prayer warriors to the home with you. In fact, never go out to bless a home alone. Always take someone with you. If you are a male, bring a female, just in case a manifestation occurs in a female at the house. If you are a husband-and-wife team like Lisa and me, you are all set.

I recommend a team of four to pray in a home where there is demonic activity. This is because the spirits will start hopping from room to room to avoid being blessed. Start with an initial walk-through and then bless the house. In a single-story house, have as many people in different rooms as possible and bless the house. In a two-story house, position two team members upstairs and two downstairs as you bless the home.

To be clear, the people on your team need to be prayer warriors who know their authority over evil spirits. Remember: this is war. Give yourself at least two hours or more for a good house blessing. The blessing doesn't take two hours, but you may need additional time on the premises in the event a spirit manifests through someone and deliverance is required.

Pray over the house, covered in the blood Jesus. Make sure, through prayer, that the home is the property of and blessing of the Holy Spirit. Any spirits then find themselves in a home that belongs to the King of kings and Lord of lords. They must leave under the authority of His Word.

Blessing a house is the start of what I call launching the counteroffensive campaign. This is your spiritual D-Day, your Battle of Normandy, so to speak. Other battles will ensue afterwards. For now, you are establishing the spiritual beachhead. It's the beginning of taking back the house and those who live in the house. If the people call you two days after a house blessing and report frantically that they slept well right after the blessing, but the activity started up again, don't be alarmed. This happens. But now the house is under the covering of the blood of Christ. It's time for the people in the house to learn their Kingdom authority. If they are Christians they *must* stand on their authority! If they just accepted Jesus while witnessing signs and wonders during the house blessing, I am more likely to offer more assistance, because new converts need to learn about their authority. It is our ministry's duty to help equip them to walk in their authority.

Do you see the difference? I cannot fight battles for discipled Christians; God already gave them authority. If they don't use it, they are in effect relinquishing their dominion to the enemy. Under those circumstances, the demons will not leave their house. However, I will participate in prayer time that they arrange and I will help them become prayer warriors. In the end, it is on their authority alone that the demons will finally leave.

As I said, our team of intercessors consists of people who know their authority in Jesus. The M16 intercessors blanket the people we assist in prayer; they pray in order to protect these people, their families, and their property. The intercessors pray for them to see their authority in Jesus. The most effective approach to spiritual warfare is for the families living in the affected homes to fight back. Once they learn how to wield their spiritual authority in wisdom and understanding, they can fight the enemy whenever he tries to attack them.

Dealing With Defiled Objects

Demonic oppression in a household can manifest from defiled objects. Such manifestations can come from something as blatantly demonic as a pentagram to something as harmless as an old family heirloom. It can come from Grandpa's Freemasonry book or a Jehovah's Witness Bible.

The hardest part is ridding yourself of demonically tainted family heirlooms. Yet, Scripture tells us we must part ways with these items. If we don't, we are willfully accepting the demonic activity they generate. Know this: God will not inhabit a defiled environment.

No, but the sacrifices of pagans are offered to demons, not to God, and I do not want you to be participants with demons. You cannot drink the cup of the Lord and the cup of demons too; you cannot have a part in both the Lord's table and the table of demons (1 Corinthians 10:20-21).

Furniture and paintings can be defiled as well. How were they defiled in the first place? I don't know, but I know they can be defiled. First Samuel 5 gives us an example of a defiled object, the statue of Dagon. The Ark of the Covenant was stored in Dagon's temple. The next morning, the people found the statue lying face down on the ground before the Ark.

False idols and gods are demons. Anything that is worshiped other than God is demonic. In my humble opinion, the face-down statue of Dagon is an example of what Philippians 2:10-11 tells us: every knee, including satan's, will bow to the Lord Jesus Christ, to the glory of God the Father.

So what do you do with these objects? Pray over them of course! If it's a little trinket or idol pray over it, bind the demonic power in it, repent for owning the item, and then destroy it. Use your Kingdom authority over it!

If it's a larger object like a bed or a painting that was an expensive purchase at the antique store perhaps, try praying over the object and see if you can consecrate the item back to God. Ask the Holy Spirit if the item is cleansed. You can feel in your spirit if it is or isn't.

If the item is an obvious source of complete, concentrated evil I suggest praying as you did before with the trinket, but this time with a prayer team. A few friends who are prayer warriors will suffice. Pray over the item and attack it and bind the darkness in the item. Next, destroy the item, smashing it into pieces that will fit nicely into an incinerator. Then incinerate the item.

Prayer to Bind a Defiled Object

Here's a prayer you can use when praying over an item that the Holy Spirit has revealed as being defiled:

Holy Spirit, I thank You for revealing this defiled object. I want You in my home and nothing else. In this home we will serve no other God but You. Thank You, Jesus, for Your work on the cross and for defeating satan.

Lord, forgive me for bringing into my house an object that harbors an evil spirit. What is bound on earth is bound in Heaven. I bind this demon now with my authority in Jesus Christ.

In Jesus' name I bind you demon. You are never to interfere in my family's life again.

What is released on earth is released in Heaven. Lord, I ask that You release blessings and favor on my family and break any and all assignments this object has brought upon us, in Jesus' name! Thank You, Jesus.

Leaving the Hitchhikers Behind

Always pray and clean yourself off when leaving a site with demonic activity. You don't want any demonic hitchhikers following you home. And they will try. If this is your first house blessing, I suggest you put a post-it note on your steering wheel to remind you to pray off the hitchhikers when you return to your car. The ideal place to pray off any "cling-ons" is actually before leaving the premises. Pray this with the family whose home you have blessed.

Oppression can follow you home and manifest as activity in your house. This activity can include a dose of oppression on your family members, nightmares, or even manifestations. This is spiritual warfare and the enemy has power. This is why I also bless my house regularly and make sure nothing is in defilement.

My home, which belongs to the Holy Spirit, is my sanctuary, covered in the blood of Jesus. When I go home after cleaning myself and others off, I know that I am in a blessed place where it is safe to take off my prayer holster and hang it up. We need our rest in the Lord, too.

It is important to tell you that I do have spiritual activity at my house, but it is angelic. Lisa and I have had guest speakers over to our house for meetings and they remark on the angelic activity. If you see a spirit in your home, listen to your armor and ask whether the spirit is from God. I know the difference between my Father's warriors and the powers of darkness.

Before we continue, here's a prayer example you can use to spiritually clean off your team after you have blessed a house or done deliverance work:

Thank You, Jesus, for this victory. No weapon formed against us shall prosper. Satan and his army were defeated at the cross. Jesus, we ask that You clean off from us all unclean spirits now.

In Jesus' name, we forbid any form of retribution. You will not touch our homes, families, or pets. You will not cause any financial or property damage. You are bound and forbidden from any form of retaliation, in Jesus' name.

Lord, we ask that You release warring angels to protect us during this time and to cancel any and all assignments of the enemy. For this we thank You in advance, in Jesus' name.

A Haunting or a Calling?

Lisa and I have worked on several cases involving children who experienced supernatural activity while in their early teen years.

The typical scenario involves youth group worship leaders and intercessors. The enemy may manifest using fear in an attempt to derail these young people in their callings. These kids have reported seeing shadows or even manifestations of spirits in their rooms. It makes their parents uneasy, because these are usually kids who are very stable in their home and church environments.

What often happens is that God allows these young people to see into the spirit realm. It would be easy to overreact; but it is very important not to quench the Holy Spirit when He is working on a child's gifting.

> *Do not put out the Spirit's fire; do not treat prophecies with contempt. Test everything. Hold on to the good. Avoid every kind of evil* (1 Thessalonians 5:19-22).

By this I mean, don't pray the spirits away from the child and command them never to be seen again. The Holy Spirit may be training the child to see spirits; He may be developing a gift in the child for use in His Kingdom.

However, if a spirit manifests and harms the child, this is obviously not a situation that is being allowed by God. This is demonic oppression and must be dealt with at a high level of warfare. The point I want to make is that, if a child is faithful and has a relationship with Jesus, make sure you understand what is happening. If the spirits appear and the child tells them to leave, it may be the Holy Spirit training the child in the use of his or her Kingdom authority. The child will need to speak to the heavenly Father and learn whether this is the case.

The key point is that a relationship between the heavenly Father and the child is already established in faith. Sometimes Christians go off the deep end when demonic activity is involved. They may lack understanding and yet be the first ones to give advice when they themselves are significantly ill-informed.

Keep in mind that the Holy Spirit will stir the hearts of young people and allow a little tribulation to grow them into their callings.

God typically summons His warriors in this manner. He takes them by the hand and shows them His signs and wonders.

Taking Back Your Own Home

David killed the bear and then the lion before he slew the giant Philistine, named Goliath (see 1 Sam. 17:37). If you have activity in your house and you are frightened, take back the house in baby steps. Recover the TV that keeps switching off and on even while it's unplugged. (Satan seems to enjoy manipulating electrical devices.) Lay hands on it and bind the enemy from interfering with it.

Speak into the spirit realm with conviction and authority! Have you ever had an acquaintance steal something from you? Did you get angry and demand it back from the person? Of course you did! Well, that's the tone of this prayer. You don't need to shout at the spirits; they hear you. Just speak with your authority!

> *Father, I thank You for Your glory and for Your Son's work on the cross, which has given me this victory. I give all the glory to You in this battle, in the name of Jesus Christ,*
>
> *I bind the television set from the forces of darkness. You are not to touch this piece of equipment. I submit to the authority of Jesus Christ, and in Jesus' name I bind you! You are never to touch the TV (microwave, radio, etc.), in Jesus' name!*

If the television switches on, bind it and take it back. Bless, anoint, and consecrate it and any other items back to the Holy Spirit. If the bed is vibrating, bind the enemy that is shaking the bed, and take it back. Win some small victories to build up your faith. Then start taking back a room, and then a house.

I once had to bind the fire alarms in my house because demons were trying to torment my entire family with them—at 4:00 in the morning. As God led me into spiritual warfare, my house was a war zone. Now it's a sanctuary under the protection of the blood of Jesus Christ. In the midst of warfare, we have incursions into our homes. But we exercise our authority and order the spirits to leave.

By now, almost everyone has seen the Pixar movie, *Monster's Inc.* In the spirit realm, we have found that physical doors (especially, closet doors) can be gateways to the spirit realm. Bind the closet if it is a doorway or entry point for evil. Use this prayer, if you like:

> *In Jesus' name I bind this doorway of evil. I order it permanently closed to all evil spirits. What is bound in Heaven is bound on earth. What is released in Heaven is released on earth. Lord release Your warring angels to protect me and seal this door, in Jesus' name!*

You are at war. Win some victories and start taking back your house! When you experience victories you build up your faith and are able to stand on it later. Standing on faith is standing on your authority. When the demon growls or moans in the middle of the night, bind it and shut it up, in the name of Jesus. You can use those exact words! Read Scripture in the middle of the night—out loud.

When a demon wakes me up at 2 A.M., I call it story time. I think to myself, "You want me up? OK—I'll read some Scripture to you."

From our experience we know that the reading of Scripture *burns* demons! Now, the activity is not as much fun for the demon. What you are doing is speaking into the spirit realm through Scripture, and standing on your faith.

Please note *we don't speak to demons* or ask them their names. Never talk with demons! In my experience they always lie. Always talk to Jesus! I speak to the Father, Son, and Holy Spirit. I could care less what the demons' names are. You tell the demons what to do. They have to go!

Summary

A haunting is a divine evangelistic appointment, although the people calling for your assistance may not see it that way at first. God wins these battles every time when those being tormented give their lives to Jesus. Still, many will reject Him as their Lord and Savior. Some will even use their torment to draw sympathy from others.

No matter what case of demonic activity you are called to address, you must listen to the Holy Spirit. The Holy Spirit might even tell you not to go to the house and pray, because the people are not ready to be healed. It is not that God is withholding deliverance; He wants to heal them now. Yet, sometimes, the person in bondage doesn't want to ask for the healing. You can see that listening to the Holy Spirit is crucial in spiritual warfare.

Don't rush into a situation without first praying and talking to the Holy Spirit. God might tell you to take along a few extra people to pray with you. He may also give you more revelation through your dreams as you wait on Him. God is always victorious; some cases just take a lot of time and prayer.

Always, always, clean yourself off with prayer and make sure you don't bring home any hitchhiking spirits. Cancel any assignments the enemy has set against you and your team. Be sensitive to the leading of the Holy Spirit and you will experience total victory.

Endnote

1. Gabriele Amorth, *An Exorcist Tells His Story*, (San Francisco:Ignatius Press, 1999), 125.

CHAPTER 7

THE MIRACLE
OF A REPENTING HEART

*Therefore confess your sins to each other and pray for each
other so that you may be healed. The prayer of a righteous
man is powerful and effective* (James 5:16).

When the Holy Spirit heals, He heals the body, soul, and spirit. At a prayer meeting, Lisa and I met a woman who said she was suffering from depression. She also said her health wasn't so good. Lisa and I laid hands on her and prayed.

As the Holy Spirit invaded this prayer session, He revealed two words to me: *son* and *addiction*. I quietly asked the woman about what the Holy Spirit told me. She tried to keep her composure, but started to cry. She told us that she lost her son to addiction years earlier and blamed herself for not doing more for him. The Holy Spirit permeated her life and the root of her depression right there. She needed to hear that she was forgiven. At that point, she just fell down to the ground and cried. The light of Jesus Christ infiltrated her darkness and all the self-hatred deep inside that kept her blaming herself. All of it had to come up.

We finished praying for the woman and left her lying on the floor for a good 20 minutes. She was now under the care of the

Holy Spirit. When God invades the problem and heals His children of depression, He goes straight to the root of it and prunes it at the source. God is merciful and gentle when He touches a person with His grace.

> *For this is what the high and lofty One says—He who lives forever, whose name is holy: "I live in a high and holy place, but also with him who is contrite and lowly in spirit, to revive the spirit of the lowly and to revive the heart of the contrite"* (Isaiah 57:15).

We briefly touched on the topic of healing in our discussion of spiritual authority. In deliverance prayer ministry, we have seen incredible, unexpected healings that came when the Holy Spirit led the individual to repentance.

This is where your deliverance prayer team ministry needs to be comprised of people of good character who have a high degree of sensitivity toward the emotions of those requesting prayer. These are delicate issues. The Holy Spirit may reveal, through a word of knowledge, an area of suppressed darkness that needs to surface for healing to be released.

Now, if you get frustrated while praying for someone and decide the person needs to repent of his or her sins, this is not a word of knowledge. The word of knowledge I'm talking about serves a different purpose, although it involves repentance. "Now aren't we supposed to be forgiven once and for all?" you might ask.

Yes. We know from Scripture that we are forgiven by the Father and we are told He hurls our iniquities into the depths of the sea (see Mic. 7:19). However, we don't always allow ourselves to be forgiven. This is where the Holy Spirit reveals darkness that needs to surface and be thrown out. He will give a word of knowledge—it might even come to several people in the prayer group around the same time.

Our unforgiveness isn't always aimed at ourselves. There are also instances in which we Christians choose not to forgive others. This is a dangerous thing—it can fester and literally eat away at us on the inside.

THE MIRACLE OF A REPENTING HEART

I Don't Want to Forgive

It is astonishing to me just how often the Holy Spirit reveals that the person I'm praying for (who was previously unknown to me) needs to forgive someone.

The person's immediate response is often a spiteful, "No!" Mind you, these are Christians I am praying for. At a house meeting I was praying with a gentleman who was suffering from strange back pains. I'd never met the man, so I didn't know much else about him. As I prayed for healing, the Holy Spirit told me the guy needed to forgive his ex-wife. His response was, "No, I don't."

I prayed for him some more, wrapped it up, and moved on to another person. I know the voice of the Holy Spirit; this man for sure needed to forgive his ex-wife. Later in the evening, the person who was leading the ministry called out my name and asked me to pray over the same man again—for forgiveness issues. The guy looked at me and laughed. I was irritated because there were other people in the room who needed prayer and were willing to forgive others, as the Scripture commands:

> Bear with each other and forgive whatever grievances you may have against one another. Forgive as the Lord forgave you (Colossians 3:13).

Most of the folks there were willing to forgive and be healed. The man in this example, however, was one of the sympathy seekers I mention time and time again. They don't want to be healed. Their demons just want to talk, talk, talk, and suck the life out of other Christians. That's the assignment of these demons.

Time after time, I have seen oppressed people who lacked the capacity to forgive their own family members. The root of their oppression is the very anger they refuse to release through forgiveness. But what does the Word of God say about forgiveness? In Matthew 18:21-22, Jesus told Peter that he should forgive a brother who has sinned against him 70 times seven times!

There is no hall pass allowing Christians to choose whom to forgive or not forgive. The point Jesus made is that you need to forgive others—period!

I remember during a prayer meeting when a young college girl asked me to pray for her. The Holy Spirit told me she needed to forgive both her parents. She vehemently responded, "No! I don't want to."

I don't know how many times my prayer is shut down by the spiritual immaturity of adult Christians. No matter what you think your parents have done to you, they are no longer the issue once you become an adult. The Scripture says we must honor our mother and father, regardless of their state of mind.

What does the Gospel of Matthew call Christians who do not forgive? He calls them contemptible and wicked servants (see Matt. 18:32 AMP). God also says He will turn these people over to their tormentors, the jailers—the demons. Even if you don't want to forgive someone who hurt you, please hear me: I have learned in deliverance ministry that absolute evil and hurt are real. I have seen manifestations of the demonic. In order to be set free, you must forgive!

> *Then his master called him and said to him, You contemptible and wicked attendant! I forgave and cancelled all that [great] debt of yours because you begged me to. And should you not have had pity and mercy on your fellow attendant, as I had pity and mercy on you? And in wrath his master turned him over to the torturers (the jailers), till he should pay all that he owed. So also My heavenly Father will deal with every one of you if you do not freely forgive your brother from your heart his offenses* (Matthew 18:32-35 AMP).

Praying Against Bipolar Disorder and Depression

One of the first deliverance encounters the Holy Spirit led me into involved a generational curse. The root was anger, generations of unforgiveness, and severe depression.

What we have seen in our experience with bipolar disorder and depression is that demonic oppression is always involved. Sickness, disease, and death are from satan.

Be very careful when you pray for people with mental disorders. Satan has done enough damage to them; you want to be sure your team does them good. Make certain you have more experienced people on your prayer team for these cases. They will grasp onto every word you pray whether you know what you said or not. They will obsess on all the wounds the Holy Spirit reveals to you. My advice is not to share what the Holy Spirit reveals unless it is absolutely necessary. The last thing these folks need is to take home another thing to obsess on.

We typically have one or two people from our deliverance prayer team minister to the person suffering from a mental disorder. It is not uncommon for oppressing spirits to make themselves known during this prayer time, whether by speaking to us or causing manifestations of mental issues. The point is to keep people calm as they are being prayed for and just let the Holy Spirit heal them.

Voices do get shut down. It takes lots of prayer. Little by little, through multiple prayer sessions you will see small victories. Just remember: never allow the people being prayed for to turn prayer time into a counseling or pity-me session. Demons often try these tricks in order to keep healing prayers from being released.

The victims of demonic activity whom you are trying to help are there *for prayer.* If they want your ear so you can feel sorry for them, they came to the wrong place. Many times, interruptions by people being prayed for are a sign that they don't want to be set free. At that point, they are wasting your team's time.

This is strictly a time for healing. It is a quiet and relaxing time in which they can receive prayer and get touched by the Holy Spirit. The Holy Spirit will reveal to the mentally ill exactly what is needed to make them whole. It is a slow, but powerful healing process that includes repentance.

Some people who are receiving prayer decide they don't need their medication anymore. Hallelujah! But it is not the prayer team's place to tell them this. People with bipolar disorder and depression are usually under medical care. Let this decision be between the doctor and the patient. Often, doctors are dumbfounded by the changes they see in the patient. When that happens, they often recommend a lower dosage of medication or even agree to stop the medication altogether. This is an individual thing; it is a step for people in accepting responsibility for their healing and walking in the life Jesus has planned for them.

Arthritis, Anger, and Bitterness

On a beautiful June night, while walking through the Tenderloin District of San Francisco, our Night Strike team came across a wheelchair-bound woman named Diane.

One of our prayer team members, Samantha (Sam) Brinegar, asked if she could pray for the woman. Diane said she had some pain in her feet and wanted Sam to pray for healing. Sam knelt down in front of the wheelchair and laid hands on Diane's feet. She used her authority in Jesus and commanded healing into Diane's body.

I stood next to Diane's wheelchair and watched as Sam prayed. A few seconds into the prayer, I noticed that the fingers on Diane's left hand began gnarling and twisting. I had seen this before when we prayed for people with arthritis. The spirits involved with someone's arthritis often respond to healing prayers for other ailments or conditions the person has. The spirit afflicting the arthritis reacts to the divine "medication" entering the body—the Holy Spirit!

I asked Diane if she had arthritis. She looked at me, bewildered as to how I knew that, and said, "Yes." Jimi Merrell was also on the team that night; he held her hand and prayed. The Holy Spirit revealed to Jimi that there was some bitterness toward some people Diane knew. Forgiveness needed to be released for these people.

People—and especially women—who live in the streets have it very hard. They experience a great deal of verbal, physical, and sexual abuse. It is almost a normal way of life for the homeless women we encounter. This shouldn't be. Nevertheless it is; therefore, when we ask people on the streets to forgive, it often falls on deaf ears.

There can be even more long-term consequences where arthritis is concerned. We have seen that when an arthritic person chooses not to forgive, arthritis can travel upward through the family line in the form of a generational curse. I know some very spiritual and extremely forgiving people who have suffered horrible rheumatoid arthritis that came, not from unforgiveness in their lives, but from an inherited generational curse.

I know firsthand of a woman who prayed and took authority over that curse. She is seeing victories in her battle to be completely healed. Through prayer, there has been a significant improvement in her health.

With arthritis, you may see an instant healing, healing over time with lots of prayer, or no healing whatsoever. Always pray and expect healing, no matter if it is your first time or your hundredth time praying for the same person. Each time, pray from Heaven with your Kingdom authority. Lay hands on people if possible, especially hold their hands if it isn't too painful and pray with them.

Healing prayers are always a calm form of spiritual warfare. The intent isn't to elevate their blood pressure, but to relax them so the Holy Spirit can invade the situation.

Demonic Bondage and Forgiveness

During one case in which our M16 team went out to bless a home marked by spiritual activity, the young woman who lived there said she was psychic and was learning to use her gift.

As we blessed the house, the spirit that was in the house began to manifest in the woman. The prayer team and I prayed over her and started pulling spirits off her. When the house settled into a climate of peace (through the Holy Spirit and our prayers) we wrapped up our session and headed home.

The next morning, I shot an e-mail to a friend who is also my mentor. He immediately replied with a word of knowledge that the demonic spirit in the woman's house intended to return that night. The woman involved in this case needed to forgive someone.

As I returned to focus on my day job, I forgot about my friend's email. Late in that evening, I received a phone call: the spirit had returned and we were needed right away. I immediately remembered what my friend said in the e-mail.

Lisa and I spent nearly three hours on that deliverance. We cut through the spirits with the power and authority of the Holy Spirit to get the woman to repent for an unresolved matter in her life.

Dealing with demonic oppression is multi-layered. In this particular case, the spiritual gateway into this woman's life was opened up through her training in psychic practices. The demon spirit found the darkness inside her and latched onto it. If I had just asked the woman to repent for using powers of darkness, it wouldn't have evicted the spirits entirely.

These monsters are legalistic. That is why you should never ask them their names. They lie; and if you call out the wrong demon, your deliverance session will become that much harder for you. Rely on the gifts of the Spirit. The Holy Spirit will reveal the underlying sin these demons have used as their nest. In this case, psychic practices opened the gateway, but unforgiveness was where the demon settled in. That nest was revealed and cleaned out.

Forgiving Yourself; Self-Hatred

Evil has no respect for age. Satan attacks children with the full intention of scarring the body, mind, and spirit. These horrible attacks include molestation, rejection by parents, physical and verbal abuse by parents, and the loss of siblings. When the healthy life of a child is invaded by these evils, self-hatred is one of the horrible scars that manifests in the mind.

This is not the only entry point for self-hatred. This evil can invade the lives of adults through rape and spousal abuse (both physical and verbal). Verbal attacks can be as devastating and scarring as acts of rape. Lisa and I worked with women who were in environments of continual verbal abuse from spouses or fathers. These women were crippled in their future relationships. They have been brutally convinced they are not able to succeed at anything.

During prayer, if the Holy Spirit reveals to me and others that a man has broken down a woman's will by speaking curses over her, I will stand in, as a man, and ask forgiveness for the evil that was spoken over her. These women have never heard the repentant voice of a man asking their forgiveness. Nor have they believed they ever would hear such a voice.

The asking for forgiveness in this stage of prayer is powerful and releases a lot of darkness that is bottled up in these tormented individuals. At this type of moment in prayer, you can see the Holy Spirit rush into these people's lives.

Anorexia and other self-inflicted wounds, such as cutting, are physical manifestations of self-hatred and anger. I have, through a prayer team, prayed for several women with anorexia; the spirit physically manifested itself and was driven out through prayer.

Anorexia can be tricky; the spirit will leave, but may return several times before being completely cast out. There is another spirit that must be driven out and that is anger. The Gospel of Mark refers to anorexia and demonic oppression with the healing of the boy with the evil spirit.

Whenever it seizes him, it throws him to the ground. He foams at the mouth, gnashes his teeth and becomes rigid. I asked Your disciples to drive out the spirit, but they could not (Mark 9:18).

The King James Version uses the words *pineth away* in place of *becomes rigid*. The Amplified Bible says the boy was *wasting away*. The demons were interfering with the boy's ability to eat. This is anorexia.

The practice of cutting and hurting oneself is another demonic oppression. In most cases, the demon is present too in the form of voices that are heard in the head. In some cases, the demon appears in the form of a friendly ghost spirit. Sometimes the "ghost" even manifests as a lover. We know what a ghost is—a demon.

> *You shall not make any cuttings in your flesh for the dead nor print or tattoo any marks upon you; I am the Lord* (Leviticus 19:28 AMP).

An example of cutting is found in the Gospel of Mark. It was one of the traits of the demon-possessed man in the region of the Gerasenes:

> *Night and day among the tombs and in the hills he would cry out and cut himself with stones* (Mark 5:5).

The voices heard by cutters can be shut down. Freedom can be reached through deliverance prayer and by blessing the person under spiritual attack. These open the door to healing for those plagued by self-hatred.

Repentance is part of the healing process. Below is a prayer of repentance for self-hatred. If you need to repent of this sin, I recommend having a friend pray with you and lay hands on you as you pray. Let the Holy Spirit do His work. Have your friend pray for the Holy Spirit to fill you as you pray this prayer aloud. As the darkness leaves, your friend praying with you will ask the Holy Spirit to occupy the vacated premises. Continue to pray together as the Spirit leads you.

Prayer of Repentance for Self-hatred

Heavenly Father, I thank You for each new and wonderful day. I thank You that You loved me so much that You sent Your son, Jesus, to save me. You knew me before I was born. You knew me in my mother's womb. I recognize that I am beautifully and wonderfully created.

I repent for having had thoughts of being anything less than Your perfect creation. I repent for hating the way I see myself; I repent of my eating disorder and of wanting to hurt myself; I repent of cutting myself; and I repent of my depression. Right now, I want the light of Jesus Christ to invade my darkness. Jesus, I take every unclean thought toward myself captive and leave it at the foot of the cross.

From this day forward, I choose to live a life closer to You, my Father in Heaven. My thoughts about myself will be healthy and godly. I know that lies are from the enemy. I repent of the self-hatred that kept me in the darkness instead of in Your light. In Jesus' name I come to You and ask to be made whole. Amen.

Forgiving Others

I have covered in detail the power to release healing by forgiving others. Revenge and retribution are dangerous avenues Christians should never consider pursuing. There is a saying that describes revenge perfectly: "Revenge is like drinking poison and waiting for someone else to die."

Revenge festers and eats away at you. A good example is that of a man who goes through a brutal divorce because of his own infidelity, and then blames his ex-wife for being evil. In deliverance ministry, as I mentioned previously, I rarely see a bitter, divorced husband take responsibility for his infidelity.

Infidelity is evil and comes with consequences. These men rarely face up to their own sin; they instead choose to blame their wives who often expected only love and commitment out of the relationship. This anger manifests in sin that slowly devours them mentally, physically, and spiritually.

Retribution is something I will never seek. I was on the streets of San Francisco one evening on Night Strike and my team came across a demon-possessed man. I tried to bind the demon so I

could speak to the man in bondage. This man had a fully compromised will; I could not reach him. He needed massive deliverance and it wasn't going to happen on the street.

The spirit controlling him identified itself as the spirit of retribution. If spirits lie, why did I believe this one was the spirit of
retribution? This event occurred during a season of my training
by the Holy Spirit, where an authority was imposed on spirits to
force them to give me their names without me asking it of them.
It always happened during my street ministry. The Holy Spirit
wanted to show me first hand what spirits were out on the streets
of San Francisco. Then one day, this season ended and the spirits ceased this strange behavior on the streets. I believed it was
to be one of the spirits of judgment sent to the city and waiting
for its time to be released. This was something I picked up in
the prophetic while my son and I stood in front of him. When I
looked into this spirit's eyes, I saw pure, unadulterated evil. The
man's eyes were rolled up in the back of his head. He was walking around with nothing but the whites of his eyes showing. Witnessing this first hand and seeing this man's condition were all I
needed to convince me *never* to seek retribution.

Releasing forgiveness, for the right reasons and on the right
people, has incredible impact in healing ministry. A lot of times
the demonic oppression is sent packing and its afflictions must
leave with it. The greatest healings we have seen are those in
which the doctors were unable to provide any further medical
assistance or comfort. That is when a testimony is ripe for the
releasing!

Prayer for Forgiving Others

*Heavenly Father, I thank You for this day. I come to You and
ask You to forgive me for not forgiving others. I repent for not
forgiving my mother and father and not honoring them. I repent
for not forgiving my son or daughter. I repent for not forgiving
my in-laws. I repent for not forgiving any and all family members. I repent for not forgiving my ex-wife/husband. I repent for
not forgiving a friend. I repent for not forgiving others who hurt*

someone I loved. I repent for not forgiving others in the Body of Christ. I repent for not forgiving medical professionals.

I repent for having thoughts of retribution and seeking acts of revenge. I repent of the feelings of rejection and guilt that entered my life by not forgiving. From this day forward, I choose to repent of my sin of unforgiveness toward others. I renounce and cancel any word curse spoken against these individuals, in the name of Jesus. I speak blessing over them and over their families, in Jesus' name! Amen.

Forgiving God

Many times, Christians are deceived by an untimely death. I have heard many Christians ask, "Why, God, did You give my loved one cancer?"

God did not give your loved one cancer; the enemy did. I know a lot of cancer survivors who are alive today because of a miraculous healing touch from God. I also know a lot of people who went on to Heaven and were not healed here on earth. This is a great mystery.

Time and time again, I have seen a spirit of death wrap itself around a healthy family and squeeze the spiritual life out of it. I have noticed a common thread: often this happens to families that are very close and loving. It can begin when one sibling dies from a horrible affliction or commits suicide or dies from a drug overdose. The other sibling, whether younger or older, exhibits extreme rebellion toward God and is very angry.

This behavior needs to be dealt with immediately. Once the grieving sibling turns away from God, the door is wide open to demonic attack. In extreme cases, the sibling is so distraught as to take oaths and welcome in the enemy as a way to get even with God. The blessed life quickly becomes a cursed life because the individual didn't deal with grief in a healthy manner.

Older children are harder for parents to influence; but if your children live under your roof, make sure you enforce the rules prohibiting anything demonic in your house. Do whatever you can to stop the spiral away from God. If it is a spirit of death, it won't stop until it curses and consumes a family line. However, these curses can be broken when the lie of the enemy is revealed.

Jesus came into the world to destroy the works of the devil! We must recognize who our true enemy is. I am aware of a case in which Jesus appeared in a dream and told a terminally ill young boy that he would receive a miraculous healing. He told his family and church and they were excited about the news. The boy passed on to eternal life a few months later.

Why did Jesus appear to the boy in the dream and grant him a healing? Satan and his minions can masquerade as angels of light, as Jesus or the Virgin Mary—you name it. There is no limit to satan's level of hatred for mankind. He wants us all dead, including your precious little children. When you are angry at God I suggest you try talking to Him and calming yourself down. God will heal you during your time of grief. Grief is a finite process; we can recover from grief while we are here on earth. Seeking to hate God, on the other hand, is eternal damnation.

The same is true for people who are going through a horrible season in life. When things are really difficult, take time to understand what God is showing you through the trial. You may become angry and curse God for the struggle, when His intent is to pull you closer and deeper in Him. This kind of season is often called *The Dark Night of the Soul*. The name is taken from a poem of the same name written by a 16th century Roman Catholic believer, Saint John of the Cross.

Back in 2007, some letters of Mother Teresa's were released in which she described how she had experienced the dark night of the soul. The dark night of the soul is a mystical theology term, that comes from the writings of Saint John of the Cross, from the 1500s. Mother Teresa's dark night of the soul is mentioned briefly in an online Time article, Mother Teresa's Crisis of Faith, August 23, 2007[1].The misinformed media ran with the story, saying that Mother Teresa had lost her faith in God. That is not what she said in the letters. They were deep spiritual documents of how God used hardship in her life to bring her deeper into Him.

Prayer for Forgiving God

Heavenly Father, I thank You that You're merciful. I thank You for Your grace. I thank You that Your Son, Jesus, died on the cross to take away my sins and curses. I come to You in humility and ask You to forgive me for being angry at You. I repent for being angry with You, God, over the untimely death of a loved one. I repent for being angry with You, God, for my unhealthy physical and mental condition. I know sickness and death come from the enemy.

I repent for blaming You for my poor financial condition. I repent for listening to the counsel of the enemy. I repent of the word curses and vows that came out of my mouth while I was angry with You. I renounce the word curses and vows and cancel them now, in the name of Jesus Christ.

Lord from this day forward I will put no other God before You. As for me and my household, we will worship You, Lord. This I pray, in Jesus' name. Amen.

Summary

Repentance is one of the most powerful gifts God gave us in releasing the power of the Holy Spirit's healing. When praying for people, always speak to God and ask Him what is going on. He may tell you it is nothing. That's OK. Jesus is the one who heals, not us. He heals all.

Another tip: I usually quietly check with prayer team members to see if they pick up on the same word I am getting. Many times we do receive the same word. This is why it is so important to listen to the Holy Spirit during prayer.

Never go down a forgiveness check list and interrupt the prayer session with questions like:

Are you angry at yourself?

Are you angry at someone else?

Are you angry at God?

Are you allergic to shellfish?

It's absurd to pray in this manner. Just relax and make sure the environment is relaxed. Then let the Holy Spirit run the healing prayer session. The important thing is for the person who needs prayer to lay his or her burdens down at the foot of the cross and release them, forever, to God.

Endnote

1. *Time.* "Mother Teresas Crisis of Faith," August 23, 2007.   http://www,time.com/time/worid/article/ 0,8599,1655415,00.html (accessed August 22, 2010).

CHAPTER 8

WITCHCRAFT AND VOODOO

When this became known to the Jews and Greeks living in
Ephesus, they were all seized with fear, and the name of the
Lord Jesus was held in high honor. Many of those who believed
now came and openly confessed their evil deeds. A number who
had practiced sorcery brought their scrolls together and burned
them publicly. When they calculated the value of the scrolls, the
total came to fifty thousand drachmas. In this way the word of
the Lord spread widely and grew in power (Acts 19:17-20).

I f you are going to be involved in a successful deliverance ministry, you are going to cross paths with the occult sooner or later. I have many testimonies in dealing with the occult. The good news is that, whenever the person being attacked realizes that Jesus already won the battle, the curses are broken! Yes, I am speaking about authority in Christ again.

One of the more interesting battles I have participated in involved voodoo. A person in Switzerland was being attacked by the spirit of African witchcraft. She was a young African hairdresser named Edna. The rival beautician in town was also from Africa and decided to level the playing field of competition by using black magic.

How does a California boy get a divine appointment from Switzerland? Well, it went like this: One Friday evening in October, I

was in San Francisco setting up teams for Night Strike. Bob Johnson, who runs City Ministries and Night Strike, approached me
and asked me out of the blue, "How good is your French?"

I gave Bob a puzzled look. Then I asked him to repeat the
question. Bob asked again, "How good is your French?"

I told him I had four years of French in high school, but that
was back before electricity was invented. I didn't remember my
French classes at all except for reading French. Bob said he had
some friends in France who needed help fighting demonic activity and witchcraft.

"France, huh?" I didn't immediately tell Bob, "No!" But I
didn't say, "Yes," either. I needed time to pray and think about
this one. Bob said he would give me the contact information and
I could follow up. That is Bob's way of saying he heard a yes.

After wrapping up Night Strike and heading home, I remember praying to God about this case. "God, if this came to my
doorstep because You want me to be part of it, I need to know
You are in it with me!" I was clearly thrown off by the fact I was in
California and the people I needed to help were in France.

When Sunday night rolled around, Lisa and I went to the
Kingdom of Grace Maranatha prayer and healing meeting. We
are part of the Kingdom of Grace prayer team and pray for people who come for healing. You will remember that Gary Paltridge
is a friend and is the minster at Kingdom of Grace. He asked
me to pray for a particular gentleman that night; he said the
young man needed to be set free from—you guessed it—African
witchcraft.

This was the second time in the same weekend that a spiritual battle with African witchcraft was assigned to me. A coinci-
dence? Not likely. After two hours of praying, this young man was
almost completely free of the majority of the witchcraft demons.
After one or two more meetings, he was completely free.

What Gary pointed out to me during this prayer battle was
how many nasty demons were removed in two hours. The Holy

Spirit was showing me that He was with me during a spiritual battle. I walked away from this battle knowing that distance wasn't an issue. The battle didn't require proximity; it required faith and authority!

On Monday, I followed up and called the overseas husband and wife team, Jerry and Barbara, who had requested help with deliverance prayer. They were actually in Switzerland, but very near the French border. Barbara's hair stylist, Edna, was the young Nigerian woman being attacked by voodoo. Edna's house had snakes and spirits manifesting in it. She had become ill and couldn't eat; her skin had developed a strange rash.

Edna learned from one of her friends that a competitor in town had sought the aid of a voodoo priest in Nigeria to drive Edna out of business. The situation became so dire that Edna sent her son to live with relatives in France to get him out of the spiritual war zone.

Lisa and I spoke with Jerry and Barbara and immediately mobilized to equip them with spiritual warfare information. These people knew their authority in Jesus Christ; this made them the perfect people for the job. Lisa worked with Barbara on how to bless homes. We wanted to immediately stabilize Edna's home environment. We found out that, because the spiritual activity at her home had gotten so bad, she had moved out and was living in an apartment with her friend.

The plan was to spiritually bless wherever Edna was currently living and prepare for a deliverance session over the phone on the upcoming Saturday. I immediately began fasting and going into intercession with Jesus.

Through the week, we worked with Jim and Barbara. We gave them material on breaking generational curses, including witchcraft curses. We knew we needed a translator. Edna spoke some English and I spoke some French. We needed someone who spoke both French and English fluently.

An interesting side note is that, during my times of intercession, I get some cool "download dreams." In one dream I was given a leather-bound book on Edna's life. I flipped through it and looked at the pictures. It looked like a personal photo scrapbook of Edna's with her own comments handwritten in French. In the dream, one photo caught my attention; it was the photo of a woman with blonde hair. Keep this side note in mind; it comes into play later.

Throughout the week, Jerry and I exchanged e-mails of the material I sent him that was being translated into French. We also found an interpreter; it turned out to be the woman who was letting Edna stay at her place.

By Thursday, I believe, Jerry and Barbara had completed the spiritual house blessing and had blessed the apartment where Edna was currently residing. We found out later that the apartment building was very old and the residents saw shadows and apparitions there all the time, especially at night. However, the spiritual activity was suddenly shut down once the house had been blessed!

On Saturday, a small audience gathered in Edna's apartment in Switzerland to witness the deliverance session. They came because they had witnessed firsthand the cessation of all spiritual activity in their building. Meanwhile, I had invited my good friend, Jimi Merrell to be part of the West Coast posse gathered in California.

When it was time, I dialed Switzerland. Based on my experiences with demons hanging up the phone on me, I had already taken authority in the spirit realm and bound demonic access to the phone lines.

Jerry and Barbara orchestrated the deliverance from Switzerland as Jimi and I listened in on the speakerphone. We interjected where we felt the Holy Spirit needed us to break something off Edna, such as soul ties or anything witchcraft-related that was bringing her harm.

Edna's roommate read the deliverance prayer to her. If Edna didn't understand the sentence in English, her roommate repeated it in French. About half an hour into the prayer and deliverance, I heard a woman weeping. I quietly asked Barbara if Edna was crying. Barbara whispered back that it wasn't Edna. I asked her who was crying. She said it was the interpreter. Edna's roommate was getting delivered too!

Then I asked Barbara if Edna had blonde hair, because I had seen a blonde woman in my spiritual warfare dream. Barbara said Edna's hair wasn't blonde, but her roommate's hair was!

After the deliverance session Edna was able to eat again. Her rash disappeared in a matter of days. Barbara assisted Edna that week in unpacking her hair shop, which Edna had closed and had now re-opened for business. The woman who placed the curse on Edna was so freaked out that she went back to Nigeria to look for a more powerful witch doctor. Good luck with that! No witch doctor can compete with the Most High God.

Voodoo

I still receive e-mails now and again from Africa and Nigeria requesting help with voodoo. The people seeking my help are usually Christians. I tell them they have authority to cancel any assignments being sent against them by voodoo practitioners. If they don't realize the authority in Jesus Christ and His work on the cross—they will never be set free.

When I receive a request for help I immediately check to see if they know Jesus. If not, we share the Gospel and invite Christ into their deepest, darkest problems. If they know Jesus, then they must stand on His work and their faith. Otherwise, they will live in fear, which means handing their authority over to satan.

Witchcraft

In our mainstream media, the concept of the witch has evolved from the classic green-faced woman with a wart and a pointed black hat (like the wicked witch of the West in *The Wizard of Oz*) to someone far more palatable. In fact, the modern-day witch has a better media image than the average Christian does. Christians are stereotyped as empty-minded pursuers of a mythological person named Jesus Christ, whom they say was proven a fraud by *The Da Vinci Code* and the secrets of the Knights Templar.

The average witch on television today is a "good" witch who happens to be sexy. Only dark magic is considered evil and satanic; white magic is portrayed as being good. And the name has changed from *witch* to *Wiccan*. Some newscasts even feature Wiccans who give readings on television. We see them working side-by-side with clergy in ghost-hunting shows. The implication is that the one true God cannot resolve a problem with evil spirits, so the Wiccan steps up with a solution.

Do you see how clever satan is? He has wisdom from God like no other creation was ever given before the finished work of the cross of Christ. The Holy Spirit is the Spirit of truth but we allow ourselves to get side tracked from truth by what we see on television and Internet videos. If satan's got the media, he's got our minds and our attention. We are almost conditioned to believe Wicca and other "nice" forms of demon worship are good.

However, Scripture calls divination and witchcraft detestable:

When you enter the land the LORD your God is giving you, do not learn to imitate the detestable ways of the nations there. Let no one be found among you who sacrifices his son or daughter in the fire, who practices divination or sorcery, interprets omens, engages in witchcraft, or casts spells, or who is a medium or spiritist or who consults the dead. Anyone who does these things is detestable to the LORD, and because of these detestable practices the LORD your God will drive out those nations before you. You must be blameless before the LORD your God (Deuteronomy 18:9-13).

Whether it is white magic or black magic, it is detestable to God!

Witchcraft and Defilement in Our Homes

The Scripture tells us to avoid witchcraft at all levels. This includes movies and books, such as the Harry Potter series, that glorify witchcraft. It also includes seeking the aid of soothsayers and psychics, or dabbling in the occult on your own.

...Do not practice divination or sorcery (Leviticus 19:26).

The mainstream media like to sell white magic as a progressive alternative to Christianity. Again, satan is masquerading as an angel of light. Our society is so starved for spirituality that the population eats this stuff right up.

I told you about my mother's collection of books from the psychic, Sylvia Brown and how my mom saw Ms. Brown on Oprah Winfrey's program. Let this be a cautionary tale. We have to filter every influence. Just because a book is being promoted on *The Oprah Show* does not mean it is harmless. I am still trying to cleanse this influence from my mom's home, even though my mom passed on some time ago.

Yes, my mother was a devout Catholic—so much so that she got upset when I ventured out in my youth to attend an Assembly of God church. My mother was well aware of the Lordship of Jesus Christ. Yet there were some areas in which she opened herself to the lies of satan. Visiting psychics and playing with tarot cards can open a doorway for the spirit of death, no matter how often you attend church!

This is a doorway far too many Christian families have opened. It happens because there is a lack of knowledge. God says that His people *are destroyed* because they lack knowledge! (See Hosea 4:6.)

When I was in junior high school, my mom taught me to read her mind to know which playing cards she was holding in her hand. To this day, I prefer not to be anywhere near a deck of cards. You are probably saying, "Oh, my. That's a dangerous way to open your child to hijacked (demonic) spiritual gifts."

You are absolutely right. It was very dangerous. Yet, how many Christian parents purchase *Harry Potter* books for their kids or take the whole family to see a *Harry Potter* movie? The series glorifies witchcraft. It is nicely packaged spiritual poison.

No matter how cute the "wrapping" might seem to be, it is completely satanic.

The *Twilight* series is another popular example of satanic deception. The *Twilight* books and movies are about demons! To become a vampire you must give up your mortal life and become possessed by a blood-drinking demon. And when you bring this stuff into your home and your mind, defilement comes with it.

> *Your eye is the lamp of your body. When your eyes are good, your whole body also is full of light. But when they are bad, your body also is full of darkness. See to it, then, that the light within you is not darkness* (Luke 11:34-35).

I don't want to turn this chapter into a *Harry Potter* commentary, but I will make one last point on the matter. In the book, *Harry Potter and the Prisoner of Azkaban*, author J.K. Rowling inverts the Scripture in Deuteronomy 18:9-13, in the form of a school syllabus. Thus the author makes everything that is detestable to God sound like fun to young readers.[1]

Here is the Hogsworth syllabus,

"Many....are unable to penetrate the veiled mysteries of the future,"..."It is a Gift granted to few...We will be covering the basic methods of Divination this year. The first term will be devoted to reading the tea leaves. Next term we shall progress to palmistry....In the summer term... we shall progress to the crystal ball—if we have finished with fire-omens..."

Comapare the syllabus to Deuteronomy and the list of detestable practices. Do you see the inverting of scripture?

> *When you enter the land the LORD your God is giving you, do not learn to imitate the detestable ways of the nations there. Let no one be found among you who sacrifices his son or daughter in the fire, who practices divination or sorcery, interprets omens, engages in witchcraft, or casts spells, or who is a medium or spiritist or who consults the dead. Anyone who does these things is detestable to the LORD, and because of these detestable*

practices the LORD your God will drive out those nations before you. You must be blameless before the LORD your God (Deuteronomy 18:9-13).

Think of it this way: Would you hang an inverted cross in your kids' room and encourage them to worship the devil? Of course not! Based on my experience, these popular books and movies bear the fingerprint of a demonic scribe.

My point is this: if you are going to go into a spiritual warfare ministry or you are in the midst of a spiritual battle involving witchcraft, you better have your house spiritually in order. Draw a line in the sand and refuse to give the devil any turf in your household.

A Christian friend once told me that I was looking to cast a demon out of every tree. The remark was in response to my warning to this person not to read *Harry Potter* to the kids. This person witnessed firsthand one of my deliverance sessions in which the Holy Spirit set a young girl free from a deaf and dumb spirit. I know I cannot have it both ways. I cannot dabble in the satanic and minister in the power of the Holy Spirit. I don't want anything in my house or my spiritual house that is in defilement to the one true God.

There is a second point you need to understand: it is the *why* part. Defiled items open toeholds and even gateways for demonic oppression. You cannot help other people when demonic oppression shows up in your own house. Case in point: My oldest son, Matt, had a 3D game that he loved, called *Oblivion*. The game involves a fantasy environment in which you cast spells and fight monsters.

When I was in the midst of a spiritual battle, the enemy used the video game to open a doorway of oppression on my son. He would walk the halls late at night like Lady Macbeth. The Holy Spirit revealed to Matt in a spiritual warfare dream that the game was the entry mechanism for the oppression.

We were fighting oppression in our own house and trying to help others. Our house was a war zone. From that point forward, we learned everything we could about removing defiled objects and keeping a home that is pleasing to God. Your home, your family, your life, and every living creature under your roof are now part of the ministry. Believe me; you don't want to learn this lesson like we did.

You *will* go through this learning experience when you enter into spiritual warfare and choose to engage the enemy. Satan was given supernatural wisdom and can see ways to attack you that you would never imagine. But satan's wisdom has its limitations. That's why you need to be talking to the Holy Spirit.

Hexes

As we pray against witchcraft and demonic oppression, we need to be aware that there are people out there who cast spells against us. This is another form of spiritual warfare that sends incoming fiery darts (see Eph. 6:16). Sometimes the darts stick into your armor. My friends and I call this "getting slimed." It is a term we borrowed from the movie *Ghostbusters*.

This is the part of the battle where it is imperative you live a healthy Christian lifestyle; are not typically depressed; don't need deliverance; and don't have a porn, alcohol, or drug addiction, for example. If you are living a stable and balanced Christian lifestyle, you will be able to recognize when you have been slimed. The hex shows up in some form of oppression, such as an addiction. If you don't have an addiction, and better yet, never have had one, and you suddenly experience unnatural, elevated cravings for sex or alcohol or a cigarette, then you know that you have just been hexed. It typically occurs during the midst of a spiritual battle, but comes on subtly. It is like a bee sting or spider bite; you don't feel a thing until the venom is released. Then the pain spikes!

This is not to be confused with the typical oppression that often accompanies a battle with the enemy. This is a specific curse that is intentionally placed on you by a person involved in witchcraft.

In the Kingdom of God, we have prayer warriors; the Wiccan world has its counterparts. They pray to establish demonic outcomes. When we walk on the streets, we believers can see each other's heavenly anointings. Wicca followers recognize the demonic "anointings" of their peers. I put the word in quotes because the anointing is for those who walk with God. The enemy always has a counterfeit version for what God has in His Kingdom.

A few days after my mother died, I went out to dinner with my father. A few days earlier, I had been in a deliverance session with Jimi Merrell and Mark Neitz. The source of the evil in that case was witchcraft. As my father and I waited for our food to be served, a beautiful woman in her early 30s walked by our table. Either she knew what her assignment was or she was a practicing white witch and didn't see what she really looked like in the spirit realm. She did take spiritual notice of me, though. That I know for sure.

As she passed our table, I saw in the spirit realm she had a thorax on her back, like a spider does. Little spiders were crawling all over the thorax. Something shot at me. I reacted too late and got slimed. In witchcraft, there is a demonic behavior I call sexually transmitted demons, or STDs. Whether you are talking about white witches who are into so-called good magic or satanic priests involved with black magic, sexual rituals are common. Demons transfer through these sexual acts.

The typical "good" witch is clueless when this happens. However, the satanic priest seeks to have sex with as many people and even animals as possible, in order to gain as many demons as possible. The woman in the restaurant had some sexually transmitted demons on her.

I was fine through dinner. For my father's benefit, I tried to act like nothing happened. But as I drove home, I was aware that some sort of enemy darts had stuck me. I started getting weird shakes and a hyper-elevated desire for sex. This is when you had better know how to call your Father in Heaven; otherwise you're in big trouble. I went home, fell to the floor, and prayed to the Father to come help me out. I remember falling asleep there and waking up to find that everything was OK. Know your authority and know how to speak with God.

During other times of battle, I have been slimed with depression. Once, I was slimed in a spiritual warfare dream against a witch, and the assignment manifested outside my dream. I prayed and went to church that day. What broke that assignment was a good old-fashioned confession and repenting session with God. The witchcraft assignment broke off me immediately.

We need to cover the bases before doing spiritual warfare. If you have any unresolved addictions, I strongly urge you to get free of them before you enter a deliverance ministry. This isn't a game, and the enemy has power.

You need to be on your toes in both your natural life and your spiritual life. Being alert helps you to know when you are being attacked. Then you can dive into prayer immediately. I have encountered people whom I call spiritual hypochondriacs. They are not on their toes. Instead, they imagine themselves to be under attack by just about everything.

This is oppression in the form of a spirit of fear. For instance, I shared with one person I was helping that my cars usually take a beating when I fight witchcraft. The enemy knows he can't bring it to my house so I have cases where the enemy just beats up my cars in a temper tantrum. After mentioning the car thing, I started getting e-mails from this individual. He wrote, "Mike, you were right. The cigarette lighter in my car broke today and now my radio knob fell off."

This is not what I mean by getting your car beat up. This is normal wear and tear. It is a classic example of the kinds of things I see oppressed people obsess over when I tell them what to expect when fighting a battle. They use the counsel I give them as a checklist. Then they go down the list to make sure they're experiencing all of the items I told them to look out for.

Let me give you an insight: this person is one of those sympathy-seekers I have mentioned often in this book. The spiritual activity they describe exists more as an obsession in their minds than a matter of reality. They need to seek Jesus and salvation. The point I want to make is that we have people in our churches who operate this way. They might want to join a deliverance team, but they are in need of deliverance.

Every deliverance team needs people who are eating solid food and are mature in their walk with Jesus. This is imperative because they will be required to stand on their own faith and fight the enemy.

Fighting Witchcraft

The number one thing I do when I know I am going into a fight with witchcraft is *fast*. A Daniel fast is fine (see Dan. 1:12). Go into intercession with God at least five days before the battle begins. Speak with God and ask the Holy Spirit for revelation on the matter.

I would only bring Holy Spirit-filled Christians into the fight. I have been castigated by those who are steeped in the technical aspects of theology; they assure me that you don't have to be a Spirit-filled Christian to enter this fight or drive out demons. That is true, but would you go into a fight like that lacking communications with headquarters? Wouldn't the fight be a lot easier if you were receiving tactical information straight from the commander of the Lord's army?

M16 Ministries has its own intercessors who pray with us and for us when we go into battle. The intercessors pray for protection—both for the people we are helping and for us. They pray to surround all of us with the protection of the Lord's angels. They pray to protect our property, families, pets, and cars.

Some of your friends who are Spirit-filled and already know they have the gift for intercession would make a great prayer team. Remember this: there are prayer warriors, which is a common term for a person who respectfully prays or intercedes frequently, and there are pray-er *warriors* who are spiritual combat veterans. Our team experiences attacks from the enemy; each of us has had to fight our own battles at home while praying to stay in the battle at hand.

When you pray against witchcraft, make sure your prayers into the spirit realm aren't curses. Pray blessings and pray for the witch to have a Jesus encounter. Jesus doesn't want any of His people to go to hell. Praying curses and harm is Christian witchcraft. You can go to war against the witch's curses, but at the same time pray for the witch. Here's how I would pray for an individual who is being attacked:

> *Jesus, I thank You for this victory. I thank You that You took on my sin and died for me. I thank You that You defeated satan and his angels. I pray, Jesus, that You release mighty warring angels to surround (name the person under attack).*
>
> *Jesus, I pray Your protecting blood over (name the person under attack), their family, and their home. Any assignment of witchcraft shall be broken in this person's life, in Jesus' name. Evil spirits, you have no authority in this matter. I order you out of every aspect of this person's life. By the authority in Jesus Christ you are to leave (name the person under attack) now. I speak the assignment over them and their household to be broken. No weapon formed against (name) shall prosper.*
>
> *Jesus, release blessings and favor from Heaven on this person and on their family. I bless the family line and pray to protect it from curses. I pray a blessing on the one coming against me (the witch) and ask that the one true God is revealed to them. I ask You, Jesus, to touch this person in their dreams and their thoughts so they can see Your love. I pray for this person to see Your glory and have a repenting heart, in Jesus' name.*

Dealing With Those Who Are Cursed

Your first course of action in these cases is to determine whether the person is really being attacked by witchcraft. It might be someone you already know. Knowing the person may be helpful. But do not be misled by the fact that they attend your church.

I have learned that some churchgoers masquerade as Christians on Sunday. They are completely different people at home.

Most people I help are not people I know. I meet them only over the phone; but I can tell after a call whether they are sincere and have a genuine spiritual problem involving witchcraft or some other spiritual activity.

Make sure the person you are praying for wants a full healing from the curses now. What do I mean by this? Simply asking people if they want to be healed isn't enough. They will always say, "Yes," and bawl their eyes out. But are they willing to forgive individuals at this place and time? If they are not, they need to work on themselves until they get to that point.

I learned this lesson the hard way. It is the point I was making earlier regarding my cars getting beat up. It was because I fought in the spirit realm by myself. The Holy Spirit showed me that I needed to put together an intercessor team to assist in all aspects of the battle. I realized that I needed to protect myself, and others, from retaliation if the person we were working with was in agreement with his or her own demons to stay in bondage. In this case, the person I prayed for stayed in bondage, even though there had been a miraculous, spiritual jailbreak. An angel can open the jail door, but that doesn't always mean the spiritual captive will step outside his or her own cell.

With witchcraft, the spirits get retaliatory when this occurs. That is why I spend a lot of time helping others to learn to fight for themselves. In the case of those who resist forgiving others, just pray with them and speak to them about the importance of forgiveness. God says we must forgive others seventy times seven times (see Matt. 18:22). If not, He will leave us to our jailers.

At times, I have had to tell people that they are at a point in battle where they can no longer pick and choose which Scriptures they want to live by. I explain that they are past that stage and must now live by the whole of God's Word. What I am saying is this: "Do you want to be healed?" If so, we must live by the

Scripture and do as Jesus instructed us: confess and forgive. A lot of people can't and because of this they don't see the glory in a victory. They end up inviting satan in, instead of Jesus.

Jesus never said, "Now, now, that's OK. Some people don't need to be forgiven because they are beyond redemption."

No! Jesus said we must forgive! I know there is evil in the world. I have a ministry solely based on fighting evil. But the charter of any ministry is sharing and living the Gospel of Jesus Christ. When you forgive and repent, the forces of darkness are powerless. It's not complicated and it isn't a formula or a ritual.

> *Bless those who persecute you; bless and do not curse* (Romans 12:14).

The only power witchcraft has is fear. God is faith and satan is fear. People under attack by witchcraft need to hear the Gospel of Jesus Christ so the Holy Spirit can come in and heal. If these people are not Christians and they reject the Gospel being offered, there isn't really much more you can give them. It is Jesus who heals, not us.

Lisa and I have been involved in cases where the Holy Spirit broke open the treasure chest with signs and wonders, and *still* the people rejected the Gospel. You can lead a horse to water, but you can't make him drink. It's the type of situation in natural warfare when the Navy Seals radio in for an extraction and have no choice but to leave the prisoners behind.

You have probably noticed that I mention often the hard truth that you cannot "rescue" everyone. This upsets people when I speak at different Christian venues. It is not that I am being mean. With Jesus, I know I am *guaranteed* a victory. It's why I do what I do. I am *guaranteed* a victory! It's the people who sometimes reject Jesus and the victory. Sadly, the ones who reject His offer are often lifelong Christians who know better. Yet they choose to live a life of defeat.

So, forgiveness is essential to deliverance. Here's an example of how to pray for forgiveness:

Jesus, I thank You for this victory. I thank You for taking on my sin and dying for me. I thank You for defeating satan and his angels. I ask for Your mercy and grace right now. I am sorry that I chose not to release forgiveness to people. I choose now to forgive (name of witch, person, people, church, etc.). I release forgiveness now and I ask You to forgive me as I forgive them.

Please forgive me for having these thoughts. They have eaten away the inside of me. Jesus, I invite Your light to shine into my darkness. I want Your light to shine all through me into the deepest part of me. I want to release blessing on (name), so that they, too, receive Your Kingdom. Blessed are the merciful for they will be shown mercy. Blessed are they whose transgressions are forgiven, whose sins are covered. I pray this from my heart, in Jesus' name.

Christian Witchcraft

This is a good place to discuss Christian witchcraft at greater length. We need to understand what happens when we return a curse with a curse. In First Peter we are told not to repay evil with evil:

Do not repay evil with evil or insult with insult, but with bless-ing, because to this you were called so that you may inherit a blessing (1 Peter 3:9).

Why does Peter warn us this way? Because, even when we talk to God, what comes out of our mouths can curse instead of bless. This is a form of Christian witchcraft. For example, when you pray, "Lord, teach that witch a good lesson. You know what I mean!" That is Christian witchcraft—you are proclaiming a curse on the witch.

If Jesus walked into a psychic shop, He would say, "Follow Me." That is something very different from cursing the psychic or witch. So, when you speak or pray curses, who is listening? Satan and his army.

> *From the fruit of his lips a man enjoys good things, but the unfaithful have a craving for violence. He who guards his lips guards his life, but he who speaks rashly will come to ruin. The sluggard craves and gets nothing, but the desires of the diligent are fully satisfied* (Proverbs 13:2-4).

Guard your lips. Never, ever speak rashly, whether during spiritual warfare or at any other time.

Witchcraft, Soul Ties, and Generational Curses

There is a topic I speak about when I am in churches; it is one I have already mentioned briefly in this chapter. The subject is *sexually transmitted demons*, or STDs. I will speak on this at greater length in Chapter 12, but it is a witchcraft-related topic that fits in here.

I was involved in a case in which a supposedly Christian man had willfully cheated on his wife with a witch. During sexual intercourse, the witch loaded up the man with demons. During the deliverance session, every part of the man's body that had received an intimate touch from the witch was ice cold. There were frigid demonic fingerprints where they had hooked arms or held hands. All of the cold spots on the man's body had been entry points for the demons.

Any sex outside of the confines of marriage is an abomination to God. Evil takes hold of this and runs with it. I have stories that would scare young people into pre-marital abstinence. What results from sex out of wedlock are soul ties. Soul ties are demons that cling and are hard to pull off without full repentance.

A generational curse is another interesting pattern in which witchcraft can invade a family line. I have met people who were adopted as children and learned later in life that their birth parents were practicing witches. Some of these people endured horrific childhood experiences based on soul ties to the parents that took the form of generational curses. These experiences include spirit activity, seeing shadows, and even levitation.

The soul tie and the generational curse are broken through prayer. The Holy Spirit can break this off in one touch by Him. Have a prayer session and invite the Holy Spirit in to take over the prayer meeting.

Ritual Abuse

Ritual abuse and multiple personality disorder come up a lot with the topic of satanism. Ritual abuse is sexual abuse that is committed in satanic worship. In some cases, children of satanic priests have their minds divided up into multiple personalities that provide homes for demons.

Unfortunately, the Church is making the healing of ritual abuse more complicated than it has to be. Some people try to turn deliverance into counseling sessions and then put time frames on the deliverance prayer. What I encounter often in this situation is that people don't consider the miracles, which I have seen, where the Holy Spirit will heal someone instantaneously. We always consider counseling or long deliverances as the norm because that's how the human mind reasons. We put God in a box and give the Almighty a timeline in which to heal. We like to fall back on the concept that the human mind is like an onion and has layers. Jesus would rather heal us in one prayer session, which, from what I have seen, Jesus prefers to do if we allow Him to have His way. Forget about the root cause charts and analysis. We don't heal people, Jesus does!

Have a time of worship, invite the Holy Spirit in and let Him heal people! The best thing for us to do as deliverance ministers is to sit and listen to stories of those abused as they tell them. Give them ample time to tell their story and pray with them afterwards to break off what was revealed. Don't be surprised at how little print I have devoted to this topic. There are many books that cover ritual abuse in depth. Suffice to say that each deliverance session is unique to the individual. There is no formula or road map to heal these people. The key to healing is the Holy Spirit. And the healing happens quicker than most books suggest.

Native American Shaman Witchcraft

I have received calls from people wanting to know what to do when they encounter Native American witchcraft. Some people have called the local Indian councils only to find that no one returns their call.

I am amazed by the universal, Unitarian strain of spiritual political correctness that says Jesus can't go to heal people on Indian sacred grounds. I say, "Why not?"

Usually, the people I speak to about this already have religious spirits. It is difficult to convince them that the Creator of the universe can handle this type of situation. Jesus can surely cancel the assignments of demons posing as Indian witch doctors! Yet, many ghost hunters resort to demonic solutions. In the ghost-hunting television shows, psychics use what they perceive to be Indian shaman techniques to drive out Indian spirits from a haunting, even though the lead cast member is a practicing Catholic.

A particular show makes this point about techniques in almost every episode. It is mind-boggling to see this expert in the supernatural reduce Jesus to a demi-god when dealing with Native American spirit hauntings. The charismatic Roman Catholics who go out on the streets with me would call on Jesus if they were on this paranormal show. They know He has it covered; and they know that the problem isn't a Native American ghost—it's a demon!

If the experts on these shows would spend more time with Jesus, they would be able to catch and broadcast some incredible spiritual happenings. But that is not what the enemy wants. In fact, it would be counterproductive to his plan.

Tackling shaman witchcraft is no different from any other form of witchcraft. Just use the same prayers and approaches I have already provided. Witchcraft is witchcraft; it's all satan masquerading as something else.

Renouncing Involvement in Witchcraft

Witchcraft can enter family lines directly through the speaking of vows (witchcraft, satanism, Freemasonry, New Age, psychics, yoga, and eastern religions, to name a few) and the physical practice of witchcraft. It can also sneak into the family tree as a generational curse.

As with any curse, the generational curse can be renounced and made void through the blood of Christ and His work on the cross. The enemy has been crushed!

The following prayer assumes that the person being prayed for has accepted Jesus Christ as Savior. It should be read with someone (or a prayer team) in the room with you to make sure you pray the whole thing and renounce the enemy. The enemy is clever at having us jump over words when we're renouncing curses.

Prayer to Renounce Witchcraft

On this day, I declared Jesus Christ to be my Lord and Savior. I believe in the triune God—the Father, the Son, and the Holy Spirit. I believe Jesus took my sins and curses to the cross. The enemy is defeated!

Forgive me, Lord, for my involvement in witchcraft. Forgive me for seeking ungodly powers, for necromancing, and for participation in rituals and ritual sex. Forgive me for seeking to hurt or control others with these ungodly powers. Forgive me for seeking out-of-body experiences and allowing evil spirits to enter my being.

I repent of my involvement in all aspects of witchcraft. I renounce satan and his false powers and teachings. I renounce satan and all vows made to him. I cancel all curses and spells and speak them to be broken. I ask that these curses be replaced by blessings, in Jesus' name!

In the name of Jesus, I bind all demonic spirits in my life. I command satan to loose his hold over my life and my future generations. Jesus, cover me now in Your cleansing blood. Jesus, I receive You into my heart today. I receive Your freedom and forgiveness. I pray all of this in Your name, Jesus. Amen.

Summary

You can see from the opening testimony in this chapter that I use the same tactics for voodoo, shamanism, satanism, and witchcraft. They are different manifestations of the same satanic masquerade. No single demonic practice is greater in power than any other. And all are under the authority of Jesus Christ! Remember, *every* knee will bow.

Always be very careful of the fight that you step into. Pray to God for revelation and pray to God for the approach you must take in each battle. Remember that each turn in the battle is an opportunity to share the Gospel and show that God is real.

Most of all, make absolutely sure the person you are helping wants to be set free. Some people grow comfortable being damaged goods; the enemy has taught them that many people will pay attention to them because of the attacks they experience. These people must want to be set free from any coexistence with the demonic realm.

When demons know the person you are trying to help is in a relationship of coexistence, they will divert their energy to attack you or your property. Why? Because the demons know they are safe. They know the person you are trying to help doesn't want them evicted.

Endnote

1. J.K.Rowling, *Harry Potter and the Prisoner of Azkaban* (Scholastic, 1999), 80

CHAPTER 9

NIGHTMARES AND THINGS
THAT GO BUMP IN THE NIGHT

*For God does speak—now one way, now another—though
man may not perceive it. In a dream, in a vision of the night,
when deep sleep falls on men as they slumber in their beds,
He may speak in their ears... (Job 33:14-16).*

Personally I find dreams are one of the most fascinating ways
in which God can speak to us. Whenever People tell me that
God doesn't speak to them, I usually ask them about their
dreams. God shows up in our dreams, but seldom does He appear
with a cloud of witnesses proclaiming He is God. He is a lot more
personal than that when it comes to talking to His kids.

Even though I spent more than 30 years as a prisoner to a
fear of the dark, God would speak to me in my dreams to help
me fight and overcome my fears. I had violent nightmares with
demons, but, strangely enough, I enjoyed these dreams. No matter how scary or insurmountable the odds were, I always fought
back in these dreams. There would always be some small victory
that God used to build me up and awaken me from the demonic
oppression I hadn't yet realized I was under.

I often reflect back to November 2006; it was the pivot point
at which Jesus kicked me in the pants and drafted me into

spiritual warfare. Just months earlier, I had a series of spiritual warfare dreams that some people would dismiss as nightmares. Although these dreams scared the crud out of me, I awoke from them feeling exhilarated and wanting more.

The series of dreams I had back then would go something like this: I would enter a house that I knew was spiritually "active." I would instinctively go to the room where I knew the evil spirit was manifesting. It was a bedroom with no furniture except for an old antique hutch. Voices and growling would emanate from the hutch. The room would become cold and I could see my own breath. I would try to pray, but I couldn't speak. I would try to fight and force my voice to pray out loud. Only I couldn't. The hutch would start to shake violently; growls would come out of it. Under the power of an invisible force, I would be shoved to the floor. The demons would force me to bow to them. I wouldn't give in.

The dream series finally broke one night when I was again forced to bow to the invisible demons. I couldn't speak, but this time I reached out with my hand toward the hutch and drew the symbol of the cross. I suddenly snapped out of the dream and gasped as I awoke. I never had that dream again.

As I write this and look back on this series of dreams, I see information that I didn't see at the time. I believe the reason I couldn't pray in the dream was because I didn't have my prayer language yet. I wasn't baptized in the Holy Spirit until December of 2006. Now I no longer experience the sensation of not being able to pray in my dreams. In fact, I now pray in my dreams exclusively with my prayer language. The other interesting item to note is that, prior to my ministry of spiritual warfare, the demons in my dreams were invisible. Now I can see them in their entirety.

To show the difference the equipping of the Holy Spirit makes in our dreams, I will share with you a dream I had a few weeks ago. For the sake of context, time-wise, this dream came three years after the dreams of the demonic hutch. This recent dream took place in the house where I lived when I was in high school. It's been 25 years since I lived in that house.

In the dream, I went into my old bedroom where I saw a shadow manifesting on the wall. I turned around and locked the door behind me, which left me in the darkness with the shadow. As I prayed in my prayer language, light began to enter the room from the place where I was standing. I watched the spirit as it fled from the light being prayed into the room and dissolved into the wall.

Are you up for a quick dream analysis? This was a generational dream. I say that because it took place in the house I lived in during my high school years. The content pertains to me, my past, and my family. I went into the bedroom where I slept in fear as a young man. I confronted the spirit of fear and locked it in the room with me. I wasn't about to leave; it had to leave! The spirit and its enveloping darkness were driven out by the light of Jesus. I allowed the light of Jesus to invade my darkness. This is a spiritual warfare deliverance dream.

As I mentioned early on, my family lived in several homes with spiritual activity, mostly during my childhood years. In one home, I saw shadows and heard voices in the hallway at night. The spirits never came into my room, but stayed in the hallway. That was a real problem when I needed to relieve my bladder at 2:00 A.M. You remember the routine I shared earlier: I would throw on the light in my room, bolt to the light switch in the hallway, and then run to the bathroom. My mother would get up and ask me what I was doing with every light on in the house.

Assignments in Dreams

It's not uncommon for worship leaders, intercessors, and people called to spiritual warfare to have horrible nightmares. When people start to confide in Lisa and me about their dreams, we listen and try to identify the spiritual gift that God is stirring up or the demons are trying to derail. Many times a spirit of fear has an assignment to stop people from reaching their spiritual potential. The spirit of fear can effectively achieve this through nightmares. Job 4 is a scriptural reference to the spirit of fear coming to Job in his dreams.

Amid disquieting dreams in the night, when deep sleep falls on men, fear and trembling seized me and made all my bones shake. A spirit glided past my face, and the hair on my body stood on end (Job 4:13-15).

From time to time, I get to minister with Bob Johnson Ministries as he preaches at different churches in the San Francisco Bay Area. It's a kind of family road trip for the Night Strike crew. On one such outing, Bob introduced me to a young lady who was suffering from horrible nightmares. The very reason the woman had come to the service that night was a divine appointment. She had been angry at God and didn't want any more church. Daddy in Heaven, being ever so understanding to our needs, led this woman to a service at this new church on this particular Sunday evening.

No matter how angry we are at God, He is always willing to work with us. This young lady came to the service, heard the message, and got delivered. Our team returned to the church three nights later, only to learn that she had been having horrible dreams with demons. I asked her to tell me more about the dreams she was having. She said the dream started with her in a house. She was holding a present and wanted to go outside with it, but there were demons at the front door. They wouldn't let her exit the house.

To me, the spiritual warfare dream was obvious. The woman was holding a present, which is also known as a gift! The demons didn't want her stepping out with her gifts of the Spirit. Once I explained to her how simple the dream was, she looked back at me and asked, "What's my gift?"

At that moment, Bob Johnson was walking around the church foyer, hugging people and giving them prophetic words. Right on cue, he came over to where the young lady and I were standing.

Bob asked, "Did you talk to her? Anything?"

I told Bob, "Yes. We figured out the meaning of the nightmares."

Bob said "Good, because she has a prophetic gift."

NIGHTMARES, THINGS THAT GO BUMP IN THE NIGHT 191

I looked at the young lady and said, "Well then, there you have it."

She smiled. Then I prayed with her to bind the spirit of fear that was coming to her at night.

If you routinely experience spiritual warfare dreams that carry an assignment of fear, I recommend praying before you go to bed. Walk around your bedroom praying and binding the spirit of fear from coming into your room. Pray over your bed and pray over your pillow. Ask God for revelation of anything He might be trying to show you through your dreams. Then, as you tuck in for the night, dive into the Bible. Fill your mind and spirit with the good stuff from Daddy in Heaven.

From Dreams to Manifestations and Attacks

M16 Ministries has worked with quite a few people who have experienced nightmares that manifest into physical attacks. We have heard it all—people have been choked, dragged out of bed, pelted with items being thrown at them, and even levitated. These people confide in our team about details they are reluctant to share with their counselors or pastors. Usually, they hesitate to tell others because they realize their churches don't believe in the supernatural. Many have been taught that what happened in the Book of Acts was for the original apostles only.

This belief system enters the Church through many doorways. One consistent thread our ministry has encountered is the spirit of fear. This spirit erects strongholds in those who have witnessed or been victims of violent or tragic events. When you attempt to help these people, their issues can become blurred, because they don't always share all the details.

For instance, an adult man may be ashamed of a childhood molestation that was inflicted by a grown man. Satan loves destroying the lives of children. The age of accountability has nothing to do with the age at which satan attacks. As I mentioned before he'll head right to the womb if it means being able to destroy one more life.

Other common cases involve boys or girls who lived in homes that were spiritually chaotic and loaded with spiritual activity, including lots of arguing. Everyone in the family is aware of the spiritual activity and manifestations in the house. Most of the family members stick it out and become accustomed to living in a war zone. Often, however, one child will decide that they have had enough and will voluntarily leave the home to go live with a caring friend. The attacks continue under the new roof, even though the child is separated from his or her family. The attacks include nightmares, sleep deprivation, and manifestations with moving objects.

Young people in these situations need a deliverance ministry to surround and pray for them. They need to be touched by the healing hand of the Holy Spirit. They also need to learn about their spiritual authority. Without this knowledge, the activity will eventually resume.

Kids are not as fragile as we adults think. My favorite part of this ministry is teaching kids about their Kingdom authority. They get it and they run with it. Many adults never get it, mainly because they have discovered the sympathy they can get if they continue to live as victims.

Below is a prayer you can use to pray in your room and over your bed. If your room is a mess, I strongly recommend cleaning it up. Demons love chaos. Don't make your room a nest for demonic rats.

Prayer for Protection in Sleep and Dreams

Holy Spirit I ask You to make Your presence known in my room tonight. Invade my sleep and give me dreams from You. Give me a deep, relaxing, peaceful sleep, in Jesus' name.

I bind the spirit of fear from attacking me. You are not to enter my dreams. You are not to enter my room. You are not to enter my home. This home belongs to the Holy Spirit. I ask that Jesus would release mighty angels from Heaven and post them around my room. I choose to put no other God before You. No weapon formed against me shall prosper, in Jesus' name.

Jesus, thank You for the victory. Father, thank You for sending Your Holy Spirit. Amen.

See You in Your Dreams

Just as we can see evil people in the spirit realm, so can evil people see us in our spiritual form. Have you ever walked by someone and gotten the feeling that he or she is evil? Well, that person can walk by you and sense that you are godly.

I have had people walk up to me and say that they will see me in my dreams. My response is, "No you won't." I say this to break the assignment of shamans and witches *immediately*. Their words are spoken as curses that might seem innocent to those who are unaware. Such words are spoken in order for demons to enter your dreams.

It wasn't more than a month into my new walk in spiritual warfare when God sent me to the frontlines. It was the last week in 2006 and a missionary team from my church had just returned from Ethiopia. It was a pastoral team that went out to equip missionaries. One of the Ethiopian missionaries who received training then went out to a jungle village and had a power encounter with a witch doctor. As powerful as the witch doctor's magic was, it wasn't on a par with the power of Jesus.

During a power encounter, you need to understand that it is all out war with forces of darkness that are well-connected through a demonic communications network. Demons knew where this man had been trained, who trained him, and what churches were involved with the outreach. The demons sent out counterstrike orders of retaliation. The counterstrike came in the form of curses and the summoning of witches and shamans.

Being a fresh recruit with Jesus' special forces who attended one of the churches listed on the retaliation order, I was suited up, dropped behind enemy lines, and sent to neutralize the threat—in the dream realm where battles of this magnitude are fought.

I was sent to a small, two-room cabin in a swamp. I stepped into the first room of the cabin and found no one in it. I walked into the next room; there I saw an old woman stirring a cauldron. She seemed surprised to see me. I looked at her and stepped near to see what was inside the cauldron. It was boiling and churning. Human bones rose to the surface; as the bones boiled, they started taking on flesh. The flesh-covered bones were then joined one to another and people emerged from the cauldron.

I remember thinking, "This is too weird for me." So I decided to bolt!

As I ran toward the first room and the door, one of the fleshy monsters leaped out of the cauldron in the form of a bald, obese man wearing coveralls. He overtook me before I could make it to the door. He grabbed my hand and stopped me. His strength was incredible; I couldn't break his grip. With a hideous smile, he forced me to the ground to bow down to him.

I refused and struggled to break free. The demon pulled a box cutter out of his pocket and sliced my hand with it. I felt the pain, even in the dream. I looked back at the witch; she was laughing at me. I looked her straight in the eye and told her that I knew she was in Louisiana. I was immediately ripped from the dream. I awoke with what has become the all–too-common gasp for air.

I returned to sleep, awoke the next morning, and went about my business. I noticed that my mind was doing something weird; it was fixating on rhymes and sayings and repeating them over and over excessively. It was nuts. The witch had done something to me. She had slimed me on my way out of the dream. Now what was I to do?

I realized that the encounter in the dream was between two real people. I sat down and read some e-mails. The pastor of the church had sent a notice to the church body about another incredible power encounter that had happened the previous day: an Ethiopian missionary converted a village in God's glory!

Our pastor wanted us to fast and have a prayer meeting that evening. I knew somehow this was all tied together. But at this time I was still a private first class in the 1st Dream-Borne Assault

Team; I was on a need-to-know basis. (I actually think God had a good laugh sending in a new recruit to foil the plans of the enemy.)

That evening, I went to the church prayer meeting; the annoying, repetitive mind-hex virus was still running in my head. The irony here was that no one showed up at the prayer service except for the pastors, their wives, and two of the church's prayer warriors. So what brought me to the prayer meeting? I didn't want to talk about it.

One of the pastors opened the prayer service and then invited us all to have a confession between the Lord and ourselves. I did as the pastor suggested and learned an important piece of tactical information that night: it was the healing power of repentance to neutralize hexes and spiritual attacks. As soon as I repented, the hex broke. This was just a simple confession as I released things I felt I needed to bring to Jesus about my own personal behavior from the week.

The dream served another purpose: it became my calling card from God to go visit Ethiopia, where I met my brother who had the power encounter. While I was there, I videotaped his testimony of a dream he'd had.

Dreams are an important part of spiritual warfare, yet there isn't much material out there on the subject of the battles waged in dreams. As I see it, many of my spiritual warfare dreams are training videos in which I learn about the spirit realm. There's a lot I don't yet understand about dreams, but I can say based on my experiences, that my warfare dreams have not been Freudian in nature.

Fighting Back

Another important point I would like to drive home about spiritual warfare dreams is this: don't be a victim in your own dreams. If you are being attacked in your dreams, begin taking your life back during the day. Get baptized in the Holy Spirit and develop your prayer language. Start preparing yourself for a fight in the dreams and pray in your prayer language as much as possible. Pray for others and witness small victories that build your faith. Let your spirit get built up through your authority in Christ and through Scripture.

It is your spirit that is being attacked in your nightmares. Turn your spirit man into a warrior and it will surface in your dreams. Don't let your mind govern your dreams. I know that sounds a lot like a goofy self-help book. The point is that the playing field is leveled in the dream realm. You can throw a bus at the demon, run after him, and grab him by the neck. Let him hear your prayer language. Pound on him, whatever—just break the demon's assignment. Understand that when you are being attacked, the demons are relying on you to use your mind. However, your mind is for use in the physical realm. Fight with your spirit.

One spiritual warfare dream I had took place in a house of spirits. I wandered into one room that had lights on. When I entered, I saw my youngest son sitting on a couch, in a trance. Next to him was a Native American shaman (witchcraft) demon. The demon was proud of his prize and smiled at me.

This was the first time that I became so mad in a spiritual dream that I wanted to tear apart the demon with my bare hands. When I started praying in tongues, the demon told me the ways of my God had no effect on him. As I continued to pray, the demon summoned his wolf to attack me from behind. I felt the teeth of the wolf tear into my back and try to rip off my flesh.

Even that didn't stop my rage. I was determined that the demon was not going to carry out his assignment against my youngest son. I reached behind myself, grabbed the wolf's head, and ripped it off my back. The demon prayed in native chants as I fought the wolf. I finally muscled the wolf into a headlock and proceeded to choke the life out of it. As the wolf gasped its last breath, I saw the shaman dissolve and go into the wolf. The assignment on my son was broken—and my spiritual dreams were changed forever. In every spiritual warfare dream I have had since that one, I have killed the demons, violently, and broken the assignments.

If your children are having nightmares and are too old to be crawling into bed with you, teach them to pray themselves back into the dream and kill the enemy. This also goes for adults who are tormented by spirits in their dreams. Ask the Holy Spirit to put you back into that dream so you can take care of that evil spirit.

When I hear shamans tell me they will see me in my dreams, I break the assignment. But under my breath I ask do they really want to see me in my dreams? God showed me my authority; it works just the same in the physical realm as it does in the spirit realm. Use your authority and turn yourself into a warrior. You are only a victim of your dreams as long as you want to be.

Summary

For me the subject of spiritual warfare dreams is exciting. If you're experiencing nightmares take back your room, your bed, and your dreams through prayer and Scripture. When these dreams produce manifestations in the physical realm (a clock radio going berserk; the TV switching on or off; fire alarms going off or growling and clawing), ask the Holy Spirit to help you take back your ground. Spend time in the Word before you go to bed. Like God told Joshua, you need to possess the land (your bedroom)!

CHAPTER 10

CASTING OUT DEMONS

...God did not spare angels when they sinned, but sent them to hell, putting them into gloomy dungeons to be held for judgment... (2 Peter 2:4).

I am going to open this chapter with a word of caution and a disclaimer. I know that many people who enter the deliverance ministry do so primarily on the basis of casting out demons. Then their ministry fails to bear fruit and they wonder why.

The reason is that deliverance ministry is not about casting out demons; it is about sharing the Gospel of Jesus Christ and making the sick and brokenhearted whole through Him. Too many people are chasing miracles and not chasing the love of the Father. Take a look at what the Scripture says:

And these signs will accompany those who believe: In My name they will drive out demons; they will speak in new tongues; they will pick up snakes with their hands; and when they drink deadly poison, it will not hurt them at all; they will place their hands on sick people, and they will get well (Mark 16:17-18, emphasis added).

When do these signs accompany those who believe? When you preach the Gospel and share it with someone. The Father likes to give His children exquisite gifts. When Jesus went through the villages, He didn't look for demons to cast out or people to heal. People came to Him to be healed. It was part of His ministry of saving people. The Scripture tells us people gathered around Jesus to hear Him preach. But they also brought the sick because their faith was strong enough to believe that Jesus would heal them or their loved ones and make them whole again.

Rejoice! Your Name's Written in Heaven

The people on your prayer team who are casting out demons should be free from demonic influence and oppression. By this I mean if you have people on your prayer team who have an addiction to pornography, gambling, alcohol, tobacco, or drugs, they should not be on the team.

Be wary also of prideful people. Those who boast about the healings received by people they have prayed for should take a look at their own pride issues. Jesus said in Luke 10:20 that we should rejoice, not because we have authority over demons, but because we have a relationship with the Father. It is the Father in Heaven who gave us the authority. We have authority over spirits because we have a deep-rooted relationship with the Father and our names are written in His Book of Life in Heaven.

Sons of Sceva and the Chief Priest

Soon after the Holy Spirit called me out to the streets I began returning with incredible testimonies of encounters with evil spirits and my authority in Jesus over them. As you know, members of my church congregation warned me about the seven sons of Sceva from Acts 19. The people's heartfelt warnings were a curiosity to me because my experiences were the opposite of what happened to these men.

The seven sons of Sceva engaged the spirit realm and got whipped by a demon. When you look at the account in King James Version, you see an important detail not reflected in the NIV or The Message translations. That detail is the word exorcists. This title eludes to a history of these men casting out demons prior to this battle.

Then certain of the vagabond Jews, exorcists, took upon them to call over them which had evil spirits the name of the LORD Jesus, saying, We adjure you by Jesus whom Paul preacheth (Acts 19:13 KJV).

In modern terms you would call these guys itinerate deliverance ministers. They traveled from town to town, casting out demons. Why couldn't seven devout Jewish men and a chief priest drive out this demon? They were part of the old law and still living under the curse. They knew the name of Jesus had power, but they didn't understand their authority.

The name of Jesus should have been powerful enough to drive out any demon, but these exorcists weren't baptized in the Holy Spirit. The Scripture shows us they had no idea of the authority they were wielding. These two points gave the upper hand to the demon, which then seized the opportunity to beat them up.

I have received numerous e-mails from people who like to argue the point you don't need the Holy Spirit to cast out demons. My answer is yes, you can do it without the Holy Spirit, but based on my experience I wouldn't even think of going into battle without the Holy Spirit. Such a battle would be prolonged and tiring to the point that the demon could wear you out, or even beat you up.

Equipped to Cast Out Demons

There is no real way of telling if a demon is truly gone without using the gifts of the Spirit. This takes training and practical application prayer sessions to develop this skill. Most of all, it requires a deep-rooted relationship with Jesus. I have taken people on the streets with me who had all sorts of black belts in deliverance, yet could not sense a demonic presence sitting right in front of them.

I am not boasting here; I want to make a point that you need the Holy Spirit to reveal the unknown. Faith comes by hearing. I sharpened my discernment of spirits by working both on the streets and inside prayer meetings. The feelings are now a reflex by which I can determine if I am in the presence of something evil. Ironically, I have seen psychics in ghost-hunting shows mention some of these feelings; they describe them as a gift. Yes it is a gift from God; but satan hijacked their gift.

In some instances, I have seen people channel demons because they thought they were spiritually gifted psychics. They were not channeling spirits; they were in the process of becoming fully demonically oppressed. Quite a few of them are believers. A religious spirit told them not to go church because they don't need to go.

This is a common trend with religious spirits; they tell people in church that the pastor is evil or practicing witchcraft. My advice to these people is that they need to get plugged into a church right away and get help in their fight. What often happens is that these people become so besieged by religious spirits that they stop contacting M16 and opt to quietly endure lives of oppression. I have a long list of people like this for whom I pray continually. They need breakthrough and they need to get back to Jesus.

Remember: deliverance prayer ministry is one of patience and no agenda. It's about free will and timing. If you are a time management control freak you should consider something other than deliverance ministry.

I believe all Christians can cast out demons if they know their authority. However, if you're going into deliverance ministry, take the time to get equipped. There's an old cowboy saying that says, *If you're talking, you ain't learning.* Be willing to take instruction and correction as you enter this ministry. Mentoring is imperative. My mentors help me work in the prophetic, in dream interpretation, and in spiritual warfare. I meet with different prayer groups run by people I trust. By working with them and learning from them, I have earned their respect in operating in the gifts of the Spirit.

The Holy Spirit has trained me a great deal, but there are times when practical field application is necessary. That comes through street evangelism. Yes, you need to pursue the gifts and push to breakthrough and use them. How do you do this? Through lots of prayer with Father—a two-way conversation in which He speaks and you learn to listen.

It is so frustrating to me that Christians find it easy to say that God doesn't speak. That is not so! Go somewhere quiet and get into a two-way conversation with God. You *will* hear Him speak, if you are willing to listen.

Again, your equipping comes in large part from practical experience. There are deliverance teams all over now. Make sure you connect with an ethical team—one that does not videotape or make sound recordings of their sessions. Everything is personal and kept confidential for the sake of the person receiving prayer. What happens in deliverance prayer sessions stays in deliverance prayer sessions. It doesn't belong on youtube.com and it shouldn't be recorded on your cell phone. This is true whether you are ministering in church or on the streets; it's personal one-on-one time. You are helping God's people, His children, His sons and daughters.

Examine the ethics of the team and the minister before you join. Are the people who seek help being physically or verbally abused? That's a red flag right there. The Holy Spirit doesn't abuse; He invades with His peace. No one should be held down or yelled at.

Oppression and Possession

What is the difference between demonic oppression and demonic possession? Demonic oppression describes a demonic presence that causes an affliction such as an illness, disease, mental disorder, misfortune or even a perpetuated abuse on a person. Luke 13:11 tells us about a spirit of infirmity that crippled a woman for 18 years before Jesus set her free.

Job is another example of demonic oppression by which satan brings supernatural misfortune to a person's life. I just mentioned mental illness; allow me to caution that it is a category best handled by a mature deliverance team. I mentioned earlier that many church counselors abandon their *faith* for *learned human reasoning.* As a result, they have little or no success helping those suffering from depression or bipolar disorder.

When the trained medical and counseling communities are no longer effective, it is a good time to introduce healing prayer. Prayer should be *incorporated* by every Christian church, to give the Father in Heaven the opportunity to heal His children.

If you are familiar with books on exorcism, you are aware there are varying degrees of oppression. In deliverance I lump them all into one. If it is obsession, it is oppression; if it is misfortune, it is oppression; if it is infirmity, it is oppression.

A Christian can have demonic oppression. Paul had demonic oppression; the demons had an assignment to interfere with Paul's ministry:

> *To keep me from becoming conceited because of these surpassingly great revelations, there was given me a thorn in my flesh, a messenger of Satan, to torment me* (2 Corinthians 12:7).

Do you know a Christian with depression? This is a demonic oppression and should be prayed for. Forget what the know-it-all in your church congregation thinks. The common solution for depression is medication. I have seen many people set free from depression *and* their medication.

Anxiety is another weapon the enemy uses against the Church. My wife Lisa had horrible anxiety attacks about going into San Francisco. We didn't realize it back then, but it was one of the enemy's assignments on us to prevent us from ministering in the city. Lisa received prayer at Kingdom of Grace Maranatha and had that assignment officially cancelled and sent back to the enemy. The arthritis in her hands also left when she received her healing. The assignment designed to stop us from doing God's work failed!

Demons are nasty distributors of mental and physical illness. They'll stop at nothing to prevent you from reaching your God-given destiny. Demonic oppression attacks the body and soul (the mind) simultaneously.

Demonic possession is the next degree in severity after demonic oppression. Demonic possession is where the person's *will* is *completely* compromised. This typically occurs when a person willfully submits and gives an oath to satan. It also happens to children who are given over to satan. The Roman Catholic Church has defined possession as a state in which a demon takes possession of a body and even makes the person say things they don't want to say.[1] Possession can also take over parts of the body and cause the possessed person to strike someone.

There is a fine line here; I have seen oppressed people exhibit these tendencies, too. I have worked with demonically-oppressed Christians who have evil spirits speaking through them (demons manipulating their bodies). This is where I take issue with the Roman Catholic Church; they label this as always indicating demonic possession. But, as I mentioned earlier, cling-ons (the oppressing spirits that cause oppression in Christians) are capable of producing these actions. They can be prayed off.

The Roman Catholic Church labels another category of demonic attack: it is called *demonic subjugation*. This is a special case of demonic possession where people willfully give themselves to satan.[2] The key point here is to know which definitions are being used by the groups with whom you operate. If you are a charismatic Catholic deliverance minister working with an exorcist, learn the Roman Catholic Church definitions. For the Pentecostals, we either have cases of demonic oppression or the more rare demonic possession. But it is good for all deliverance ministers to be aware of the definitions used by our Roman Catholic brothers and sisters.

If I am ever invited to train exorcists at the Vatican, I will need to use their definitions. You need to be speaking the same vocabulary with your team. If you are on a Catholic deliverance prayer team, it may make more sense to adopt the vocabulary of the diocese to assist in the event an exorcism is required.

Now I am about to upset a lot of Christians: I have witnessed a member of a strong Christian family who was demon possessed. Regardless of his family background, I don't believe this young man ever truly accepted Jesus as his Savior. He suffered severe demonic oppression (Job-like oppression) during his youth. The family was active in church and so was he. The oppression became so severe after the suicide of a family member, that the young man became angry at God, rebelled against Him, and gave an oath to satan.

That is when the nightmare started. The young man was eventually institutionalized. There were so many demons in him that the spiritual battle to cast them out took a long time. But Jesus is always victorious.

Let me add the highlight of his testimony: During his early 20s, he was delivered through prayer. M16's intercessor prayer team, an intercessor team from his parents' church, the pastor of the church, and the Kingdom of Grace ministry all prayed for him.

The enemy was badly beaten up by the volume and length of intercession and fasting we threw at him. The young man walked into the prayer room of his own free will a few months later.

I mentioned that he had grown up in a strong Christian family. Yet, evil happened! After he renounced satan and witchcraft, we talked with the young man about accepting Jesus. We wanted to be sure he was sanctified in the event the enemy surfaced. We did not want demons returning to an empty house.

His salvation at this point was crucial. The young man freely asked Jesus into his heart and his deliverance was very peaceful. The enemy was present and he was broken. He did not put up a fight. Not all experiences in deliverance from possession go like this. The Holy Spirit had it covered.

Horrible things can happen during demonic oppression and possession. Depending upon the severity of the situation, it can be a long tough road to clear out people's houses and restore them to physical, mental, and spiritual health.

Remember our rule of thumb: it is the Father, Son, and the Holy Spirit who heal these individuals, and not us.

Binding

Chapter 3, "Authority in Christ," is your Binding 101 course. Now you have graduated to Binding 201. To bind a demon is to use your Kingdom authority over it. Binding is probably one of the most overused or abused prayers in spiritual warfare.

When I observe something irrational, I ask God if it is His doing or a spirit manifesting. I don't want to make the mistake of binding something that is His doing! For example, when I see a Christian shaking, I consider the fact that it may be the way that person responds to the presence of the Holy Spirit. It might also be the way the person was trained to behave in the Spirit's presence.

There are people who bind what they don't understand. They neglect to ask the Holy Spirit whether the thing they are trying to bind is His doing. You cannot bind the Holy Spirit!

The reason for binding a demon is found in the Gospel of Mark:

No man can enter into a strong man's house, and spoil his goods, except he will first bind the strong man; and then he will spoil his house (Mark 3:27 KJV).

To bind the strong man (which is a demon), is to tie him up. You need to use your Kingdom authority and tie up the strong man with prayer. When should you bind the demon? The best time is when you see it manifesting.

I have also prayed to bind doorways into church buildings when I knew people with demonic oppression were going to enter through them. I do something similar with people who want to worship God but are attacked by demons that seek to interfere with their worship. Binding the doorways and praying over the seats keeps the demons shut up during the service.

Prior to any deliverance prayer meetings, I strongly recommend that you have your team arrive early and work in the prophetic to bind any spirits of which the Holy Spirit warns you in advance.

If you are in a prayer meeting or a church service and you see a demon manifesting, you need to bind it right away. This will help to minimize the show the demon wants to put on in order to disrupt the meeting or service. This will also protect from harm those who may need to escort out anyone through whom demons are manifesting. I physically speak out to the demon, with authority, and notify them that they are bound. Sometimes I read from Ecclesiastes:

> *Though one may be overpowered, two can defend themselves. A cord of three strands is not quickly broken* (Ecclesiastes 4:12).

When we bind spirits, we speak from Heaven with our Kingdom authority in Jesus Christ. We can bind something in Heaven with our authority and we can release from Heaven with our authority.

> *I will give you the keys of the kingdom of heaven;* **whatever you bind on earth will be bound in heaven,** *and whatever you loose on earth will be loosed in heaven* (Matthew 16:19, emphasis added).

Jesus repeated this phrase again in a different context, this time referring to what we should do if a brother sins against us:

> *I tell you the truth,* **whatever you bind on earth will be bound in heaven,** *and whatever you loose on earth will be loosed in heaven* (Matthew 18:18, emphasis added).

We have the authority to bind and loose things in Heaven. You can bind the demon and ask Jesus to release healing and angels.

There is one very important point I want to make about binding the enemy: I have read so many horror stories about misinformed people acting in fear and beating up people they believed to be demon possessed. I have had demons take a slug at me, but I have never retaliated in the physical. These are demons using people's bodies to strike at me. God and His angels have protected me in every instance and I have never been clocked by a demon. When the demon tries to strike me, I up the attack in the spirit realm with prayer and binding of the evil spirit. I have never, ever, used physical force on a person for whom I was praying for deliverance.

The Strong Man's Armor

Revelations on the strong man can be found in the Gospel of Luke:

When a strong man, fully armed, guards his own house, his possessions are safe. But when someone stronger attacks and overpowers him, he takes away the armor in which the man trusted and divides up the spoils (Luke 11:21-22).

The only things we truly know about the demonic and their powers can be found in the Scriptures. When the demon is overpowered, it loses its armor. The "someone stronger" refers to Jesus and His work on the cross overpowering the forces of darkness.

Are we being given an inside tip that demons have power, but no armor?

Salvation and Spirit-Filling

When dealing with severe demonic oppression and demonic possession, please make sure the person being prayed for is saved! When working in extreme cases like these, I am already in intercession with God. There is no need to act irrationally and move immediately into the deliverance prayer ministry. It is for situations like these that M16 Ministries has an intercessor team.

Pray for the possessed person's protection by the Holy Spirit as you and your team fast and counsel with the Father in Heaven. You might receive word not to proceed with a deliverance prayer session because the person is not saved. Several people in your ministry team may hear the same word from God. The Holy Spirit is giving this message to you for a reason.

> *Then it says, "I will return to the house I left." When it arrives, it finds the house unoccupied, swept clean and put in order. Then it goes and takes with it seven other spirits more wicked than itself, and they go in and live there. And the final condition of that man is worse than the first. That is how it will be with this wicked generation* (Matthew 12:44-45).

If people aren't saved and the spirits are evicted, they can return with more spirits that will make matters worse than before. Take the time to reach people so they can receive salvation. This is pivotal in winning the battle that has already been won for them. A salvation prayer is provided in Appendix A.

As you evict spirits, have a prayer team member pray for the person to be Spirit-filled. The infilling makes sure the house is not left unoccupied! Remember that you can lead someone in the baptism of the Holy Spirit with the laying on of hands. A prayer is provide in Appendix B.

The Dry Arid Place

Luke 11:24 reveals another curiosity about what happens to demons when they are bound and cast out. They go to a dry, arid place:

> *When an evil spirit comes out of a man, it goes through arid places seeking rest and does not find it. Then it says, "I will return to the house I left." When it arrives, it finds the house swept clean and put in order. Then it goes and takes seven other spirits more wicked than itself, and they go in and live*

there. And the final condition of that man is worse than the first (Luke 11:24-26).

When I order a demon to leave I command it this way:

Take your afflictions and your oppression to the foot of the cross. Go now where the Holy Spirit tells you to go!

I use this because it makes the demon go where the Holy Spirit is ordering the evil spirit to go. I used to order the spirits to go to hell. But I wasn't sure if I was allowed to sentence judgment on the demons at this point in time. I do know that the saints will judge the angels:

Do you not know that we will judge angels? How much more the things of this life! (1 Corinthians 6:3).

The Book of Revelation also talks about this:

I saw thrones on which were seated those who had been given authority to judge. And I saw the souls of those who had been beheaded because of their testimony for Jesus and because of the word of God. They had not worshiped the beast or his image and had not received his mark on their foreheads or their hands. They came to life and reigned with Christ a thousand years (Revelation 20:4).

We will judge the angels that rebelled, that much is certain. I simply use my authority to command the demons to depart and go where the *Holy Spirit* tells them to go. If the Holy Spirit sentences the demon to the abyss, so be it.

I used to command the demons to surrender to the angels. I did this because I saw it done a few times in my prayer sessions and I figured this was the formula to casting out demons. Then the Holy Spirit taught me a lesson (I would call this a correction). I ordered the demons to go and surrender to the army of angels that were there with me. The demon in the person I was praying for just looked at me and snarled. It knew I tripped up and that I wasn't in unity with the Holy Spirit on this.

The Holy Spirit helped me during the fumble and instructed me to tell the demon to go where the Holy Spirit orders it to go.

Do they go to hell or do they go to the dry arid place? This is a good question. Through Kingdom of Grace ministries I have witnessed a demon cast out of someone surface in another person. We were not the ones who cast this demon out the first time. God revealed to the deliverance team that this demon was expelled from one person and came into this individual. I suspect this is a case where the demon is cast out and wanders to the dry arid place wandering around for another body to occupy.

I have also seen demons leaving kicking and screaming knowing full well their destination was a deep dark pit with chains. I have learned to order the demon to go where the Holy Spirit tells the spirit to go.

What about our passage from Luke 11 that speaks of demons returning with seven more even worse spirits? I have had several cases with prayer teams and M16 Ministries where we have kicked out evil spirits and counseled the people on what to do, only to have our advice fall on deaf ears. The advice was to receive salvation—especially since the person had already witnessed the power of Jesus Christ.

We don't leave people empty-handed; we work with them and help them to seek Jesus. Those who reject our counsel are often dumbfounded at what they experience and witness when, just days after being delivered, they fall back into the lifestyle that caused their demonic oppression. But this time, it is worse.

Guess who fields the emergency phone call? Sometimes, even after this consultation over the phone, people are reluctant to change their ways. The only change they want is to be rid of the problem. In that case, M16 ministries can't help them. They are adults; we provided explicit instructions on what must happen. It is up to them to choose a change in lifestyle, or what Jesus called full repentance.

After this kind of phone call, I eventually part ways with the person and pray for release. You cannot tell adults how to make up their minds. God created man with a free will. But, does this mean you should avoid casting demons out of non-Christians?

No. A lot more people ask Jesus into their lives in these situations than reject Him.

Ironically, those who end up with more evil spirits than before tend to be people who already know Jesus but have fallen off the wagon and refuse to meet the Father halfway.

There is another circumstance under which demons return. I see it when working with Christians who are just learning to exercise their authority. Here, it is not a case of their refusing God or rejecting Christ. This situation occurs when spirits return just to test whether the people really know how to exercise authority. The people then need to stand firm and drive out the spirits again, sending a message to the spirit realm that they are standing on their faith and the work of Jesus on the cross.

The enemy will always try to derail Christians who are learning to walk in their authority. Lisa and I both experienced this firsthand. Complete freedom is achieved by standing firm and enforcing your authority.

Testing for the Presence of a Spirit

I entered the deliverance ministry through the back door. As a trained scientist, I am always skeptical when I see someone manifest a demon. A lot of people learned how they should look when they're being delivered, so they act it out in order to get attention.

If I suspect someone is acting out being delivered, I just move on. First John 4:1 tells us to test the spirits. I do several things when I see a possible spirit manifestation. First, I walk up behind the person without showing myself and I hold my Bible inches from the person's spine so the individual cannot feel any contact. If a spirit is manifesting, it will abruptly jerk the person's body away from my Bible.

When this happens, I step away from the person and open my Bible to Revelation 20. Very quietly, under my breath I begin to read to the person. I keep my voice low enough so that the person cannot physically hear me:

> And the devil that deceived them was cast into the lake of fire and brimstone, where the beast and the false prophet are, and shall be tormented day and night for ever and ever (Revelation 20:10 KJV).

Demons will howl or snarl when they hear this. Another good Scripture for testing the spirits is from Isaiah 66. It talks about the lake of fire:

> "As the new heavens and the new earth that I make will endure before Me," declares the Lord, "so will your name and descendants endure. From one New Moon to another and from one Sabbath to another, all mankind will come and bow down before Me," says the Lord. "And they will go out and look upon the dead bodies of those who rebelled against Me; their worm will not die, nor will their fire be quenched, and they will be loathsome to all mankind" (Isaiah 66:22-24).

You can also ask the Holy Spirit to reveal any demons that may be present. Pray in silence or in tongues and see what happens. During this time, pray for the Holy Spirit to surround you and the person you are praying for. Demons cannot stand the presence of the Holy Spirit.

Developing Prayer Team "Special Ops"

A church prayer team is an ideal place to put together a deliverance ministry. Some churches are not on board with deliverance ministry. In fact, some church congregations fear the movement of the Holy Spirit. God will send His leaders to these churches to move things along and get the ball rolling.

It is not the position of a layperson to enforce a deliverance ministry on a church or cause division in the church. This is rebellion and God says rebellion is like witchcraft (see 1 Sam. 15:23). If you want to pursue a deliverance prayer team, you are free to do so outside of the church, in your own house meetings.

Meet outside the church; make sure the prayer sessions are productive and do not negatively impact your home church in any way.

Our M16 team trains churches. We have had great testimonies from those we have trained. One pastor shared about a woman whom he believed was demonized. She would walk back and forth in front of his church on Sundays and never come in. I was informed that the Sunday after our ministry team trained this pastor and his intercessors, this woman walked into his church and was set free from demonic oppression. Training and prayer impartation are great ways to jumpstart a ministry. If it is at all possible, continue to provide mentoring over the longer term.

The Bible has provided us with everything we need to cast out demons, live a Christian lifestyle, and deeply seek the heavenly Father. Live your life like you are living in Heaven and exercise your Kingdom authority in the earth. To do so is to live on your faith and pull the invisible realm into the physical.

This, then, is how you should pray: "Our Father in heaven, hallowed be Your name, Your kingdom come, Your will be done on earth as it is in heaven" (Matthew 6:9-10).

You live on earth as you do in Heaven, according to the Lord's Prayer in the Gospel of Matthew. When it comes time to cast out demons, the powers of darkness will put your authority and your faith to the test. They will force you to prove that you truly have faith and know your Kingdom authority.

I have yet to have a deliverance prayer session in which the casting out of a demon is wrapped up in a matter of minutes. My first deliverance prayer session took four-and-one-half hours! More than a dozen demons were evicted! Jesus (and possibly the apostle Paul) could do this instantly. I don't know anyone like that. Nor do I know of anyone yet who can heal people just by casting his shadow, as Peter did. I would love to be able to do that, but for now, it takes some time and effort. The important

216 A Field Guide to Spiritual Welfare

thing is that we see victories for all the people who leave their inner darkness at the foot of the cross!

A typical deliverance for someone with moderate to severe demonic oppression may require two to three hour-long sessions (once you get up and running and understand what tricks the demons are going to pull). Don't be surprised if you need to wrap up a session and schedule another appointment. You may have cast out some nasty demons, but a few may remain. It's OK to pause and schedule more deliverance prayer sessions down the road.

That being said, the Holy Spirit can also give people a full healing in one session if they are willing to be healed, willing to truly resolve their unforgiveness issues, and willing to repent of their ways. It all depends on how the Spirit leads you and what He tells you during the session.

Some deliverance prayer may only require a few minutes of heavenly intervention. Let's look at a case where there is a minor demonic oppression of anxiety attacks and no other deep-rooted spiritual weeds intertwined. An example would be a person you know who has anxiety even though the family is from generations of true Christian believers. They are Christians 24/7 and have no major family issues. In other words, there are no deep-rooted spiritual weeds of divorce, rejection, alcoholism, and other spirits that congregate in generations of dysfunctional families.

Instead, we have a Christian with a cling-on, a spirit of anxiety that needs to be prayed off. Often, these people can receive a few minutes of prayer and then walk in their authority. This is not a gauge of how to pray for Christians and the demonically oppressed. I want you to see that each prayer session is different. Some people may only require a few minutes of your time; others may require a year of continuous prayer. My advice is to take your time and move forward without an agenda as to how long a healing should take. When it comes to healing, the Holy Spirit caters to the needs of each individual.

Summary

I strongly urge those seeking to enter this ministry to pray for qualified Holy Spirit-filled mentors. I recommend getting equipped by participating on a prayer team. Then pray to God about when you should be released into ministry. There are many forms of deliverance martial arts (a term I use for the various popular forms of deliverance ministry taking shape today) out there right now. Whatever you choose, make sure you know the voice of the Holy Spirit and know how to use your spiritual discernment. You don't need a fancy title for your deliverance style to cast out demons. But you should seek the Father and the baptism in the Holy Spirit!

Casting out a demon can be instantaneous or can take from several hours to several sessions. Communicate with the Holy Spirit and Jesus only, and never with the evil spirits. Bind them and tell them to shut up. Order them to the foot of the cross and tell them to go where the Holy Spirit is ordering them to go. Things may get a bit tense, but this is the sign that a demon is losing the fight. The evil spirit knows the Holy Spirit is going to have another glorious victory!

Endnotes

1. Gabriele Amorth, *An Exorcist Tells His Story* (San Francisco: Ignatius Press, 1999), 33.

2. Gabriele Amorth, *An Exorcist Tells His Story* (San Francisco: Ignatius Press, 1999), 34.

CHAPTER 11

GENERATIONAL CURSES

The Lord's curse is on the house of the wicked, but He blesses the home of the righteous (Proverbs 3:33).

All my life, I suffered from a horrible affliction of allergies and asthma. As a child, I enjoyed the beautiful, warm weather of springtime. I loved playing outside; yet, as much as I loved it, I also loathed it. Flowers would bloom and pollen was everywhere, which meant a respiratory nightmare for me.

I remember the dreadful allergy attacks I would get from mowing the lawn. Immediately after mowing, I would run inside and take a shower. I would rinse off the contaminants and inhale the steam to get some relief.

In elementary school, I absolutely despised the Presidential Physical Fitness tests they would conduct. And when did they do it? In the spring, of course! I was one of the fastest runners in my school. I could outrun anybody. But during the springtime fitness tests, my lungs would fill with pollen as I ran. My heart and lungs would burn; I would have to bow out of the race and focus on regulating my gasps for air. As a result, I could never defend my title as the fastest runner at my elementary school.

My mother had severe asthma and, in later years, suffered from emphysema. These afflictions nearly immobilized her near the end of her life. As I watched my mom struggle in those final years, I couldn't help wondering if I would follow in her footsteps and be tethered to an oxygen bottle.

In the back of my mind something in my DNA told me I needed to do something about this. The issue was a ticking time bomb for me. Asthma isn't a laughing matter. In fact, my mom was hit so badly by it that whenever anyone showed the slightest sign of hay fever, Mom would inevitably say, "You better go get checked for asthma!"

I mastered outsmarting the hay fever that would come in the spring. In northern California, the rains that usher in spring arrive in February. As long as I had started a regimen of over-the-counter medication, I could narrowly avoid needing an asthma inhaler prescription. I would do OK as long as I remembered to take my allergy medication each night before bed. If I forgot, I paid the consequences the next morning with horrendous, violent sneezing. If I didn't start the medication in February I paid the price in spring by going to the doctor and getting a prescription for an inhaler.

One of our friends on the Kingdom of Grace prayer team was prayed for and cured of asthma. It didn't occur to me off the bat to ask for prayer for my own healing. I was a prisoner to my own medicated remedy. Then God started speaking to me by sending me to pray for strangers on the streets of San Francisco. He would give me a word of knowledge that the individual standing in front of me suffered from asthma. The person would be bewildered to see that I, a stranger, knew about the condition and would pray for healing. Through this process, God revealed to me that I needed to ask and receive prayer for my own asthma! It felt hypocritical for me to ask other people whether I could pray for their asthma, while I had never asked God to fully heal me of the affliction.

I remember one December, telling God that I wanted to be free from asthma, just like my friend from Kingdom of Grace.

God told me to step out in faith and said that I was being cured. However, when the rains of February came, I returned to my yearly self-imprisonment of over-the-counter medications. Even though I wanted the full healing and even though God told me I was healed, I figured I would test the reality of my healing and cover my bases, just in case I wasn't healed.

My plan was to take one allergy pill every other night and see what happened. That's not stepping out in faith. What happened next was shocking: the medication I had used for years suddenly caused a reaction. I could no longer take it! I panicked. Not listening to God, I came up with a new plan to take the medication even less frequently, in the hopes that any reaction would be insignificant.

What happened was that I got so busy, I forgot the medicine altogether. I went for a whole week without taking any and I felt perfectly fine! I figured I would go another week without medication. A week turned into a month; I got through spring with only the most minor allergic reactions. It was nothing like my past history. I knew from years of experience that, unless I medicated myself from February on, I would be curled up on the couch, gasping and wheezing with my inhaler beside me.

All of that changed! I went through the summer without any medication. In September, I went on mission trip to Guyana with Mark Neitz and Jason Amarant, from City Ministries Night Strike. Both Jason and Mark had an episode of allergy with congestion. We were in South America in springtime. Mark commented about how nice it would be to not have allergies. I answered that it was very nice and explained about my healing.

I now know that my allergy and asthma problem was a generational curse. It was passed on to me from my mom. What was the root cause? I don't know. But I am incredibly grateful for the glory of God that removed it from my life.

I mentioned earlier that I live in the radical middle when it comes to my spirituality. I am careful to guard the words of the

Scripture and make sure they are not being twisted or taken out of context. When God led me by the hand to seek deeper things, I stumbled into this strange area of spiritual warfare called generational curses. These curses are forms of demonic oppression that can enter family lines through the sins of one's ancestors. The consequences of ancestral sins can perpetuate nearly indefinitely, unless the sin is revoked. The notion that generational sins could infiltrate families and even enter the lives of Christian family members completely defied my notion of living free in Jesus.

For my first 38 years, first as a Roman Catholic youth and later as an Assembly of God member, I never heard one word about generational curses. That is, not until God called me into spiritual warfare. Then I began visiting charismatic churches to hear guest speakers teach on deliverance. The peculiar topic of generational curses (especially those affecting Freemasons) became a favorite subject.

Now, I know I just lost credibility with those who are seeking deeper things like I was. "Come on," some say, "the Freemasons? Our founding fathers were Freemasons and they were all incredible men of God!" I had the same thoughts. I would listen intently through the deliverance portion of the guest speakers' talks, but turn into a skeptic during the generational curse discussion.

The whole notion that peoples could have curses upon them for generations sounded insane. For me it seemed like too much free association and linking of medical problems with misfortune. Surely, a Christian living under the works of the cross and the blood of Jesus could not be living under a curse!

Therefore, there is now no condemnation for those who are in Christ Jesus, because through Christ Jesus the law of the Spirit of life set me free from the law of sin and death (Romans 8:1-2).

This is the crux of the New Covenant under which we live—so how is it even possible for a generational curse to exist?

Legalism of Evil Spirits

The Holy Spirit changed my mind on this topic. I went through some "interesting" spiritual seasons with my Friday Night Strikes on the streets of San Francisco. For several months, I was having weird experiences in which the Holy Spirit would order spirits in people on the streets to walk up to me and identify themselves. They would come up to me out of the blue and say things like: "I am a Freemason of the 33rd Degree," or "I am molestation," or "I am sado-masochistic bondage."

These are a few of the spirits that approached me, identified themselves, and walked off into the crowds on the street. For a while, I grew accustomed to this; then the strange events ceased as suddenly as they had started.

I eventually understood that these events were for my edification. God was revealing strongholds that were generational. Perhaps the most interesting thing was the number of people who identified with the spirit of the Freemason of the 33rd Degree. Because I see the physical realm through a "math lens," I believe God wanted to show me how statistically prevalent the curse was. The subject clearly warranted further consideration.

The Holy Spirit revealed the generational curse as a matter of demonic legalism. Satan is a lawyer; if he thinks he has any legal authority over you, he will seize it and do his best to keep it.

A lot of the information from Christian books and websites over-complicates the issue. I've seen prayers that include literal checklists of curses ranging from financial curses, to disease curses, to death curses, and so on. It's pretty simple: a generational curse is the legalistic means by which the demonic realm makes acquisition of a family line. The curse consists of the unrepented sin of our ancestors. It travels down the family line—but can be broken through the blood of Jesus Christ!

Entry Points for Generational Curses

The primary entry points for generational curses are spoken oaths to ungodly spirits (religions, the occult, and organizations with an occult hierarchy). Sexual perversion (including adultery, rape, and molestation) is another entry point.

The first deliverance case the Holy Spirit brought me into involved a generational curse. I didn't realize it at the time, because I didn't know what a generational curse was. It was the first time I sat down and "read someone's mail" (charismatic slang for receiving a word of knowledge). It freaked me out. I didn't understand what was happening, but God had it covered and He had a plan. I met with a gentleman named Thomas and received a huge download from the Holy Spirit about his life—both his current situation and family history. Not surprisingly, Thomas had no intention of sharing this very personal information with me. He had been physically and verbally abused by his father; his father even made several attempts to kill Thomas when he was a child.

Thomas grew up living a lie. The focus of his life was to conceal the problems of his past. This was a big factor in Thomas' bipolar condition. Another unfortunate result was that Thomas had no capacity to love his children, because he never experienced real love in his childhood. He and his family attended church, but the charade was effective only on Sunday morning. Their family life was a dysfunctional powder keg that finally exploded.

Thomas sat in church for years and yet never really heard the message of the Gospel. When I worked with him, demonic religious spirits would twist every Scripture I tried to use to help him. The spirit activity was so bizarre that Thomas never realized that the red print in the Bible marked the words of Jesus!

Thomas could have been healed, but he chose to remain in bondage. "What?" you ask.

Yes, you read that correctly; sometimes people don't want to be rid of their demons. Demons will add something to people that they feel they are lacking. Infidelity, perversion, power, strength, courage, boldness—these were things Thomas believed he could not have in the absence of these demons. He believed the lie that he could not cope without them.

OK, so this sounds like a case of demonic oppression right? Yes, it is. But it becomes generational when the rejected children choose anger over forgiveness and choose not to honor the offending parents. The result is a demonic toehold that eventually becomes a stronghold.

There are many cases like this in our own churches. In counseling circles, it is called a *dysfunctional family*. Yet, these people need more than counseling. They need deliverance prayer. The sad part is that not everyone in the family will want to be delivered. Just sitting the family in a room and praying deliverance over them is not enough.

Not all dysfunctional families are under a generational curse. As a deliverance prayer team member or minister, you should never run up to one of these family members and say, "You have a generational curse."

There are multiple dynamics in dysfunctional families. Generational curses are often involved. I recommend letting the family or family members come to you. You need to unwind the ball of yarn in the spirit realm and see what is revealed. This involves praying to the Holy Spirit, and asking if someone in this situation wants to be healed.

Oppressed people may pretend they want to be healed, while every aspect of their life and behavior says they don't. When the oppressed don't want to be healed but you keep trying to help them, the demons play games and suck the life out of you. (Does this sound like anything found in one of those deliverance books or Web sites?)

I refer to generational curses as demonic shrapnel grenades. There is lots of collateral damage; only those who truly want to be saved in the grace and mercy of Jesus Christ will be rescued. Remember: it is Jesus who heals these families, but they must want to be healed.

The Freemason Curse

The Freemason and 33rd Degree phenomenon I kept experiencing on the streets needed some investigating. I considered the Freemason curse to be something of fiction. I saw it as a Dan Brown novel with some Templar Knights and Illuminati intrigue thrown in. In actuality, the trail unraveled like the skin on an onion. I started meeting people whom I believed to be levelheaded and who showed me birth defects that resulted from oaths taken by their fathers, grandfathers, or other ancestors. These people knew precisely which oath caused the curse.

As if this weren't information enough to sway me, there was more. Some of the demonic spirits would manifest in deliverance sessions and would again spout something about oaths in Freemason rituals. But remember rule one when working with demons: when they speak, their language is lies.

In a deliverance session, I cannot let anything a demon says sway me. It could be demonic misinformation. But in this case, the information was too staggering to dismiss as out of hand. The Freemasons do perform rituals and take oaths that symbolize death. I have no intention of perpetuating a conspiracy theory, but something about this is spiritually tainted. Furthermore, we Christians are not to swear any oaths that bind us with death and harm. It is a very bad idea.

There is a lot of material out there on generational curses and the Freemasons. It is difficult, however, to find reliable, factual information on the subject. One book, *Freemasonry-Death in the Family*, by Yvonne Kitchen, seems to be well researched on the matter.[1] In my personal research, however, I needed to understand what was going on with the spirits identifying themselves as the 33rd Degree. I know this: the 33rd Degree Freemason office is blasphemous and applies the title *King of Kings and Lord of Lords*. The title alone should be a big red flag to any Christian.

The ceremony of the 33rd Degree involves satanic rituals such as drinking wine (which represents the poison hemlock) out of a skull. This is a form of satanic communion with an oath of death. Hemlock is used in high-order satanic rituals and the casting of spells.[2]

You don't have to be a conspiracy nut to realize there is something bad going on in Freemasonry. The rites may seem harmless early on, but as you work your way up the veil of evil, the truth is revealed. Of course, voluntarily participating in "fun" black rituals is still sin and rebellion against God.

The LORD is slow to anger, abounding in love and forgiving sin and rebellion. Yet He does not leave the guilty unpunished; He punishes the children for the sin of the fathers to the third and fourth generation (Numbers 14:18).

I am now aware of many birth defects that are associated with death vows made in Freemason rituals. Satan is legalistic; generational curses are commonly initiated from vows or oaths such as these. My word of advice: do not participate in organizations that require vows or oaths.

No Other Gods Before You

When I speak at Bay Area workshops, many African-American and Chinese-American church pastors and members attend. I joke that there are no demons in Caucasian churches. Of course, that's not true; although many such churches like to think so.

Chinese- and African-American churches tend to have a better handle on what is going on spiritually in their churches. They know that there is demonic activity in their churches. They are aware that African witchcraft, slavery, Eastern religions, idolatry, and anger can generate generational curses in their communities.

The Chinese church members I have spoken with at our classes in the San Francisco Bay Area have witnessed manifestations of Eastern religion demons. At an M16 Ministries talk, a woman shared that her church delivered her from possession by an Eastern religion demon.

This kind of activity occurs in all Eastern cultures. In my early walk, I prayed with Christians from India who knew they were experiencing a generational curse from their ancestors' religious practices. Many of these rituals included violent sexual acts. You can imagine the enemy's glee at such opportunities to oppress and possess people. For me, the evidence is overwhelming: generational curses are valid issues for deliverance prayer ministry.

Here on our own turf, we must deal with the generational curse of idolatry. Even atheism is idolatry; in this case the antichrist spirit is idolized and must be removed from the family line.

> *You shall not make for yourself an idol in the form of anything in heaven above or on the earth beneath or in the waters below. You shall not bow down to them or worship them; for I, the Lord your God, am a jealous God, punishing the children for the sin of the fathers to the third and fourth generation of those who hate Me, but showing love to a thousand [generations] of those who love Me and keep My commandments* (Exodus 20:4-6).

We have seen firsthand in our ministry how a spirit from a generational curse can manifest in a person. This spirit (or spirits) must be driven out and the void must be filled with the Holy Spirit. Individuals must also turn from their sin and live lives in the New Covenant of Jesus Christ. If individuals choose not to live a blessed lifestyle or backslide to their old ways, the doorway opens for more demons to enter in.

Lisa and I have witnessed this in several people we have ministered to. As you know, we walk away from those who reject a lifestyle in Jesus. They are adults and are capable of making their own decisions. It is astounding the degree of poor decision-making many Christians attain to.

God gave us free will.

The Occult

While speaking at a church in Assosa, Ethiopia, I shared the supernatural experiences of a Night Strike team working in San Francisco. I thought it was an interesting twist for an American to speak to Africans on miracles, signs, and wonders in America, since Africans have more of a grid for understanding the occult and spirit activity.

I mentioned my experiences on the streets with generational curses. All of a sudden, I saw congregation members open their notebooks and begin to jot down notes. I was puzzled and asked Pastor Tobe afterwards what the interest was in generational curses. He told me that, in Ethiopia, it is common to pray deliverance prayers to remove demons associated with Egyptian sorcery.

In the San Francisco Bay Area, one-third of M16 Ministries deals with witchcraft or the occult. The occult cases commonly involve people with generational curses or practitioners who have left the occult. Other memorable cases involve generational curses affecting adopted children. Some of these babies are put up for adoption by women practicing Wicca. Many of them eventually experience horrible demonic manifestations that they are afraid to share or reveal to anybody. Although they were not raised by their biological parents, they are affected by their parents' involvement in sin and rebellion.

The first step for people in this situation is to embrace *their* authority in Jesus. Christians who understand their authority can remove this curse and live free from it. Satan is legalistic; he needs to have his eviction papers served to him by *you*. A prayer team is extremely effective in helping break the curse, but they cannot make the curse go away. You must break the hold the curse has over your family.

This goes back to the message of free will. Your family will be in bondage to the curse for as long as you want it to be. A prayer team is effective when the demons challenge your authority. Yet, you must be steadfast in your authority and speak the curse to be broken. During your prayer time talk to Jesus and renounce the iniquities of your ancestors.

The following prayer can be used to break various types of generational curses. Just insert into the prayer the specific type of curse you need to break:

> *Jesus, thank You for Your work on the cross and for defeating satan and his army. I thank You for giving Your life for my family and me so that we can have eternal life. I take authority over my family's involvement in (witchcraft, Freemasonry, occult, adultery, etc.) and repent today for the sins that have entered my family line as a result. I renounce satan and order him out of all aspects of my life and my family's life. I choose for my family generations to be blessed by You, Jesus. My family will put no other God before You. I speak in my authority and demand the curse of witchcraft (Freemasonry, occult, adultery, etc.) to be broken from my family line, in Jesus' name!*

It is also important to bless your house. You can do this yourself, using your authority. Spiritually cleanse the house by getting rid of anything that stands in defilement to God. This includes stuffed witch toys (they may look cute, but they are demonic), Harry Potter items, rock posters, any music that glorifies satan, any explicitly demonic items, or items related to Freemasonry, the occult, or any other sin. Get rid of it! Cleanse the house of these items and repent for having them in your house. Then bless your home.

Sexual Perversion and Generational Curses

The most common form of sexual generational curse I have seen is adultery. Any kind of sexual perversion opens the door for other spirits to enter in as well. These include fear, suicide, death, anger, infirmity, religion, rejection, and rejection of the Holy Spirit, to name a few.

We have seen the generational curse of sexual perversion enter when a sexual predator molests a child and appears to get away with it. Such acts do not go unnoticed by demons, however. They watch and then seize the family line. Sexual perversion enters the sons and daughters.

The child who was molested by a sexual predator may try to keep silent about the horrific event. Self-hatred envelopes the child and opens a doorway to self-mutilation, anorexia, and obesity. Some will even become sexual predators themselves, expanding the reach of the curse and making matters worse in their own lives. Those who have lived this nightmare can carry it clear into adulthood; some end up taking their own lives.

Deliverance prayer ministry is extremely effective in helping those who were sexually molested or raped. It will require some very private prayer time, however. If you are praying for a woman who was sexually assaulted, take a maximum of three women ministers into the prayer room. Let the woman receiving prayer tell you what happened to her. Often, deliverance starts when the secret is released. Breaking this tormented silence allows light to touch the darkness that was hidden in the heart for years. Then you can pray, ordering the spirits out of the woman's life and breaking the curse that held her bound.

As always, the prayer team must really listen to the Holy Spirit. It is God who heals, not the prayer team!

Molestation is not the only cause of generational curses of sexual perversion. More subtle forms of perversion, such as infidelity, can affect the family line. When a spouse discovers infidelity, anger and bitterness usually enters the picture. The curse compounds and spreads in any direction it can. The children become angry with their parents and choose not to honor them. As a child rejects a parent, the parent also rejects the child. The child also learns not to trust his or her own spouse later in life. You can see how growing up in a family so brutally torn apart by sexual sin can lead to more infidelity, pornography, and even homosexuality and other issues of perversion.

Prayer can break this pattern of perversion, whatever the cause!

Physical Ailments and Generational Curses

Earlier, I mentioned birth defects relating to Freemason oaths. A variety of ailments can result from different types of generational curses. Some are connected to family patterns of anger and bitterness. You may see arthritis, diabetes, heart disease, bipolar disorder, or migraines, for example.

Often, you will find multiple family members experiencing the same physical manifestations. This is a sign of a generational curse. Some families descending from the former Nazi Germany exhibit inexplicable forms of mental illness, particularly among male family members. Bear in mind that the Nazi regime was a manifestation of the little horn that arose on the beast in Daniel (see Dan. 7). Nazism sprang from an antichrist spirit. This curse needs to be removed from the family line.

Strange physical ailments can also surface from family curses set in motion by forms of sexual perversion including pedophilia, rape, molestation, or murder. As I said earlier, Grandpa may have seemed to get away with his sin. Maybe no one knew about it but Grandpa and the people he assaulted; maybe someone in the family had an inkling. Whatever the case may be, the demons saw it and invaded the family inheritance on the grounds that a legal door was opened by sin.

We have witnessed startling healings through prophetic words and the releasing of forgiveness upon family members. Take Grandpa's case. Let's suppose that a family member knew about what he did, but said nothing. Now, in prayer, the person who guarded Grandpa's secret is startled when the Holy Spirit brings the secret to light. Suddenly, chronic back pain ceases or a digestive disorder goes away.

It's remarkable to see all the afflictions demons take with them when they leave. The prayer team may not even know about the ailments at first (or at all) because they are praying for some other aspect in the person's life. Through the prophetic and the word of knowledge, however, these may be revealed.

A word of caution: Make sure you have some experiences under your belt to operate at this level of the prophetic and the word of knowledge. By that I mean that you must be listening to the Holy Spirit, learn to know His voice, and know how to operate in humility.

Removing the Curse

In my opinion, many Christian books and media on generational curses give a lot of legalistic and doctrinal babble for removing them. It's actually quite simple: apply the Gospel of Jesus Christ!

> *Therefore, there is now no condemnation for those who are in Christ Jesus, because through Christ Jesus the law of the Spirit of life set me free from the law of sin and death* (Romans 8:1-2).

Use your Kingdom authority over the curse! You can take the matter into your own hands and renounce the curse from your family line. Tell the demons there is no assignment over your family because Jesus Christ died at the cross and you are living under the New Covenant. They have no hold over you or your family. Take the authority and the responsibility for living free in the law of the Spirit of life.

Bad things happen to us; so do the good things. That's why this is spiritual warfare: there are difficult skirmishes and there are victories! I have seen people set free in a few hours because they embraced their freedom and also chose to forgive. I have also seen people drag their spiritual chains, rattling them from one prayer meeting to the next, seeming to look for freedom, and deliverance.

It always comes down to a matter of free will. Count your small victories and start kicking the darkness out of your family and your home. Parents, become responsible adults and take authority and dominion over your home. You can receive healing just by living free of generational bondage—if you take the responsibility and ownership of the family sins and repent of them.

Fathers shall not be put to death for their children, nor children put to death for their fathers; each is to die for his own sin (Deuteronomy 24:16).

The notion that you must suffer for the sins of your ancestors is a demonic power grab designed to usurp your authority. You will be judged for your own sins and not the sins of your grandfathers. For some, it is easier to say they are under a generational curse than to put the effort into grabbing the reins of their dysfunctional family and their disrespectful children.

Some people have lived as victims for so long that they don't want the responsibility that accompanies healing and a life of wholeness.

Summary

Generational curses can transcend family lineage. They can enter from vows and oaths, sexual attacks, the occult, and participation in ungodly religions.

For our ministry, it is truly amazing to see the numbers of lives that have been set free from generational curses. Each person who stepped into his or her freedom in Jesus Christ did so by making a choice. In the end, the exercise of a person's free will is the make-or-break element. Choose freedom over bondage and you will see the healing begin and the generational curse break.

The heavenly Father helps us in so many amazing ways. His one and only Son died on the cross so we could be free!

Endnotes

1. Yvonne Kitchen, *Freemasonry-Death in the Family* (Victoria, Australia: Fruitful Vine Publishing, 2002), 125.

2. Yvonne Kitchen, *Freemasonry-Death in the Family* (Victoria, Australia: Fruitful Vine Publishing, 2002), 126.

CHAPTER 12

SEXUALLY TRANSMITTED DEMONS

*Therefore God gave them over in the sinful desires of their
hearts to sexual impurity for the degrading of their bodies
with one another* (Romans 1:24).

One of the strangest and most peculiar aspects of deliverance, I feel, is the subject of sexually transmitted demons. I call them STDs.

We touched on STDs earlier. We saw that demons literally have the ability to hop from one body to another through acts of both voluntary and involuntary sex. I was first made aware of this during a deliverance prayer session. I shared a little bit about this case in Chapter 8.

If you remember, a man with a Christian upbringing cheated on his wife with a witch. He followed his lust to the point where he involved himself in ritual sex acts with the woman. He got loaded up with dozens of demons from these sexual encounters. Although he was the first case like this that I had seen, we have since prayed for over a hundred deliverances from demons that were transferred through these practices.

In this case a husband and wife, Sean and Cindy, came out to Night Strike to minister with us and serve the poor. My friend, Jimi Merrell, also went out with us that night. Jimi and I first stopped off at City Ministries to meet up with Mark Neitz and see whether we could offer a lift to anyone else who would be joining us.

Mark introduced Jimi and me to Sean and Cindy. He told us they were going to spend the night in town and wondered whether Jimi and I would be available the next morning for deliverance prayer. We said that we would and then drove off to minister to God's people on the streets.

The next morning I returned to the City Ministries building, prepared for a generational-curse-breaking session. Jimi showed up shortly after me with a Starbucks coffee and a story about how the barista asked him twice what he was planning to do that day. With a streak of boldness, Jimi said he and his friends were going to pray to break the hold of evil spirits off a man's life. The gal was intrigued. I mention her now because, when Jimi returned to Starbucks a few weeks later, she asked him about the prayer session and was led to Jesus through that conversation!

When all of us had arrived for the deliverance session, Mark, Jimi, and I invited Sean and Cindy into the prayer room. We started the interview with Sean and asked him what was going on in his life. He said he had several spirits that would surface and take over his body. When we asked him how he knew they were spirits, Cindy jumped in and answered, "They're spirits, all right. He walks around all night long and different spirits talk through him the whole time."

Jimi asked Sean how many spirits he thought were oppressing him. Sean thought there were dozens. We surmised immediately that this wasn't an ordinary curse-breaking prayer session. We were going into major combat. Mark opened in prayer. Nearly immediately, a spirit manifested in Sean, who was sitting in a large chair across from us.

Sean said, "Oh no," and his head shot back. When his head rolled back, it was not Sean but a demonic spirit looking back at us. We bound the spirit right away using the following Scripture:

And if one prevail against him, two shall withstand him; and a threefold cord is not quickly broken (Ecclesiastes 4:12 KJV).

The spirit was immediately bound and glared back at us. Jimi ordered the spirit to leave. In unison, Mark, Jimi, and I again ordered the spirit to leave. The spirit raised Sean's hand toward me and extended his middle finger in my direction. I reached into my pocket, pulled out my anointing oil, and blessed the hand. The spirit immediately retracted the finger and the hand. (That moment lives in infamy; whenever Jimi and I speak at the same function, he brings up the incident and tells the people what to do when a demon spirit gives this improper salute.)

The spirit wasn't about to leave, but appeared to have been kicked out by another, bigger spirit that was seeking to avert seizure by an angel that was in the room with us. Jimi saw the angel's reflection in the glass of a fish tank several times. Unfortunately, I had my back to the tank at the time.

I believe it was Mark who then turned to ask Cindy if she knew how Sean got loaded up with so many demons. Cindy replied that Sean had been unfaithful. She said he'd had an affair with a witch which lasted for some time. Sean and Cindy were professing Christians. I have mentioned before that I have witnessed Christians doing things that go beyond any rhyme or reason. Sean's first bad choice was to have an affair. The stakes were raised by having an affair with a woman involved in black magic.

Mark, Jimi, and I got an education that day on how witches spread and collect demons through sexual rituals. Remember that Sean willfully participated in these rituals with his witch mistress. It was a costly affair!

As you learned in Chapter 8, the witch's intimate touch left spiritual fingerprints on Sean's body. Any place she touched him intimately (to hold hands, etc.) left a cold spot on his body. We could only guess what was going with the other parts of his body where the contact was even more intimate.

Throughout the deliverance session, demons created all sorts of distractions to keep us from praying for Sean's freedom. On several occasions, the roof of the building creaked loudly, as though it were being pulled down on us. At one point, while Mark, Jimi, and I prayed in our prayer language, a manifesting demon declared in foul language that it hated the gift of tongues.

Some other noteworthy spirits surfaced that day. One spirit caused Sean to behave like a female; this demon identified itself as Brenda. Brenda got the boot from the same darker spirit that ejected the middle-finger-waving spirit earlier. Whenever angels came to collect spirits, this "bigger" spirit would defend itself by causing chaos and kicking out the lesser spirits. I have never witnessed anything like this in any deliverance session since.

When we got to the point where we knew we were talking to Sean and not manifested spirits, I began the work of curse-breaking. I had Sean renounce satan and witchcraft. All along the way, as we made incremental progress, "new" spirits would surface to interfere with our breaking of the curse. The three of us had to pray in unity over the course of four hours to kick out most of the spirits Sean had picked up from the witch.

When we got down to the last spirit—the nasty one—Mark received a word of knowledge that Sean's father had left an emotional hook in Sean's back. This hook was the demon's stronghold: it was the father's rejection. Now how did we jump from the sex rituals to the father's rejection? I want you to see how complicated the human consciousness can be. The root cause of Sean's adultery went all the way back to fatherly rejection!

To remove this stronghold, Mark reached out in a prophetic manner and pulled out the hook. Sean had his back to Mark and couldn't see what Mark was doing; yet Jimi and I saw Sean being lifted out of the chair as though someone were removing a physical hook from deep in his back.

Sean's rejection stronghold had compounded into other strongholds. One of these strongholds led him to the affair with the witch, where many demons gained entry through ritual sex and adultery.

Let's be perfectly clear about this: just because Sean had strongholds doesn't mean the devil made him do what he did. Sean committed adultery knowingly and of his own free will.

Soul Ties

The word *soul* refers to the mind, emotions, and will. A *soul tie* is the binding of our mind and emotions to something that can influence our behavior. A soul tie can also affect our will and the choices we make. The Bible makes references to good and bad soul ties. In Genesis 2:24, God describes His plan for a godly soul tie relationship—it is called *marriage*. God spoke His plan for marriage into existence in the Garden of Eden:

> *For this reason a man will leave his father and mother and be united to his wife, and they will become one flesh* (Genesis 2:24).

His Word is very specific about how we are to conduct ourselves in sexual relationships. The sex act is permitted only between a man and the woman to whom he is married. The institution of marriage was created by God, in part as a divine plan for procreation. It permits the joining of flesh between a man and a woman; it also allows the continuation of the human race.

Yet, Ephesians 5 reveals a higher meaning and purpose to God's one-flesh plan of marriage. The union of marriage is the earthly model of our heavenly union with Christ:

> *"For this reason a man will leave his father and mother and be united to his wife, and the two will become one flesh." This is a profound mystery—but I am talking about Christ and the church* (Ephesians 5:31-32).

This passage explains the larger spiritual aspect of our sexuality. As a man and a woman unite, they become one flesh. Likewise, their souls become united through sexual intercourse.

For better or worse, souls are bound together in every sexual relationship. In Paul's first epistle to the Corinthians, God describes a bad soul tie in which a man has joined himself with a prostitute:

> *Do you not know that your bodies are members of Christ Himself? Shall I then take the members of Christ and unite them with a prostitute? Never! Do you not know that he who unites himself with a prostitute is one with her in body? For it is said, "The two will become one flesh." But he who unites himself with the Lord is one with Him in spirit* (1 Corinthians 6:15-17).

We live in a promiscuous society. The number of soul ties from casual encounters with opposite-sex partners is staggering. Add to that the number of soul ties that slip in through homosexual relationships.

Studies have shown that the average heterosexual male in a steady, married, but promiscuous relationship, in the Netherlands, can have as many as eight relationships per year. A homosexual male can have as many as several hundred.[1] No matter how you look at the numbers, they get really big really fast—especially because you can take on soul ties with people you have never even met.

Here's how this works: Imagine that you are a single woman who has had one sexual encounter this year. Let's assume that your one-night stand was with a promiscuous man who had intercourse with eight other women over the course of the year. For the sake of argument, imagine that each of these women had sex with as many as eight men that year.

Your one-night stand did not expose you to one soul tie with your only partner. When you had sex with him, you were exposed to all of the soul ties from all of his sexual encounters. In this case, you can take on as many as 64 soul ties, mostly with people you will never meet—and we are singling out just one year's worth of promiscuous sexual activity!

Keep in mind that some homosexuals engage in casual opposite-sex relationships from time to time. Now consider what happens if your one-night stand involves a man who has slept with another woman who, in turn, had relations with a homosexual man. There's no telling what kind of exponential exposure to soul ties you would be risking. Notice that we have not even taken into account the possibilities of exposure to sexually transmitted diseases.

Generational curses propagate through the joining of the flesh, a soul tie. Some generational curses manifest in the physical realm as hereditary disease or affliction. The curse can also manifest spiritually with tormenting voices, or depression, for example. The curse can manifest in a stronger aspect with demonic manifestation and torment.

We have already learned that any vow taken by an ancestor in any ungodly ritual, such as in Freemasonry or satanism, can travel down the family line until the vow is renounced. These are all forms of demonic oppression passed along through sexual activity and the resulting sexual soul ties. (I believe a better word for this would be *flesh ties*.)

Lisa and I have ministered to Christian women who have been divorced from husbands with drug addictions or histories of incarceration for rape. The passing of demons through intercourse was not inhibited by the fact that these women were legitimately married to these men. Curses were still passed to them through the sexual relations they had with their husbands.

We both remember well a woman named Keri, a sweet, pleasant, Christian woman who was also a grandmother. Keri attended church regularly and loved Jesus. One night when we prayed for her, a spirit manifested that wasn't Keri. It was an angry, bitter spirit that tried to pretend it hadn't manifested. I was sitting next to Keri. The spirit looked at me from the corner of Keri's eyes. Keri's lips (now conveying the demon's facial expression) tightened and started twitching. Her hands balled up in a manner that is customary with a spirit of bitterness and anger.

One of Keri's hands started to make a fist. I know the spirit had every intention of striking me. I bound the spirit and ordered it to release Keri's hands and leave. The spirit boldly answered, "No! She's ours." This is the standard answer spirits give; it is another reason I don't speak to them.

I then bound the spirit, forcing it to shut up. The spirit just stared at me and twitched its lip. I ordered the spirit to leave again. This time, the spirit faked an epileptic fit and tried to make Keri gag on her own tongue. I ordered the demon to stop the fake seizure and release the tongue. The spirit did so, but still wouldn't leave.

After some time, I shut down the prayer as we were locked in a stand-off with the demon. When Keri returned to us, I asked her what was going on. She told us that her first husband was a violent, convicted rapist. When she was young and single, she allowed the man to have his way with her, even though she knew premarital sex was wrong. Little did Keri know that he was a predator who was raping women while he was dating her.

Keri said the manifestations started happening around the time she was having sex with the man she was yet to marry. This is another situation involving compounding strongholds. Deep down inside, Keri never really forgave herself or her ex-husband. To this day, she lives with this torment. Freedom is just a short forgiveness prayer away, but as long as Keri chooses bitterness and torment over forgiveness and freedom, she will deal with demons.

This case demonstrates the importance of knowing whom you are going to marry. Too many couples feel that because they're already having sex and living together, they have found the right reason to get married. In fact, this is the worse methodology you could use to determine whom your future spouse should be. Know the person you are marrying and know his or her generational history, including the medical conditions present in the family line. There is a perfectly good reason for the socially accepted year-long engagement before getting married. In this time the man and woman should learn full well whom they are marrying. Remember: you cannot change a person when you get married. Your spouse's habits will only get worse! The good news is curses can be broken. I would recommend any engaged couple to be prayed over for blessing and curse removal. This is even more important if there is any repeated history of abuse or illness on either side of the two families joining to become one through marriage.

Prayer to Break Soul Ties

Heavenly Father, I thank You for loving me. I confess my sin of being sexually impure and worldly. I ask for Your forgiveness of my sexual promiscuity. I repent of my own sexual sins and of the soul ties that I received through these sins.

I take ownership of my family line, in the past and the future. I renounce and break all soul ties from my body. I renounce satan's hold on me through these impure acts. I also renounce ties to witchcraft. In Jesus' name, I ask You to release me from all unclean spirits that I received. In Jesus' name I also ask You to remove all unclean spirits from my children. Release me, my family, and my future generations from the spirits of perversion and religion.

From this day forward I want to live blessed under the covering of the blood of Jesus Christ. I pray this in Your precious name. Amen.

Ritual Abuse (Satanism, Witchcraft, and Tantric)

I remember watching a show on television a few years back about how Wiccans celebrate Halloween in Salem, Massachusetts. The television cameras followed a woman into her house and showed the Halloween "festivities" engaged in that night. The entire family and the woman's guests conducted their rituals while naked. Several children were present in these rituals because the television show and the Wiccans considered this to be a family gathering. It was presented by the media with a serious tone, as a sacred time for the Wiccans. Can you imagine the media frenzy and insinuations of molestation that would have ensued if this celebration had been conducted by Roman Catholic priests or Protestant ministers?

246   A *Field Guide to Spiritual Welfare*

Practically speaking, these Wiccan parents handed their children over to satan. The kids were being involuntarily led into rituals that glorified him. They obviously believed they were worshiping some earthly god, but who is the prince of the earth, if not satan? And the nudity—it was and is a mockery of the pre-Fall absence of shame found in the Garden of Eden.

Satanic ritual abuse is another issue that surfaces in deliverance every now and again. I have seen cases in which women were left in rooms to be raped by demons. The male demon is called an *incubus*. The female version is a *succubus*.

For some reason, Christians fixate on satanic ritual abuse. Calls to deliverance ministries become more frantic when people stumble onto cases of satanic ritual abuse. It is a horrible act, but it is no worse than the horror of rape. Remember that these people have survived this far with the torment of the ritual; the Holy Spirit will protect them as He delivers them from their nightmare.

Know this: the darkness of these rituals must come up during deliverance—and it won't be pretty. Deliverance in these cases may be instantaneous; it might also require an extremely long process, due to the personality disorders that result from ritual abuse.

In the ritual cases M16 ministries has been involved in, multiple personality disorder (MPD) is prevalent. And because MPD is a result of religious practice, the person suffering from the disorder seldom trusts or wants help from Christians. Some seek the guidance of trained Roman Catholic exorcists. Yet, we have found that some MPDs are designed to be resistant to the Ritual Romana of the Catholic Church.

Because of what happened to them, these people are often afraid to try a deliverance prayer ministry. We have had people set free by deliverance who then recommend deliverance prayer ministry to others. That being said, this is a very closed and secret community that reaches outside for help.

Another form of ungodly sex practices invading our "if it feels good do it" society is tantric sex. Tantra is an ancient religion

SEXUALLY TRANSMITTED DEMONS

with roots in Hinduism and Tibetan Buddhism; it uses sexuality and most forms of pleasure as spiritual doorways to Hindu gods. Tantra is a form of yoga meditation. In yoga meditation, the practitioner stretches the body to allow the entry of demons.

Online health guides and national publications in the United States now encourage tantric sex practices as a means of experiencing heightened ecstasy. Tantric sex is also supposed to release energy as the couples engage in it. The bottom line is that these people are deceived; they are seeking spirituality and enlightenment through sex.

Tantric masters, coaches, and goddesses lead people through the practice in which intercourse with a woman is a form of goddess worship. The woman is treated as a goddess and worshiped through the sex. In tantric circles, a goddess has intercourse with many men.

These practitioners also believe that sex is sacred during the woman's period of menstruation, which is contrary to the teachings of the Old Testament:

If a man lies with her and her monthly flow touches him, he will be unclean for seven days; any bed he lies on will be unclean (Leviticus 15:24).

Keep in mind that the law was given to Moses, but grace and truth came through Jesus Christ (see John 1:17). We are not under the law, but under the New Covenant. Yet, tantric sex *is* another mockery of the Word implemented by the enemy. Tantric writings are ancient; the enemy came up with this one to counter the law of Moses.

When the practices of goddess worship and meditation enter a Christian household, they can open a doorway to the demonic. God gave us the beautiful wonder of sex so we could reproduce and share intimacy between a husband and wife. Bringing sexual rituals into the bedroom is dangerous.

Even so, don't be too surprised if you encounter godly people in your church who are practicing tantric sex. Remember: ignorance can be deadly:

*My people are destroyed from lack of knowledge. Because you
have rejected knowledge, I also reject you as My priests; because
you have ignored the law of your God, I also will ignore your
children* (Hosea 4:6).

Rape and Molestation

God is no respecter of persons (see Acts 10:34) and satan is
no respecter of age. Satan has a motto, destroy people as early in
life as possible.

Rape and molestation are silent cancers of the soul. If you
believe a Christian can't suffer demonic oppression, you need to
look no further than a person who has been molested or raped.
These cases bring me to tears nearly every time. These people
were raped by demons, too. Long after the act, the enemy con-
tinues to tell these victims how worthless they are. He tells them
they need to shut up and live with their shame in silence. The
enemy tells them they will never be able to truly love anyone
because of what happened to them. Satan may even send voices
to tell them to hurt or kill themselves. This is the voice of demonic
oppression.

I have seen too many people living under this nightmare.
It does not need to continue. It can be broken if the people are
willing to lay down their years of self-hatred at the foot of the
cross. I have seen incredible healings from rape and molestation. You know what happens then? The people who were delivered develop a healthy anger; they turn around and deliver other
people who are living the same nightmare—and all of it happens
through the Gospel of Jesus Christ!

The deliverance of a person from rape or molestation can
be instantaneous or over a long period of time. God has no calendar or agenda and meets people where they are at in the fight.
One woman told me that her pastors prayed over her for deliverance from her torment. When nothing happened right away, the
pastors accused the woman of seeking sympathy.

Many of these people lived in torment for years; it may take a while to peel the layers of oppression off the rape and molestation "onion." Take the time that is needed; just make sure that, after each session, the person is in a better place than before. Work step by step; keep moving forward in prayer. The best use of this prayer time is to work in the prophetic. Let God the Father minister to His children.

This may sound like a broken record by now, but there is no formula by which God delivers His people. If you are a parent, you know that each and every one of your children is unique. Parenting methods that work for one child may have no effect on your other children. God knows how to father each and every one of us.

With this in mind, let me identify some types of spiritual activity you should keep an eye out for. This is not a checklist; these are just a few things to be aware of that may manifest when prayer is taking place.

The obvious spirits that tend to show up in cases of rape and molestation are self-hatred, rejection, and anger. It is also possible for rejection to have a physical manifestation in the form of scoliosis, arthritis, or some other back or neurological disorder.

When praying for these people I have them stand up so prayer team members can lay hands on them from both the front and the back. In some cases of rape and molestation, I have walked behind the people I am praying for and held my Bible about an inch away from their lower back or spine. Sometimes, they jerk away from me, without even knowing that I was standing behind them. You might even be able to feel the demons move on some people's backs while you lay hands on them. This is common, but doesn't always happen! When it does, or when the person gets a back spasm or pain during the prayer, order the demon off the back. Speak firmly, but do not yell!

In Jesus' name! Unbind the back and release it. Come off the back now!

During this time, just pray over the person calmly and let the love of the Father handle the situation. Work in the prophetic, too. The Father will tell you what the person needs to lay at the foot of the cross. If your team is new at this, quietly whisper among team members to see whether they are hearing from the Spirit the same things you are. Then work together in unity to pray about that matter.

Lisa and I pray in tongues quite a bit during the deliverance. It is peaceful and quiet. There is no chaos or disruption by the demon. The deliverance will, however, be tearful as the years of pain surface and are removed from the person.

Be aware that when anger surfaces, it has a tendency to manifest in the hands. In my experience, the fingers may start twitching or even ball up as though arthritis were present.

Keep in mind that a rape victim isn't always a female. I have encountered two men who were raped while in prison. The prophetic deliverance is the most powerful and effective way to pray over any rape victim. God reveals that He is real; He shows these victims that He wants to come down fom the throne room and help them. In the cases of delivering men from rape, they too cried and allowed the pain of the defilement to come off of them.

What happens when you are in a deliverance prayer meeting and the Holy Spirit delivers a violent man who has forced himself upon women? Don't be too surprised if the person is a church leader in one of your church ministries. Rapists and molesters often have everyone fooled. They are manipulators who don't stop to consider that their behavior is demonic.

Remember that the devil didn't make him do it. Offenders choose this lifestyle on their own. The behavior probably started with a toehold in pornography. Later, it manifests into perversion, forced sex acts, deceit, self-hatred, and hatred of women.

The Father loves His children and will deliver them from such perversions, but there are consequences to these rebellious actions. God disciplined King David for his infidelity. I don't know why Christians don't think the Father will spank them harshly for their rebellious sins against their own brothers and sisters.

> *Then David said to Nathan, "I have sinned against the Lord." Nathan replied, "The LORD has taken away your sin. You are not going to die. But because by doing this you have made the enemies of the LORD show utter contempt, the son born to you will die"* (2 Samuel 12:13-14).

God will use harsh discipline when correcting His children. I was at a prayer deliverance meeting where a young man sought healing from a simple physical ailment. The spirits in this man were so manipulative they convinced him that his history of sexual assault against women would not be an issue.

However, when the glory of God moved in to heal this man, his demons of rape, manipulation, and lies were attacked. They manifested with a vengeance. It was one of the most seemingly torturous deliverances I have ever participated in. As the demons were driven out, they tormented him with the same pain he had inflicted upon his victims.

All the darkness had to come out and all the lies of his false Christian lifestyle surfaced. Was he forgiven? Yes. In the prophetic, all his sins were revealed. He was in such pain from the demonic manifestations that he willfully renounced every sin that was revealed to the deliverance team members.

There are consequences for our actions. God will hand us over to our tormentors if we choose a rebellious and ungodly lifestyle. Deliverance in these cases takes some time. This young man needed to make some immediate decisions about how to spend the rest of his life: walk with Jesus and be healed or return to the lie and live in torment.

God heals us all—if we let His light into our darkness.

One last topic I have encountered in ministry is initiation gang rape and gang-instigated sex. Vows and oaths are pledged in gangs, even though some of these kids are Christians who attend church and actively participate in youth groups.

Some kids are forced into having sex in their junior high years! For the young boys, it is the gang's rite of passage into manhood. For the girls, it is a vow of loyalty to the gang. The pledge is kept by having sex with a gang member. Such vows, pledges, violence, and sexual promiscuity all point to demonic activity.

Many demons of anger, violence, and hatred (to name a few) are associated with gang activity. In the two cases of gang-related sex initiation I have seen, a deaf and dumb spirit manifested in the girls. They weren't permanently deaf or mute; they became that way only when the demons manifested.

These two cases stemmed from separate incidents occurring about a year apart in two different towns. In one incident, the girl approached me for help because she realized that an angry, confrontational side of her was emerging. She was a good student at school but blew up one day and verbally lashed out at her teacher. She knew that wasn't her nature at all. It scared her.

The girl said nothing about her gang involvement. I prayed for her at two separate meetings; in both meetings, she was slain in the spirit. The second time the Holy Spirit came over her, the unclean spirit couldn't take it. The girl lay on the floor while the spirit stared at me with a silent, evil grimace.

Then I received a word of knowledge regarding the gang initiation sex she'd had with her boyfriend, who was a gang member. I didn't elaborate on the details; I was sensitive to the fact that I was talking to a child. The demon, who cared little about the girl's age, quit smiling after I shared what the Holy Spirit revealed. After nearly two hours of prayer, the young girl was set free from the deaf and dumb spirit and a few other demons. Once the spiritual point of entry for the deaf and dumb spirit was identified, all of the strongholds were torn down.

When Jesus saw that a crowd was running to the scene, He rebuked the evil spirit. "You deaf and mute spirit," He said, "I command you, come out of him and never enter him again" (Mark 9:25).

This was the case in which Jesus' disciples asked Jesus why they couldn't cast this demon out and Jesus replied, *"This kind can come out only by prayer"* (Mark 9:29).

The King James Version of this Scripture says it can come out only by prayer and fasting! In my experience with deaf and dumb spirits, it helps to work in the prophetic with the Holy Spirit and let Him reveal the entry point of the demons. I don't really talk to demons anyway, so if it is deaf and dumb, I prefer the "dumb" part.

In the most bizarre case I remember, the demon acted out a lot of stuff as though the deliverance team were participating in a game of charades. This was what the second young girl did. When this happens, it is very distracting. Use your authority to bind the hands and feet in the spirit realm. The demon is just trying to distract the prayer team from focusing on the Holy Spirit. These demons leave, through fasting, prayer, and the prophetic. I would recommend working in all three, although I have seen deliverance through just prayer and the prophetic. It did take several sessions, however.

Abortion

We live in an age in which the media and our schools encourage sex out of marriage. If a new life results from this sex, abortion is the widely recommended resolution to the problem. Our immoral society sees having a baby as an unfair form of punishment to the young, unwed mother. (Do you recognize the words of our country's highest elected official?)

Abortion of an unwanted child—or any child—is an abomination to God. Any Christian who believes abortion is a valid method of population or birth control is living under the lie of the demon Molech, which was identified in in Scripture:

He desecrated Topheth, which was in the Valley of Ben Hinnom, so no one could use it to sacrifice his son or daughter in the fire to Molech (2 Kings 23:10).

God informs us in Scripture that we are not to sacrifice our babies.

> *The people of Judah have done evil in My eyes, declares the LORD. They have set up their detestable idols in the house that bears My Name and have defiled it. They have built the high places of Topheth in the Valley of Ben Hinnom to burn their sons and daughters in the fire—something I did not command, nor did it enter My mind. So beware, the days are coming, declares the LORD when people will no longer call it Topheth or the Valley of Ben Hinnom, but the Valley of Slaughter, for they will bury the dead in Topheth until there is no more room. Then the carcasses of this people will become food for the birds of the air and the beasts of the earth, and there will be no one to frighten them away* (Jeremiah 7:30-33).

I know the Web sites dedicated to reason will jump all over this. They will say that it is an irrational stretch to compare the sacrificial burning of babies to abortion. It is not the least bit irrational: it is the same demon in operation! Look at how society worships abortion—it's a deity. It's still Molech. There will also be consequences and judgment on these people for their actions.

So what happens when you repent of having an abortion? God forgives you. He will take the spirit of heaviness and death off of you. Here is a prayer you can pray or share with others:

> *Father in Heaven, please forgive me for having an abortion. I know it was wrong. Please free me from all soul ties stemming from this relationship. I take ownership of this sin and I fully repent of it. In Jesus' name, bring Your light into all of my darkness and heal me. I choose from this day forward to live in Your light and Your glory.*

It takes a man and a woman to conceive. There are men in church who were having pre-marital sex or committing adultery; they also need to repent for the sexual relationship and the abortion that resulted. This must be a heartfelt and life-changing repentance. Dragging someone to a deliverance meeting and forcing them to repent is not effective. It's a lot like the young man from a previous example who knew how to manipulate people. People will just say the words to get off the hook and move on without consequences. That is not how the Holy Spirit works. When He reveals through the prophetic that someone has participated in abortion, the person needs to repent of it! The truth literally sets people free.

> *Father in Heaven, please forgive me for paying for an abortion or forcing a woman into an abortion. Please free me from all soul ties stemming from this relationship. I take ownership of this sin and I fully repent of it. In Jesus' name, bring Your light into all of my darkness and heal me. I choose from this day forward to live in Your light and Your glory.*

Summary

An entire book could be devoted to the topic of sex, deliverance, and sexually transmitted demons (STDs). I covered a few topics that surface regularly during prayer meetings and private sessions.

The topics of ritual abuse and rape were both covered here. Ritual abuse is a matter that is no greater or more urgent than that of a person in your congregation who is quietly dealing with a past rape. Both of these rapes involved violence instigated by demons. Both involved the transfer of demonic oppression. There are healings for those who were victims, and there are consequences for those who willfully forced themselves upon others.

Our society still lives in a "Summer of Love" mentality. Our culture encourages sex as a form of casual pleasure with no strings attached. The sacred pillars of marriage are being torn down. God created marriage. It is an important part of His plan for His people. Society is turning this into a mockery, and this mockery is entering the Church. God has spanked His kids in the past and He will discipline us today. Let's keep God's created plan for sexuality sacred, just as He intended it to be.

Endnote

1. Maria Xiridou, et al., "The contribution of steady and casual partnership to the incidence of HIV infection amon homosexual men in Amsterdam," *AIDS 17* (2003):1031.

CHAPTER 13

PROPHETIC EVANGELISM AND DELIVERANCE PRAYER MINISTRY

Surely He took up our infirmities and carried our sorrows,
yet we considered Him stricken by God, smitten by Him,
and afflicted (Isaiah 53:4).

A lot of my inspiration comes from watching high school and college-aged believers operate in the gifts of the Spirit.

A young man named Martel took our M16 deliverance class and has worked with me on a haunting case. Martel has incredible stories of operating in the Spirit. He selects restaurants for lunch by praying and asking God where he should go to eat and have a divine encounter.

This young man has an amazing evangelistic anointing. On one Night Strike, Martel shared a story about a Friday night when he and a few friends went to the local mall. They prayed and asked the Holy Spirit to show them what and whom they should pray for in the mall. Martel sensed that they were to look for a woman with back pain who would be found in a store with the word *mark* in its name.

Armed with this key piece of prophetic information, Martel and his friends began looking for clues. One of his friends pointed out the Hallmark store, which satisfied the criterion of having the word *mark* in the store name. They entered the Hallmark store and found a woman working the cash register. Martel asked the woman if she was having back pain. The woman returned a puzzled glance and answered that she was experiencing some really bad back pain.

Martel told the woman that they were from a local church, and that God sent them to this store to pray for her. They asked the woman if it would be OK to pray for her back. She said, "Yes." So Martel and his friends prayed for her healing. When they were done, they spoke with the woman for a while and then left the store.

As it turned out, this woman was the manager of the store. The next morning, she went into work and started talking to one of her employees about how these people had prayed for her back the night before and now the pain was gone. The woman who was listening to the story started smiling and said, "I think I know who came in here last night. It sounds like Martel. He goes to my church."

The manager added, "But that wasn't the weird part. Right before they came in, I had asked God whether I should go back to church!"

Jesus instructed us, in Matthew 10:7-8, to preach the message of the Gospel, heal the sick, cleanse the lepers, raise the dead, and drive out demons. This is Jesus' mission statement for the Church's deliverance ministry. When we share the Gospel with others who are healed of their broken hearts, their sicknesses, and their oppression, these people can then go and share the Gospel with others who will also be healed.

I'll say it again: deliverance ministry has taken too much of a slant toward the casting out of demons. This is part of deliverance ministry; it is not the emphasis of deliverance ministry. Deliverance ministry is a healing ministry. Who gets healed? The broken-hearted, the sick, the terminally ill, the mentally ill, the spiritually weak—all who come to the cross looking for and accepting help.

Deliverance is an evangelism ministry that shares the Gospel of Jesus Christ. Deliverance ministry is meeting strangers on the streets, with no agenda to sway them, but instead giving them a taste of God through the gifts of the Spirit.

Have you noticed that tracts don't work as well as they used to? When you talk with strangers and give them a *word of knowledge*, you have opened a door for ministry. God will meet people where they're at in *their* lives. Once your ministry starts getting people get saved and healed, they will bring others who need ministering, too.

What do you do when a psychic, tarot card reader, or witch comes through the church doors and asks for prayer? You pray for them. When God said He would leave the 99 behind to chase the one, He was talking about all of us (see Matt. 18:12). We were all the one Jesus was chasing at one point or another. If the occult practitioners come to your church seeking prayer, I suggest you work with Jesus and pray for them. God is going to show these people how false their spiritual beliefs really are.

What do you do when this person asks Jesus into his or her life? Realize first of all that God sets divine appointments. Make sure your ministry is in step with the movement of the Holy Spirit. Be careful not to judge those who walk through the door requesting prayer. Remember that all the people who walks through that door were given a VIP invitation from the one true God who loves them.

Starting Your Own Night Strike Ministry

Bill Johnson of Bethel Redding has a fascinating story that remains stuck in the back of my mind. He said that people were calling him and asking to come out and participate in his church's mall ministry. These people spoke of evangelizing the mall the same way my friend Martel did.

Bill Johnson's official reply was that they didn't have a mall ministry; they had people who went shopping in the mall.

Putting together a Night Strike ministry can be as simple as going to a mall or a cinema multiplex on a Friday evening and seeing where the Holy Spirit leads you. These locations are good, safe places to develop and nurture the working of the gifts of the Spirit. Kingdom of Grace Ministries has young people who invade coffee shops and get other young people delivered. Your own backyard is a good place to start to develop your church's prophetic evangelism skills. Satan is at work everywhere destroying lives, including in your own picturesque hometown.

Night Strike is invading the enemy's camp and going wherever the lost are. In Night Strike, we like going to the darkest parts of town where people tell us we shouldn't go. These are places the light of Jesus needs to invade. If you are new to this, I don't recommend going to the darkest neighborhoods right off the bat. Start somewhere safe where you can put together your team, work in the prophetic, and get to know each other.

My friend Martel had the right idea. Ask the Holy Spirit which fast-food restaurant you should go to for lunch and a divine encounter. Go to the local mall and have a treasure hunt, as Bill Johnson calls it. This is where you ask the Holy Spirit for clues about the person with whom you are supposed to have a divine encounter. Martel has lots of marvelous glory stories of healings, simply because he asked God where he should go to eat.

As you gain confidence in operating in the gifts of the Spirit, you can start branching out. Go sit in a Starbucks with a couple of your friends and give some Holy Spirit-ual "readings." People who are in Starbucks on a Friday night might enjoy the demonstration of the gifts. The purpose of these expeditions is to touch them with the Holy Spirit. This is not the time to point out people's sins. It is the time to point out His love.

When you and your team feel released to start ministering in more challenging places, plan some spiritual expeditions to not-so-nice neighborhoods. The homeless hang out in these areas and are always grateful receivers of God's Word. Talk about a treasure hunt! Most people would deem these individuals untouchable and not even speak to them. Bring them some food; give them prophetic words and they will open up to you.

Many homeless people are Christians, by the way! They will allow ministry teams to pray for healing when they're sick. You need to pray for sick people to get a testimony in healing! God loves it when you minister to the poor. He really opens up the treasure chest of miracles when praying for the poor.

I love the open Heaven the Holy Spirit provides when we do our Night Strike street ministry. On those nights, the word of knowledge and the prophetic just work. When we do His work, He releases His tools for us to use.

It doesn't take much to start a prophetic evangelism and deliverance street ministry. On the streets we are first and foremost prophetic evangelists. You may be walking on the streets with your ministry team and out of the blue get a prophetic word for someone walking past you. You might tell the person, "You have a talent for writing."

The person then returns a puzzled look and asks, "How did you know that?"

You reply matter-of-factly, "Jesus pointed you out in the crowd and told me that about you."

You will most likely hear, "Wow. That is amazing!"

Through His gifts, the Holy Spirit just opened up favor for you to pray for this individual. So you ask, "Can I pray for you so that your talent will be blessed by God?"

With an opening like that from the Holy Spirit, people will seldom turn down the offer. Keep in mind this was a divine appointment set up by the Holy Spirit in the first place. The person may be a witch, a prostitute, a drug dealer, a Jehovah witness, or an atheist. Do not argue with them over any unsound religious views they present. The divine appointment was set up to touch them with the Holy Spirit. Give the person favor and respect and bless them. God is working on their salvation and you are the ambassador the Father in Heaven is using at that moment.

A veteran Night Strike team leader, Wayne LaCosse, had a word of knowledge for a woman on the streets during one night in our ministry. He told the woman that she was a practicing witch; he added that she came from a long family line of witches. The woman acknowledged that what Wayne told her was true. She also felt the power of the Holy Spirit upon her. It was like nothing she had ever felt before. The Holy Spirit engaged the woman with a word of knowledge; after talking with Wayne some more, the woman accepted Jesus. She was delivered right there on the streets.

Situations like this one always remind me of these words from the Gospel of John:

> The light shines in the darkness, but the darkness has not under-stood it (John 1:5).

The enemy will never understand the power of a repenting heart.

Don't be surprised by the ways in which the Holy Spirit will use you on the streets. In prophetic evangelism, you are the hands and feet of the Holy Spirit. Several years ago in my early days of Night Strike before I was leading teams, I was sent out with a husband and wife team, Sandy and Melody. We were ministering on Market Street in San Francisco when, all of a sudden, I had the strange sense of being aware of everything that was going on around me.

As I looked up, I saw street gang members heading my way. The looks on their faces said they meant to cause some trouble with our team. I looked over at my son. He was 13 years old at the time and was standing about 20 feet away from me, next to Sandy and Melody.

Some of our other team members noticed the motley crew coming our way. These concerned team members headed over to the team leaders. I wanted to bolt over to my son so I could protect him if necessary. The whole event played out before me in slow motion. As I began to run over to my son, I heard a voice in my head order me to stay put.

It was the Holy Spirit. I knew His voice, so I stayed right where I was and firmly planted my feet on the sidewalk. I looked up and saw the gang members dispersing through the crowd on the sidewalks. One large, African-Samoan man made eye contact with me. He meant business; I could see it in his eyes. He picked me out of the crowd and headed toward me. I could feel the Holy Spirit take over my body as the man's gaze fixed on me. I heard the word, *choose* softly echo through my head. The word wasn't for me. It was for the tank of a man heading my way. I know the Holy Spirit was telling him to choose not to engage in violence with me.

I remember having no expression of fear on my face. God took over my body, face, hands, and feet. In my conscious mind, I braced for impact with this large man. We locked into fearless eye contact. The man butted me hard with his shoulder. I didn't budge. He walked off. As his shoulder hit mine, I had an instantaneous vision of him standing in a pulpit, as a minister would, with a beautiful, young wife at his side.

The Holy Spirit transferred from me to him as he pushed past me. I felt my body control return immediately. Melody rushed over to me saying that everything was OK. She said, "I saw what happened! The Holy Spirit had to touch him."

It was great to get instant confirmation on the experience I'd just had.

I never said a word to this man, yet God touched him. Don't be at all surprised by the ways the Holy Spirit uses you and your team members to win souls. Your team will experience some incredible testimonies in this ministry!

Operating a Night Strike ministry and moving in the gifts of the Spirit brings the testimony of the gifts back to churches that thought the gifts were only for the early Church. Testimony from church members is a good, safe way to warm up a congregation to the gifts. I have worked with Night Strike participants from denominations that reject the gifts of the Spirit. They get to see the gifts of prophecy and the word of knowledge operating repeatedly throughout the night. This is a constructive way for testimonies to trickle back to home churches. Instead of our trying to convince them, the Holy Spirit is doing His work.

When you operate a Night Strike ministry for the homeless in dark neighborhoods, you are necessarily stepping up and walking by faith. I recommend scouting out a launch point for your teams. Make sure it is safe to walk to and from that point, so your teams can go and return. For the homeless ministry, we bring sandwiches with us. We have learned that providing much-needed food not only benefits the homeless; it also allows us to engage in conversation with those who would otherwise ignore us.

As we became more seasoned in the ministry, we realized that even when we ran out of food, we were able to engage people. We like to provide food, but we'll minister either way. We have developed relationships with people on the streets. We found that a lot of people seek the prophetic word that God has to offer them.

The most important thing is to let the Holy Spirit lead you as you walk the streets.

Starting a Deliverance Prayer Ministry

If your church doesn't have a deliverance ministry and you would like to start one, make sure you speak with your senior pastor first. The senior pastor must back you on this spiritual endeavor. You must have the backing of your church for this ministry.

Also keep in mind that what seems like a great idea in sharing the Gospel is actually taboo in many churches. The demonic aspects of deliverance and healing ministry frighten a lot of church members and pastors, even though the Bible explicitly states we should do this. You do not want to be in rebellion against your church leadership. The apostle Paul tells us in Scripture that we must be in alignment with the authority of the church, *"For God is not a God of disorder but of peace..."* (1 Cor. 14:33).

Let the Holy Spirit work on the church if there are areas of spiritual weakness in the body. Do not force the matter onto your home church if the senior pastor does not approve your plans. If you are not given permission by the senior pastor then that's that.

All is not lost, though. A lot of successful deliverance ministries were launched from house meetings. These are the same house meetings Jesus and the disciples used to build the Church. Having a deliverance team outside of church allows members from other churches in the area to participate. Now you have a deliverance ministry and a fellowship with other Christians that will extend beyond the walls of your church.

Whoever runs the house meeting should specifically identify who the prayer team members are and enforce that decision. You can expand your prayer team with new members as regular attendees earn the respect of others on the team. Be sure to work with new prayer team candidates. Mentor them so that the vines you plant can bear fruit.

Deliverance in a Church Service

Setting people free from their bondage belongs in the Church. However, deliverance sessions may not always belong in a church service. A new visitor who attends a church service in which people are speaking aloud in tongues, demons are manifesting with hissing and growling, or church members are weeping profusely is going to freak out!

I like to live in the radical middle. I believe in letting the Church grow with the teaching of the Gospel until miracle signs and wonders follow. Bondages can be broken in church services in a radically peaceful way, too. The senior pastor can lead the congregation in a corporate forgiveness prayer. (I have provided a corporate forgiveness prayer in Appendix C.) The pastor can invite the Holy Spirit into your meeting place and give Him free reign of the meeting. If people in the congregation are crying, it is time for an altar call of repentance.

The deliverance ministry prayer team should be released to the floor to work in unity with the Holy Spirit as He heals His Church. John G. Lake said the most powerful prayers are the ones that are accompanied by tears. This is a sign of people being set free from their oppression.

Weeping and tearful eyes are the norm in most deliverance ministry sessions. On occasion, a trapped demon may manifest. Demons prefer to hide and don't like to manifest, especially in a deliverance prayer session. When they're losing the battle they may make themselves known by manipulating the person they're oppressing. This is their effort to get the person to leave the meeting.

When a demon manifests, quietly bind the demon to silence and usher the person to a private prayer room. If it is a man, send two men to minister; if it is a woman, send two women with her. In respect of the individual who is manifesting, do this quietly. By no means should you allow the demon to disrupt the deliverance service.

Another point about service disruption: demons love cell phones. When they're about to manifest, they will use their spiritual network to have other oppressed individuals dial you in order to disrupt the service. Always make sure cell phones are shut off for these special services. When I am in a hospital praying for healing or curse-breaking, it is not uncommon for a spiritually oppressed person with whom I am working to call my cell phone. Demons have a complex communications network and they know how to use it to disrupt prayer.

Deliverance Meeting Once a Month

In light of not scaring your first-time visitors out of your congregation you can schedule a special deliverance service once a month outside of normal church service. You might schedule a Sunday evening service at, say, 6:00 P.M. and let it go until the

Holy Spirit is done, possibly around 9:30 or 10:00 P.M. Doing this protects the new visitor from being overwhelmed with visuals they don't understand.

The once-a-month meeting at church or at a house is intended for spiritual and physical healing as well as for people who want to be touched or baptized in the Holy Spirit. I am going to outline a style for holding the house meeting; I have seen this outline work well in moving with the Holy Spirit. This is not a formula for a deliverance session! The Holy Spirit moves how He wants to in these sessions. Yet, this format can be helpful in getting started. It comes from the Maranatha meetings held by Kingdom of Grace. Maranatha was launched from monthly house meetings. It grew until it needed a larger place to meet. Now Kingdom of Grace meets nearly every weekend in various cities of the San Francisco Bay Area. The meetings all started as house meetings and expanded beyond the capacity of the homes they were launched in.

This meeting format might be effective for those starting out with deliverance and healing meetings. The Holy Spirit may completely change how He wants your to meetings run. Use this as a basis for getting started and see what God does with it.

The flow of the deliverance prayer meeting usually starts with worship to God. This may go until the Holy Spirit starts moving through His people. The worship leader must be sensitive to the presence of the Holy Spirit and know how to move with the Spirit. This is extravagant worship for an audience of one—the Father in Heaven. There is a big difference between a worship session and a Sunday service worship production. For an audience of one, the worship leader is guiding the participants in inviting the Holy Spirit down from Heaven. The worship needs to be powerful, because we know from the psalmist that it binds the kings in chains:

> *May the praise of God be in their mouths and a double-edged sword in their hands, to inflict vengeance on the nations and punishment on the peoples, to bind their kings with fetters, their nobles with shackles of iron, to carry out the sentence written*

*against them. This is the glory of all His saints. Praise the
LORD* (Psalms 149:6-9).

Many enemy spirits cannot sit through extravagant worship;
they become extremely restless. Sometimes they manifest during
worship. Many times it weakens the demons' hold as they struggle
through the worship and the glorification of God.

The second portion of the meeting needs to involve sharing
the Gospel. After worship is the ideal time for this part of the
meeting. Why? Mark 16:17 tells us that signs and wonders will follow! Some people may be in attendance to get prayer for healing
even though they are not yet Christians. Peter tells us in the Book
of Acts that the Holy Spirit came for all of us.

The Maranatha Kingdom of Grace meetings host many people who have never heard the Gospel. One of the key points to
remember is *keep the Gospel simple.* Jesus didn't do anything complicated. He shared the Word of God and then healed all who
were around Him. Many people who don't know God get healed
in these meetings and leave knowing full well that there is a God
who loves them. Let the Word of God do its work. God has a lot
of things to say to His lost children.

The person preaching also needs to be aware of the movement of the Holy Spirit. Preachers in this setting need to pay
close attention to the prophetic, the word of knowledge, and the
physical signs of people being touched by the Holy Spirit. It is
common for people being healed of emotional trauma to start
crying during this time. When this happens, it is important to
move with the Spirit and let the individuals know that it is God
who is touching.

For many, this will be their first experience of God's healing touch. Help them to understand what is going on. Use the
word of knowledge and the prophetic, but operate in humility.
If God tells you that someone was molested as a child and is now
being healed, tell that person what He said. If God gives you an
age or a name, use that too, but operate in extreme sensitivity
to the people and their torment. Perhaps nothing more needs

to be said except that God is healing you now. Just be sure you acknowledge that it is God who is ministering to them.

When the prayer leader senses the Holy Spirit moving into the healing session, he or she needs to invite people who are sick or have an injury to come up for prayer. An invitation should also be extended to people who are suffering from depression and mental illness. Speak whatever you sense people may be experiencing in the room, whether headaches, knee pains, or any other ailment.

If you are the prayer leader, listen to the Holy Spirit for what He is telling you. Then release your prayer team to minister to the individuals requesting prayer. The healing session can go until the Holy Spirit is done. Don't be surprised if this lasts two or three hours. When it gets to where it is time to close the service (say, 10:00 P.M.) but you are still praying for someone, start shutting the prayer time down. (This may occur when you're praying for deliverance and healing from bondage.) Invite the person to come to the next meeting or to a private session. Let him or her know that you can continue where you left off.

Pray over individuals, bless them, and fill them with the Holy Spirit. Some healings are instant; others take more time. It is not our place to decide how quickly or how slowly a healing or deliverance should progress. It's all between God and the person being prayed for.

Deliverance in a Private Session

In some cases, private and focused attention may be needed in the areas of healing and deliverance. For example, if a demon manifests during a meeting and causes disruption, the individual is removed to a private room for further prayer ministry. Your team might pray for several hours to drive out the demons. If it gets late and you are not done casting out spirits, you can schedule a follow-up, as mentioned in the previous section.

Often, people think they have a tight leash on their demons. They believe they can keep them concealed, even in church.

But, when the Holy Spirit moves through a meeting, they cannot suppress the demonic strong man. They may be alarmed at the surfacing of the demon because they never really felt the power of the Holy Spirit before. What you need to do is to give these people the prayer team business card or contact information. Ask them to call you and schedule a private appointment.

Don't schedule an appoint right then and there. The person will almost always express the desire for an appointment. In reality, however, they may have no intention of coming at all. Either they are not ready for their deliverance or (in cases of addiction and infidelity) they like what the demon provides for them.

Yes, you read that correctly. You already know that "Christians in appearance only" may choose to coexist with demonic bondage because the destructive lifestyle it provides still seems attractive to them. In my experience, half of the people whose demons manifest during prayer never call to schedule the private session they need to get free.

Do not force these people into a session. If they choose to continue to go to church, great! At least they are still getting the Word of God. The Holy Spirit can continue to work on them during service. They may even leave the church once their secrets are exposed. Ironically, they will most likely visit more churches and play the same charade—instead of reaching for a healing through Jesus Christ.

Coming to a private session prayer meeting must be 100 percent the individual's own choosing. I have had ex-spouses, mothers-in-law, parents, and siblings try to force a deliverance session upon an adult individual. Adam and Eve were adults, yet God gave them the free will to obey Him. God treats all His children the same way. If they choose to rebel and lead a destructive lifestyle, it is their choice.

We know how much God loves us. He allowed His one and only Son, Jesus, to be tortured to death so that we might have eternal life. This love is still freely given to anyone who wants it. If an adult rejects this open hand of the Father, so be it. I have worked with really nice people who were being demonized and still rejected the hand of Jesus. As hard as it is to accept that, I have to choose to move out of their influence under the direction of the Holy Spirit.

In some cases, after some time goes by, these people will choose to go to church, simply because they got a taste of the power of the Holy Spirit and decided they wanted more of God. The Holy Spirit works with people, even those who have given up on themselves.

Always open a private session in prayer and invite the Holy Spirit into the session. Have some gentle worship or soaking music playing on low volume. You want to create a peaceful environment for the Holy Spirit to come into. After you have opened in prayer, ask the person wanting deliverance to tell you what is going on.

Do not start deliverance prayer right away. You want to hear what it is people want removed from them. It may take up to two hours of just letting them talk. This is the time for the two prayer team members to listen. If your session is with a woman, have at least one woman on your team. Likewise, for a man— have another man on the prayer team. A note on confidentiality: whatever is said must never leave the room. The information will always remain private unless the person who is delivered gives the testimony.

Satan unfairly attacks the Father's children in their youth. Many people are ashamed to discuss the sexual molestation inflicted upon them. These are dark, horrible memories that have been bottled up inside, often for decades. This darkness needs to be released. Many times in cases of severe demonic oppression, we find that the people were violently raped and demons transferred over to them through the violent act.

Again, this darkness needs to be released during this time. It may be a very tearful session, because the people are revealing the deepest darkest part of themselves. But this is often how the Holy Spirit heals people. As you have learned from previous chapters, the Holy Spirit may reveal a word of knowledge giving you the names of people who may have harmed the person for whom you are praying.

Remember that when demons manifest, you want to bind them and shut them up so you can talk with the Holy Spirit. You might remember the story I shared earlier about when the Holy Spirit revealed that we were praying for a woman whose father had been murdered. She looked at me with a startled look and then told the prayer team the murder had happened during a drug deal. She had not intended to divulge this information, but the Holy Spirit did.

Notice the simplicity in which the Holy Spirit shares information with your team. Most people expect a big prophetic download. In my case, God likes to keep it simple. He gives me images. Whether a particular session becomes a tearful time of healing or a dramatic scene of demonic manifestation, the Holy Spirit will tell you how to proceed. It isn't always pretty, but there is no shame in these meetings. There is only the supernatural love of the Father who wants to bring an end to years of torment.

Once the person for whom you are about to pray is done telling their story, the deliverance prayer ministry should start. Again, the format outlined here isn't a formula. You must move with the Spirit! A majority of the deliverance starts with the story-telling time. These are powerful times of confession and forgiveness. That is where the weight of the sessions is. Let the person lead his or herself, with the power of the Spirit, through the healing session.

Often, this is the first the person has ever revealed their deep darkness to another person. You would be surprised what people don't tell their pastors or church counselors. Yet, many will share their stories with a deliverance prayer team. That is a good thing, because the truth literally sets you free!

When the prayer session ends, fill people with the Holy Spirit and bring them back to where they can be sent home. If a healing has occurred, they will be elated. Pray for filling of the Holy

Spirit anyway. If people are suffering from severe demonic torment, more than one session will be required. Let them have a couple of days to a week before you meet again. Expect there to be hills and valleys of peace and chaos between sessions. Inform people that they will need to take responsibility over their own issues as these issues come up. This means they need to pray and adopt a healthy Christian lifestyle as the Holy Spirit moves them forward in life and healing.

The Deliverance Prayer Team Member

Now let's discuss the individual who is doing the praying for healing and deliverance.

Don't be too alarmed at the fact that some people who get delivered from torment want to join the deliverance prayer team. Many times God delivers His people and puts them into service to help others, regardless of whether the person was recently delivered or has been a Christian for many years.

First and foremost, deliverance prayer team members need to have a solid foundation in biblical truths. Do they know the Bible? Do their lifestyles reflect the Word of God? Do they have personal issues that need to be resolved? Are their family lives a complete mess? These things must be weighed and evaluated.

The prayer team member must be a person of integrity. Is this person doing it out of a love for Jesus? Or is there a desire to post a self-glorifying deliverance video on YouTube? The latter individual belongs nowhere near a deliverance ministry. My wife Lisa and I have been a part of more than 100 deliverances by both our prayer team involvement and M16 Ministries. We don't have a shred of video, audio, or photos to show what we did. This is a private time for individuals we work with. When I speak at events, I rarely record my equipping sessions, because the Holy Spirit sometimes takes over the session and delivers people. That's the way the Holy Spirit wants it. The Father wants to maintain His children's privacy and it is He who heals them. All the glory goes to the Father who loves us. We want individuals to testify to God's goodness and His glory in their time and in their way.

Therefore, as it is written: "Let him who boasts boast in the Lord" (1 Corinthians 1:31).

In plain and simple English, a prayer team member must operate in humility. He or she needs to be called by God to be in a deliverance ministry. Why? With this calling comes a responsibility to walk in integrity. Scripture tells us many will be called but few will stand up to the responsibility of the calling.

For many are called (invited and summoned), but few are chosen (Matthew 22:14 AMP).

What is the spiritual maturity of the people on your prayer team? Don't confuse earthly maturity with a spiritual maturity. A 22-year-old seeker of Christ can have a higher spiritual maturity than someone who is 20 years older.

God will take these individuals and mold them to His plans. This molding will involve breaking the soul to build up the spirit. These people will know the purpose of making sacrifices to pull themselves closer to the Father in Heaven. They understand that they must be broken by God to be used by Him. This is why many are called, but few are chosen.

On the flip side of spiritual maturity is the timing of God. A candidate may seem overwhelmingly mature and ready for the team, yet it is not God's timing. This is OK. Arriving at this conclusion means the person is spending time in prayer, conversing with and listening to God. This person has the maturity not to be pushed into a position without the blessing and release of God.

Does this vine produce fruit? A deliverance ministry will always come under fire from spiritual attack in the form of religious persons who equate miracles, signs, and wonders with witchcraft. This ministry isn't about miracles, signs, and wonder anyway; it's about saving the brokenhearted and building the Kingdom of God.

The Spirit of the Sovereign LORD is on Me, because the LORD has anointed Me to preach good news to the poor. He has sent Me to bind up the brokenhearted, to proclaim freedom for the captives and release from darkness for the prisoners (Isaiah 61:1).

Signs and wonders happen in deliverance ministry. Therefore, when such an attack comes to your ministry, what will pull the fight out of the enemy's clutches are the fruits of the Spirit (see Gal. 5:22-23). You need prayer team members who produce fruit in their church and outside of the church. Character is attacked first by those who feel they have a grasp on things and know what size box the Holy Spirit fits in. When you have prayer team members who bear fruit, you will most likely have a ministry that bears fruit, too. Let the miracles hold their own water. If they are from God, they will produce fruit.

How does this prayer team member respond to correction from God? Continually, we are being molded by our Father in Heaven. Does this person first and foremost seek a relationship with the Father? If so, the relationship will come with a desire to seek the truth.

Surely You desire truth in the inner parts; You teach me wisdom in the inmost place (Psalms 51:6).

As God speaks to His people, He will make changes in their hearts. Will the prayer team members respond to the sacrifices the Father is asking them to make?

The sacrifices of God are a broken spirit; a broken and contrite heart, O God, You will not despise (Psalms 51:17).

Spiritual growth can be painful. Romans 5 speaks about hearts being pierced through tribulations as the Father in Heaven works in His people.

Not only so, but we also rejoice in our sufferings, because we know that suffering produces perseverance; perseverance, character; and character, hope (Romans 5:3-4).

Every Christian is called, but few are chosen. Why? Because not everyone wants to persevere in order to get to the place the Father wants them to be. Matthew 14:25-33 gives us the account of Peter walking on the water. Peter saw Jesus walking on the water and said, "If that's You, Jesus, tell me to come out on the water."

Jesus responded, saying, *"Come"* (Matt. 14:29).

Jesus didn't say, "Peter, come." He invited everyone on the boat to come to Him. All the disciples on the boat were called, but only Peter responded.

M16 Equipping Churches

M16 Ministries has had its share of incredible testimonies in witnessing God's glory. Many times our ministry was part of assisting others in ministry who needed assistance or equipping. Our ministry has equipped a church in the deliverance of a church member who was demonically possessed. We equipped the church, the church intercessors, and conducted the deliverance for the person who needed to be set free.

Sometimes a church just needs a lifeline, or temporary assistance, to help them with the task the Holy Spirit has put before them. Seeing God's glory also involves seeing others get equipped so they can help others. We frequently receive requests to assist Christians outside the United States as they engage in battles with witchcraft.

We also equip individuals by showing them their authority in Jesus, so they can reclaim their lives. We helped a woman in the Caribbean named Grace who hadn't slept in over 20 years because of the relentless attack of witchcraft. M16 explained how she could bless her house; she reported getting a good night's rest for the first time in decades. Her friends said the dark circles under her eyes are starting to disappear. (There is more on her story in the next chapter.)

We also have a powerful intercessor team that is involved in praying. Our team enjoys taking on the impossible because they know that means only God can provide the solution.

> *I tell you the truth, anyone who has faith in Me will do what I have been doing. He will do even greater things than these, because I am going to the Father. And I will do whatever you ask in My name, so that the Son may bring glory to the Father. You*

may ask Me for anything in My name, and I will do it (John 14:12-14).

Summary

There is no concise format for hosting a deliverance prayer session. The most successful sessions are those that flow with the working of the Holy Spirit.

Before you select prayer team members, check the vine and the roots to see whether they are producing fruit. Make sure the people on the prayer team have the mature faith to summon that which doesn't exist and pray it into existence—a healing!

CHAPTER 14

ESTABLISHING A
BEACHHEAD: HOUSE BLESSING

The most exciting and rewarding part of M16 Ministries is witnessing firsthand the glory of God and the demolishing of the strongholds of darkness.

A perfect example comes from a case I mentioned in Chapter 13. It is the story of a Christian woman named Grace who lives on the Caribbean island of St. Lucia. Grace requested the assistance of M16 Ministries because she suffered violent, nightly demonic attacks for more than 20 years.

The cause of Grace's unrest was two witches on the island. They were trying to take her husband away from her in a strange and twisted love triangle. Grace's husband had extra-marital relationships with the witches, of which Grace was unaware. The sexual activity from the affairs made Grace the reluctant recipient of soul ties from her husband's secret promiscuity.

The soul ties passed on to Grace through her husband afforded the witches' demons supernatural access to Grace. As a result, Grace started experiencing demonic torments at night. Grace explained that she had nearly permanent black circles under her eyes from the decades of unrest and little sleep. She said that when the demons manifested, she could hear them making horrible noises on her roof. Then they would physically manifest in the form of the witches. The demons would speak curses over her, choke her, and beat her. Grace said the demons would try to push her out of her body and make her float off. But Grace said she would always fight and resist the demons. The demons never woke up her husband; therefore anything Grace might say about the nightly attacks would only make her sound crazy.

During the day, the witches would leave articles of witchcraft (limes and frogs) around Grace's home. The witches would also go as far as to make phone calls to harass Grace. On one occasion, Grace attacked one of the witches' familiar spirits that manifested into a frog. The frog leaped off and let out a laugh. That evening, the witch retaliated as a manifested demon and beat Grace in her bed.

After 20 years of torment, Grace found M16 Ministries through a divine appointment on the Internet. Grace said she had enough of the torment and needed intervention and a lot of prayer. Our ministry was unfamiliar with many of the symbols of Caribbean witchcraft. This wasn't a hindrance, however, since all the powers of darkness come from the created being satan, and all the power of creation of the universe comes from Jesus. I just needed to start speaking with Jesus.

The first objective in going on the offensive in this battle was to establish a beachhead. A beachhead is a military term; it involves the occupation of a hostile beach by a friendly army in order to accommodate the landing of more friendly troops. M16 Ministries needed Grace's house to be blessed so that we could secure the landing of the M16 intercessors' prayers and heavenly warring angels. That is what I mean by establishing our beachhead; we do it by blessing the person's home.

I e-mailed Grace instructions on how to bless her home. I also requested that she surround herself with prayer and have a couple of sisters from her church help her in her battle. This was how we established a beachhead in St. Lucia. Once I received confirmation that Grace blessed her house and had a small prayer team on hand, I moved the fight into the offensive realm; I released the M16 intercessor prayer ministry into the fight. The intercessors prayed for the witches' salvation and for them to have a Jesus encounter. Remember: hate the sin and love the sinner.

We prayed to bring the witches into the Body of Christ. We also prayed for the assignments of the demons to be cancelled. Several weeks later, I received an exciting testimony from Grace. She said she was now sleeping well and and the permanent black circles under eyes were almost completely gone! Glory to God!

House Blessing

Many Christians' first house blessing comes as a direct result of a spiritual attack of one type or another. You don't need to wait to engage in spiritual warfare before blessing your home.

Over the past decade, Lisa and I have assisted families in crisis. These are cases in which mothers and their children need a safe place to stay. We found that blessing our house and inviting the Holy Spirit into our home provided an atmosphere of peace. Families could feel this peace right away as they entered our house.

M16 Ministries also hosts house fellowship meetings for itinerant speakers. We bless our house for each event to create an atmosphere for the Holy Spirit. Many speakers who visit us are prophetic evangelists accustomed to operating in the gifts of the Spirit. We like to create a desirable atmosphere in which the Holy Spirit will dwell during these times.

Lisa and I also bless our house regularly because of the angelic spiritual activity in our home. We engage in spiritual warfare, so it goes without saying our own house is a beachhead for angels coming and going with assignments.

The house blessing is the number one request we get on our website. M16 Ministries is an equipping ministry, therefore we share information. It is the same information that was used to help Grace bless her home. We recommend that all Christian homes be cleansed of items that violate God's commands. We also encourage people to invite the Holy Spirit to indwell their homes.

Christian's whose homes have evil spirits or hauntings must never, ever seek the council of psychics, seers, diviners, or Wiccans. Seek the proper Christian prayer team to walk through the house with you, if you feel this is necessary. When blessing your house, you need to communicate with God. Allow Him to reveal to you what is going on in your home. Be aware that He talks to different people in different ways.

You may have a friend who clearly hears from God. Or you may be someone who hears from God. If you don't feel this is the case, however, don't be discouraged. There are times when God uses our nine-year-old son and his dreams to warn us of how demons are scheming to get into our house. Just listen for how God chooses to speak to you. He's God and He'll get through to you.

You should set aside time to do a thorough house cleansing. Mini-house cleansings should be carried out every so often as well. A mini-house cleansing would involve just walking the house at night before bed, for example, when checking on bedrooms and locking exterior doors.

Complete House Cleansing

The instructions here cover a complete house cleansing to be used for giving your house over to God or in preparation for spiritual warfare. You can do this by yourself or with a friend or even a prayer group. In spiritual warfare, it is advised that the head of the household (ideally both husband and wife) lead or participate in the cleansing. If husbands are unwilling, wives may still act in spiritual authority and cleanse their homes.

For spiritual warfare and the cleansing of an evil spirit from a house, I strongly suggest a curse-breaking session be conducted before the house cleansing. (This can be done immediately before the house cleansing, in a single day's session.) For curse-breaking, have the residents of the home them renounce family addictions and patterns of illness, dysfunction, and ungodly practices.

Invite in the Holy Spirit

One of the simplest ways to create a change in spiritual atmosphere is to play worship music. There is a CD by John Paul Jackson, entitled I AM: 365 Names of God that we use to change the spiritual atmosphere of a home. Play worship music that glorifies God. If the weather permits open the front door of the house and open the windows as gesture to invite in the Holy Spirit. Sit in a living room or family room and envision the glory of God. Open in prayer:

Heavenly Father, we invite You into this home today. We love You, Lord, and we invite Your Holy Spirit into this home. You are the Jehovah who provides. You have provided us with this home and this land. We consecrate this home and land back to You today. Let the Holy Spirit enter His house and His land. We will honor You today by cleansing this home. We invite Your Spirit into our hearts, minds, and bodies. Fill us with Your presence.

Give Thanks to the Lord

Take the time to thank the Lord for all He has done for your family. Thank God for the home He has provided for you and your family. Take time to reflect on ways in which God has protected you and your family in your health, finances, and any and all sources of provision and favor.

Prayer for Giving Thanks to God

Heavenly Father, we thank You for all You have blessed us with. We thank You for Your provision. You are the God who provides! We thank You for our family and Your blessings upon our family. We thank You for our home. We thank You for Your protection and for our safety. We thank You for our inheritance.

"And you also were included in Christ when you heard the word of truth, the gospel of your salvation. Having believed, you were marked in Him with a seal, the promised Holy Spirit, who is a deposit guaranteeing our inheritance until the redemption of those who are God's possession—to the praise of His glory" (Ephesians 1:13-14).

We thank You for Your sacrifice of Jesus Christ, Your Son, who showed us Your grace and mercy. "For it is by grace you have been saved, through faith—and this not from yourselves, it is the gift of God—not by works, so that no one can boast" (Ephesians 2:8-9).

We thank You for Your workmanship that created us to do good works. "For we are God's workmanship, created in Christ Jesus to do good works, which God prepared in advance for us to do" (Ephesians 2:10).

Lord we thank You for being our loving God and for being with us here today.

You may feel that the Lord is leading you into more thanksgiving prayer. That is fine. Go where the Holy Spirit leads you. He may desire more prayer time. This is a time for open communication with God.

Confession

Take this time to confess your sins to the Lord. You may do it quietly in direct conversation to the Lord or confess to your prayer partner. In the event of an evil spirit attached to a person in a home, the person must verbally confess his or her sin(s).

Jesus we thank You for the miracle of the cross and for crushing the curse of death. "For He has rescued us from the dominion of darkness and brought us into the kingdom of the Son He loves, in whom we have redemption, the forgiveness of sins" (Colossians 1:13-14).

Lord we confess our sins to You today so that we may be clean for the sanctification of this family and house.

"If we confess our sins, He is faithful and just and will forgive us our sins and purify us from all unrighteousness" (1 John 1:9).

Thank You, Lord, for Your grace and mercy. Thank You, Jesus, for suffering on the cross and saving a sinner like me.

(Confess your sins here.)

Give some time for others who are quietly confessing to God.

(End the time of confession.)

Thank You, Lord.

Bless the Threshold

Bless the front door. I use the Old Testament example from the Book of Exodus 12:7 and anoint doors in the house. I am not completely Old Testament in methodology. I use anointing oil. If you don't have anointing oil, you can use olive oil, if you have that. Whether you use any type of oil, I do recommend God-inspired Scripture reading at each door. If it's a nice day—or night, open the front door. When binding evil, speak with authority and open eyes.

Lord, I consecrate the front door of my house. "Take a bunch of hyssop, dip it into the blood in the basin and put some of the blood on the top and on both sides of the doorframe..." (Exodus 12:22).

(Touch the top center of the doorway with anointing oil. Touch each side of the door with anointing oil. Think of drawing a cross on the door—using the top and side jambs.)

"...Not one of you shall go out the door of his house until morning. When the LORD goes through the land to strike down the Egyptians, He will see the blood on the top and sides of the doorframe and will pass over that doorway, and He will not permit the destroyer to enter your houses and strike you down" (Exodus 12:22-23).

This is Your house and I bind any evil that may try to enter through this door. No darkness may enter, but only Your light. Lord, we pray over this house and everyone in it with the blood of Your Son, Jesus Christ. As we pray, Holy Spirit, reveal to us anything that is in our house that is in defilement to You.

"Now fear the LORD and serve Him with all faithfulness. Throw away the gods your forefathers worshiped beyond the River and in Egypt, and serve the Lord. But if serving the LORD seems undesirable to you, then choose for yourselves this day whom you will serve, whether the gods your forefathers served beyond the River, or the gods of the Amorites, in whose land you are living. But as for me and my household, we will serve the LORD" (Joshua 24:14-15).

Other Doors in the House

I draw the cross on each door, as instructed in Exodus, before entering each room of the house.

As I enter this room Lord, I consecrate this door to You, God. This is Your house and I bind any evil that may try to enter through this door. No darkness may enter, only Your light. I invite the Holy Spirit into this home.

Windows

I treat windows just like doors and pray over the windows. With anointing oil or olive oil I draw a cross on the sill of the window,

Holy Spirit, I pray over these windows. No evil may enter through them. No darkness may enter, only Your light.

Living Room

Living rooms tend to be where families entertain. The rooms are not usually used consistently except for special occasions. Pray that your actions and words bless and serve with graciousness that which is fitting to the Lord. Some living rooms have pianos in them. Pray over the pianos to produce only God-inspired and

God-glorifying music. Pray over furniture and sofas. Be open to the Holy Spirit pointing out a seemingly innocent object in the room that may be in defilement, such as a wooden witch doctor mask from Africa, or a statue of Buddha. God is jealous—get rid of these. Take your time in the room.

> We pray that when we entertain it would always be with gladness unto You, Lord. We pray that whoever enters this room will feel the presence and peace of the Holy Spirit. We ask that our words would lift people up and glorify You, Lord. We consecrate this room to You, Lord, for Your ministry and hospitality. "Offer hospitality to one another without grumbling. Each one should use whatever gift he has received to serve others, faithfully administering God's grace in its various forms" (1 Peter 4:9-10).

Family Room

A family room may contain many common items that can be sources of defilement. TVs, DVDs, CDs, MP3s, DVD and MP3 players are unsuspecting gateways for evil–to name a few! A family room, in some cases, could have a wet bar. The family room is where the family congregates and spends a great deal of time. Pornography in all forms should be removed from the house and from the private movie collection. I would go as far as to cancel any subscription satellite or cable channels that carry late-hour soft porn. Horror movies such as *Saw*, as well as any vampire and other demonic movies—get rid of them. Get rid of any music that dishonors God and His teaching. For families involved in spiritual warfare, none of this is optional. It should not be optional for any Christian; your practice should be to keep a pure home.

> I invite the Holy Spirit into this room. "I will give you a new heart and put a new spirit in you; I will remove from you your heart of stone and give you a heart of flesh" (Ezekiel 36:26).

> I pray into this room where our family congregates, blessings to all. Protect us, Lord, and cover us with Your feathers (see Psalms 91:4).

"He will command His angels concerning you to guard you in all your ways..." (Psalms 91:11).

Guard our mouths from what we may speak to one another. Let our tongues only be used to strengthen our family and glorify Your works in it. "You, dear children, are from God and have overcome them, because the one who is in you is greater than the one who is in the world" (1 John 4:4).

Bless this room, Lord, where our children come to play. Bless this room, Lord, where mothers and fathers come. Bless the family in this room with good times and memories to cherish. I apply Your armor over our family.

Pray over the sofa and chairs where the family sits.

Television, Stereo, DVD player, MP3 player, Cable Box

Televisions and electronics are hotspots for evil. The electronics aren't inherently evil—it is a matter of how they are used in our homes. Modern Christians have tolerated a lot of gray areas on what is evil and what isn't.

Lord, I repent, renounce and take ownership of any sinful manner in which I may have used with this (television/stereo/DVD player/MP3 player/cable box/etc.). I repent of any defilement I have brought into the house, either in media or in subscribing to it. I repent of any movies and shows that blaspheme or deny the Holy Spirit. Lord, forgive me for these sins. [Take time to consider and confess what these shows or media items are. Now, get rid of the offending media!] In Jesus' name, I close any open demonic gateways that resulted from what was watched.

Pray over the TV, stereo, DVD player, MP3 player, cable box, etc, for a moment.

Music

Lord, I repent, renounce and take ownership of any defiled music I have brought into this house. I confess my sin of listening to music that dishonors You! [Now get rid of the media! Or if you have a lot of music, make time later to sort through it.] In

Jesus' name, I close any demonic gateways that were opened by the music that was played in this house.

Wet Bar

Pray over wet bars and any alcohol in these rooms. Pray against the liquor being used as a stronghold for alcoholism.

Lord, may the hearts of the people in this house always be filled with joy. May they be drunk in Your Holy Spirit to the point of overcoming any spirit of heaviness. I pray the hearts in our family would always be cheerful and blessed, never to be crushed. "There is surely a future hope for you, and your hope will not be cut off" (Proverbs 23:18).

Bathrooms

A bathroom can be a sinister place in disguise. Think of the suicide acts that are contemplated or carried out there. Bathrooms are also hotspots for the use of pornography and lust. A bathroom is where people with elimination and eating disorders commit their sins. Please note that the deaf and dumb spirit is associated with both suicide and anorexia. The spirit of heaviness is also associated with suicide.

Lord, I pray that this room would be used for cleansing with water and purification. I speak against and bind any deaf and dumb spirit, spirit of heaviness, and spirit of perversion in this place. "Flee the evil desires of youth, and pursue righteousness, faith, love and peace, along with those who call on the Lord out of a pure heart" (2 Timothy 2:22).

Evil spirits, leave now and go where the Holy Spirit tells you to go.

In Jesus' name!

Children's Bedroom

Pray over every inch of a child's room. Remember to bless the closet doors. Stand for a moment in the room and ask the Holy Spirit to reveal to you anything you should know about the room. If the Holy Spirit reveals something to you, be a parent and get rid of it. An 18-year-old is still your child and has no business hanging a pentagram or baphomet in your house! It's not the child's room. It's the Holy Spirit's house! In the following prayer use the child's name as many times as possible.

> *"Call to Me and I will answer you and tell you great and unsearchable things you do not know"* (Jeremiah 33:3).

> *Lord, reveal to me the unseen. Reveal to me anything in this room that is in defilement. [Wait, and be sensitive to the Spirit's leading.] Lord, I pray over this bed for dreams from the Holy Spirit. I bind any spirit of fear that come to bring nightmares. This room belongs to the Holy Spirit and the child who sleeps here is a child of God.*

> *"'No weapon forged against you [name of child] will prevail, and you will refute every tongue that accuses you. This is the heritage of the servants of the LORD, and this is their vindication from Me,' declares the LORD"* (Isaiah 54:17).

> *I speak in the authority of Jesus Christ and bind any evil spirit in this room. Leave now and go where the Holy Spirit tells you to go. Lord, I bless the child who sleeps in this room. Break loose the gifts of Heaven and bless this child immensely. In Jesus' name, break loose healing, Lord. [Use your authority and specify the healing that is needed.] Lord, we thank You for this precious child. We thank You for all the gifts with which You have blessed this child. And Lord we thank You that you honor the prayers of children.*

Master Bedroom—Married

This bedroom is critical, especially in extreme cases. Evil spirits love to destroy marriages, especially through the blame game. An evil spirit's assignment will be to incite division and arguments. Pray over the room, the bed, the TV, and the bathroom.

Lord, I pray for blessings in marriage unity and strength. "Husbands, love your wives, just as Christ loved the church and gave Himself up for her" (Ephesians 5:25).

"Wives, submit to your husbands, as is fitting in the Lord. Husbands, love your wives and do not be harsh with them..." (Colossians 3:18-19).

Lord I pray over this bed that the husband finds no blame in his wife when he goes to bed. Also the wife finds no blame for any circumstance in her husband. "'In your anger do not sin': Do not let the sun go down while you are still angry..." (Ephesians 4:26).

I pray the husband sees his wife as the absolute gift from God. May the husband always find her desirable in his eyes. "Dear friends, I urge you, as aliens and strangers in the world, to abstain from sinful desires, which war against your soul" (1 Peter 2:11).

May the Holy Spirit visit them in their dreams and instruct them in the ways they require. Bless the husband and wife with wisdom in affairs of raising godly children. Bless the parents to parent with godly patience and discernment. "Fathers, do not exasperate your children..." (Ephesians 6:4).

May parents lift up their children and offer them back to God.

Lord, I pray that evil will have no hand in ruining this marriage. This husband and wife and their family will forevermore love the Lord our God and will have no other gods before You, in Jesus' name. In Jesus' name, break loose healing, Lord. [Use your authority and specify the healing that is needed.] Lord, we thank You for being the Jehovah who heals.

Master Bedroom—Single

Pray over the room, the bed, the TV and the bathroom. Pray for sexual purity.

"Call to me and I will answer you and tell you great and unsearchable things you do not know" (Jeremiah 33:3).

Lord, reveal to me the unseen. Reveal to me anything in my bedroom that is in defilement. [Wait, and be sensitive to the Spirit's leading.] Lord, I pray over my bed for dreams from the Holy Spirit. I bind any spirit of fear that comes to bring nightmares. This room belongs to the Holy Spirit.

"'No weapon forged against you will prevail, and you will refute every tongue that accuses you. This is the heritage of the servants of the Lord, and this is their vindication from Me,' declares the Lord" (Isaiah 54:17).

I speak in the authority of Jesus Christ and bind any evil spirit in this room. Leave now and go where the Holy Spirit tells you to go. Lord, bless me as I sleep in this room. Break loose the gifts of Heaven and bless me immensely. In Jesus' name, break loose healing Lord. [Use your authority and specify the specific healing that is needed.]

Closing Prayer

Take this time to thank the Lord for cleansing your home. Thank Him for indwelling your home and protecting it from evil. Thank Him for the freedom you and your family have through His Son.

In Jesus' name. Amen.

Summary

Any Christian can bless his or her home. The blessing doesn't require the presence of clergy. We should regularly bless our homes to invite the Holy Spirit to come and dwell with us in our family's life. Even our friend Grace in the Caribbean was able to change the spiritual activity in her home and take back her sleep from oppressing demons.

With electronic devices commercially available that stream Internet radio we consistently stream worship music into our house. We always want our house to honor the Lord and we always want Him to dwell in it with us. We invite the Father, the Son, and Holy Spirit to be a part of our lives, 24 hours a day, 7 days a week, for all 52 weeks of the calendar year. That's a full year of blessing with the Holy Spirit in our lives!

APPENDIXES

Appendix A

Salvation Prayer

Heavenly Father, I thank You for sending Your Son who died on the cross for my sins. I declare Jesus as my Lord and Savior.

I confess that I have lived a life of sin.

I choose to die to my worldly ways.

Today, I choose to be born again in the Spirit.

I know that Jesus died for my sins and was resurrected by the Holy Spirit.

I choose eternal life, through the Lord Jesus Christ.

I ask Jesus to come reign in my heart.

I ask the Holy Spirit to lead me in my life.

In Jesus' name, I pray. Amen.

Appendix B

Baptism of the Holy Spirit Prayer

Heavenly Father, I thank You that You love me.

I thank You for every blessing You have bestowed upon my family and me.

I believe Jesus died on the cross to take away the sins of the world.

Today I ask for the gift of the baptism of the Holy Spirit.

Jesus said, "If anyone is thirsty, let him come to Me and drink" (John 7:37).

My Father in Heaven, I am very thirsty and I have come to drink!

I believe in the Father; the Son, Jesus; and the Holy Spirit.

Let the streams of living water flow through me.

Let my spirit pray to You, Father.

Let my spirit sing to You, Father.

Let my tongue utter mysteries.

Let the gifts I receive build me up and build up Your Church.

299

I praise You, Father, and I worship You with all my heart.

I seek You, Father. Take my hand and bring me deeper into You each day.

I receive the gift of baptism of the Holy Spirit in faith.

I thank You for it.

In Jesus' name, I pray. Amen.

Appendix C

Forgiveness Prayer

Heavenly Father, thank You for sending Your Son, Jesus Christ, to defeat the works of the devil.

Jesus, I thank You for what You did for me on the cross. I know You died for the deepest darkest part of me. You have come to bring me eternal life, and it is that life that I want in the fullest. I invite Your light into my darkness.

Self-Hatred

"For You created my inmost being; You knit me together in my mother's womb" (Psalms 139:13).

Please forgive me for hating myself, for hating my body, for wanting to hurt myself, and for wanting to die.

"I praise You because I am fearfully and wonderfully made; Your works are wonderful, I know that full well" (Psalms 139:14).

Family

Please forgive me for harboring anger and resentment toward any members of my family. I choose to forgive them today.

I forgive my parents, siblings, and other relatives for their abusive actions.

I forgive my parents for rejecting me and for physically or emotionally abandoning me.

I forgive the members of my family who sexually abused me, manipulated me, or who spoke curses over me.

I choose to honor and bless my father and mother.

I break the curse of divorce in my family line. Any curse on my family, known or unknown, is broken from this day forward, in Jesus' name.

Anger

Forgive me for my thoughts of anger, temper, and fits of rage.

Forgive me for my prejudices, bitterness, and resentment.

Forgive me for blaspheming Your name; forgive me for my pride.

Forgive me for emotionally tearing down women with my words or for harboring hatred toward men.

I want to step out of this emotional darkness and into Your light.

Occult/Idolatry/Witchcraft

Forgive me for my involvement in witchcraft, the occult, and any blood covenants I have made.

Forgive me for consulting with psychics, palm readers, and Tarot card readers; forgive me for seeking supernatural powers that are not from You.

Forgive me for talking to the dead and channeling. I break all ties to the enemy now.

I renounce all pacts made with satan by my ancestors or myself.

I choose to bless all those in my lineage and my new life in You, from this day forward.

Sexual Immorality/Adultery

Forgive me for having sex outside of marriage.

Forgive me for the rape(s) I have committed.

Forgive me for blaming myself for being raped or molested as a child.

Forgive me for the self-hatred and anger I have bottled up from being sexually abused.

Forgive me for my fornication, adultery, and for feeding my feelings of lust. Forgive my pornography, sexual perversions, group sex, and sexual obsessions.

Forgive me for homosexuality or lesbianism.

Forgive me for participating in sexual acts and rituals of the occult.

Forgive my family for their ungodly participation in sexual sin and for any act(s) of incest.

Jesus, please bless me, forgive me, and wash me clean from sexual immorality.

Untimely Death

Forgive me, God, for being angry with You for the untimely death of my child, spouse, parents, siblings, or loved one(s).

Forgive me, God, for blaming You for giving my loved one a terminal illness. I recognize that sickness, death, and disease are the works of satan. They are not from You.

Forgive me for having an abortion.

Forgive me for having paid for, suggested, or forced a woman to have an abortion.

Father, heal my unresolved grief. Forgive me and my family for any curse of death that may be upon us. Bless us with life, in Jesus' name.

Religious

Forgive me for relying on works by following religious doctrines and legalisms, rather than Your grace for my salvation.

Forgive me for participating in spiritual oaths, vows, and rituals in a church that preached a false doctrine of Jesus Christ.

Forgive my family for participating in these legalisms and false doctrines. I wish to live under the covenant of the Gospel of Jesus Christ. Bless my family from this moment forward.

Sickness/Illness

Forgive me for believing the lie that, in my sickness, I was suffering for You.

Jesus, You came to destroy the works of the devil. These include sickness, death, and disease.

Father, please release my family from the curse of hereditary illness. I break all curses of sickness and disease off my family and me, in Jesus' name.

Addiction

Forgive me for my addiction(s) to alcohol, cigarettes, drugs, gluttony, pornography, (name of other addiction).

Forgive me for allowing my addictions to destroy my family.

Release my family and me from the curse and bondage of addiction, in Jesus' name.

Prayer of Repentance

Father, forgive me for blaming You, for blaming myself, and for blaming others.

I believe, receive, and request Your grace, mercy, forgiveness, and covering now. Release me from any curse as I receive Your freedom. Thank You for Your blessings and favor in my life. Amen.

PRAYER FOR BREAKING GENERATIONAL CURSES

This prayer is somewhat long; I call it the shotgun prayer. I use it when there are lots of things going on spiritually with a person, such as a long history of tragedy, illness, financial ruin, and dysfunctional family issues with a single person or family. I also use this prayer when praying with someone who is coming out of the occult, or has a history of Freemasonry, or exhibits signs of demonic manifestations.

I usually have a person to assist me when I use this curse-breaking prayer. I read the prayer aloud, slowly, and have the person being prayed for repeat the prayer lines after me. The assistant I take along needs to verify that every word is recited and spoken by the person needing prayer. It is typical during cases of demonic oppression for people to jump over the words *fear, anxiety,* or whatever word describes the root cause of their oppression. The spirits distract the person from saying these key words.

Heavenly Father, I confess the following sins and iniquities for myself and my family line.

Please forgive me and my family line.

I bind all demonic forces operating around me and my family line.

I repent and renounce the spirits of fear and anxiety, as well as their controlling factors in my life and the lives of my ancestors. I choose faith over fear.

I repent and renounce word curses spoken from my mouth, including condemnations, judgments, curses, and ungodly covenants. I break off all such curses spoken by my ancestors from my family line.

I repent and renounce guilt, shame, and condemnation.

I repent and renounce all forms of pride.

I repent and renounce my anger and bitterness. I choose to bless those toward whom I have harbored anger and bitterness.

I repent and renounce my hatred of others, including hatred against men or women or people of other skin colors. I break off these curses of hatred from myself and my family line.

I repent and renounce broken families through divorce and promiscuity. I break this curse off myself and my family.

I repent and renounce the spirit of poverty and the influence it has over my finances and the finances of my family line. I choose from this day forward to be obedient with God's provision and finances.

I repent and renounce ungodly associations, vows, covenants, and secret handshakes.

I repent and renounce all involvement in the occult, witchcraft, and the New Age by me and my family. I forgive my family of their sins and their involvement in these ungodly beliefs.

I repent and renounce having sought and used supernatural powers, levitation, out-of-body experiences, psychics, spells, rituals, and ungodly blood covenants. I break off all curses from myself and my family.

I repent and renounce the religious spirit and the spirit of rebellion.

I repent and renounce all of my involvement and my family's involvement in Freemasonry and the Daughter of the Eastern

Star. I break all curses and renounce all vows, from the 1st to the 33rd Degree of Freemasonry. I renounce all oaths of Eastern Star secrecy and silence. I forgive my family of their sins, known and unknown, and of their involvement in this.

I repent and renounce all vows, handshakes, blood oaths, and rituals of the Mormon Church. I renounce satan and his messenger spirit Morani and his false revelation. I renounce the ceremonies of the Mormon temple. I forgive my family of their sins and unknown sins and involvement in this.

I repent and renounce my involvement and my family's involvement with the Jehovah's Witnesses. I repent for all false and religious doctrines. I ask forgiveness for the rejection of the Holy Spirit. I forgive my family of their sins and unknown sins and involvement in this.

I repent and renounce all feelings of rejection from my mother, father, husband or wife, and family members. I break off the spirit of rejection in my life. I repent for feeling orphaned and unwanted. I repent for the destruction it has caused my family and me. I confess these sins and break them from my family line. Please forgive me of these sins.

I repent for feelings of hating myself. I know I was beautifully and wonderfully created. Any and all lies about my being inadequate in any way are from satan. Jesus, please forgive me for having these feelings and for wanting to hurt myself. I renounce these thoughts and break them off my family line and me.

I repent and renounce sexual sin by me and my family. Please forgive me of my sins and my family's iniquities of sexual promiscuity, ritual sex, pornography, masturbation, rape, obsessive or unnatural desires of lust, homosexuality, sexual abuse, incest, and sex with animals. I break off the assignment of the spirit of perversion and the religious spirit off me and my family line.

I break off all soul ties passed to my family and me by sex partners, adultery, and premarital sex that have entered into my family line.

I repent and renounce all word curses that I have spoken myself and from my ancestors. I replace these word curses with blessings. Please forgive me.

I repent and renounce having an abortion or being the responsible male for getting a woman pregnant and paying for the abortion. I repent of my lack of consideration of human life. I confess these sins and I ask forgiveness.

I repent and renounce word curses pronounced by me or my ancestors. I cancel these curses and replace them with blessings. Father, please forgive me and my family line.

I repent and renounce all verbal and physical abuse against myself and my family. I renounce the destruction that it has caused my family and myself. I choose to no longer be a victim and I now identify the lies of satan. Please forgive me for being a victim. I choose to live free under the miraculous work of Jesus Christ.

I repent and renounce having verbally and physically abused and harmed others. I confess my sins in these areas and I ask for forgiveness. Father, please forgive my family and me for any and all involvement in both physical and verbal abuse.

I repent and renounce any and all untimely deaths in my family. Sickness and death are from satan. I repent for blaming You, God. Please forgive me. I break off all curses and assignments of death over my family.

I repent and renounce the spirit of poverty over my family and me. I break off the assignment of poverty over my finances, my family's finances, and my manner of thinking. Please forgive me.

I repent and renounce my feelings of blame toward myself, other people, and You, God. I confess my sin of blaming others and You. Please forgive me, Lord for blaming myself, others, and You, God.

Heavenly Father, I choose to live free today. I release myself and my family from these curses, and any and all generational curses. I choose to have Your blessings released on me and my family today, and from this day forward, in Jesus' name!

ABOUT MICHAEL J. NORTON

I n the spring of 2009, Michael and Lisa Norton named their already growing ministry, M16, from the book of Mark chapter 16. M16 has been instrumental in helping people, worldwide, who have no where else to turn for spiritual warfare help. They have assisted and freed people under the attack of the occult; people with supernatural sleep deprivation, such as demonic manifestations out of dreams; demonic choking; and over a hundred cases with severe demonic oppression and several cases involving demonic possession.

M16 Ministry has an incredible intercessor team with the faith to pull miracles from Heaven and to act in the authority of Jesus Christ. The team has witnessed incredible physical healings, inner healings, and miracles of people being set free through the Glory of God.

M16 regularly participates in ministry of the homeless, witnessing to prostitutes and drug addicts in San Francisco through Bob and Kimberly Johnson Ministries, Night Strike. M16 is active in outreaches to the lost where they attend and minister at New Age and pagan fairs. M16 Ministries goes straight into the darkest parts of our land and brings the light of Jesus Christ. M16 is also active in equipping churches in spiritual warfare, both in the United States and in other countries.

To learn more about M16 go to their Web site at
http://www.m16ministries.com

In the right hands, This Book will Change Lives!

Most of the people who need this message will not be looking for this book. To change their lives, you need to put a copy of this book in their hands.

> *But others (seeds) fell into good ground, and brought forth fruit, some a hundred-fold, some sixty-fold, some thirty-fold* (Matthew 13:8).

Our ministry is constantly seeking methods to find the good ground, the people who need this anointed message to change their lives. Will you help us reach these people?

> *Remember this—a farmer who plants only a few seeds will get a small crop. But the one who plants generously will get a generous crop* (2 Corinthians 9:6).

EXTEND THIS MINISTRY BY SOWING
3 BOOKS, 5 BOOKS, 10 BOOKS, OR MORE TODAY,
AND BECOME A LIFE CHANGER!

Thank you,

Don Nori Sr., Publisher
Destiny Image
Since 1982